DON'T LIFT UP YOUR HOOD AND CUSS

To Andrew & Mary,

Two great people I am
fortunate to interact with every
two weeks.

You guys have been inter-
ested in my book, so I'm
giving you a copy.

Hope you enjoy it!

Best wishes always,
Bonnie Harrington

DON'T LIFT UP YOUR HOOD AND CUSS

A SOUTHSIDER'S JOURNEY TO REDEMPTION
THE PERSONAL MEMOIR OF AN "UNKNOWN"

BONNIE E. HARRINGTON

WINDY CITY
PUBLISHERS

DON'T LIFT UP YOUR HOOD AND CUSS
A SOUTHSIDER'S JOURNEY TO REDEMPTION
THE PERSONAL MEMOIR OF AN "UNKNOWN"

© 2017 by Bonnie E. Harrington

Windy City Publishers
2118 Plum Grove Road, #349
Rolling Meadows, IL 60008

www.windycitypublishers.com

Published in the United States of America

Paperback ISBN#:
978-1-941478-52-3

Library of Congress Control Number:
2017956022

WINDY CITY PUBLISHERS
CHICAGO

MY BOOK IS DEDICATED TO...

Chuck and Millie,
who started my journey,

And to my husband Pat,
who has accompanied me on it for 49 years.

PROLOGUE

I have read many biographies and autobiographies of celebrated people over the years, often finding myself puzzled as to why many of these people's stories merited publication? Were their lives so different and unique from the rest of us or was it their fame or infamy that made us take notice and want to know every detail of their lives?

The purpose of my book is quite simple, I want to highlight the idea that each person's life holds as much adventure and uniqueness as any 'famous' person's. The difference is that 'unknown' persons seldom get a chance to share with others the events and life lessons learned during their lives.

As such an 'unknown' person, I would like to share some of the events and experiences, good and bad, that I have had in my life. I believe that everyone can relate to them in some way. They are true life and show that each of us handles life's moments in novel and interesting ways. In the joy and coping of others with life's triumphs and tragedies, we can find hope and strength that can add quality to our own lives.

I have attempted to set down here many of the things that I will always remember, cherish, and want to share with others. My subject is daily living, nothing too foreign to anyone. This is a story of the dreams, wins and losses of an 'unknown' person presented with the hope that others might find it interesting and helpful.

CONTENTS

PART IV – CIVILIAN ADJUSTMENT

PART IV – LIFE ON FAST FORWARD

PART 1
THE GROWING YEARS

CHAPTER 1
THE WINDY CITY BLUES

To really understand a person and how he or she reacts to life, you must examine the people and the environment that helped make their life just a little different from everyone else's. I was born April 26, 1947, at Mt. Sinai Hospital in Chicago, Illinois, the first "Baby Boomer" child of Charles "Chuck" and Mildred "Millie" Rissky, both Bohemian-Polish Catholics.

Dad was a third-generation Chicago Southsider with a crop of wavy hair, a twinkle in his eye and a mother who loved to spoil him rotten. He had shipped out towards the end of World War II as a gunner's mate on board the U.S.S. *Wharton*, a troop landing ship stationed in the Philippines. Most of his time there was spent going from island to island picking up Japanese Army stragglers who didn't know the war had ended.

Mom was also a third-generation Chicago Southsider. She had a slender build, long wavy hair and a saucy personality to go with it. Mom and her mother, Ella Taraba, worked in an ammunition factory throughout WWII, while waiting patiently for their men to return from the war. On his return to civilian life, Dad went to work as a tractor-trailer brake mechanic and shortly after married Mom.

During WWII, William Taraba, Mom's father, was drafted into the U.S. Navy at age 32. He worked his way up to First Class Petty Officer aboard the U.S.S. *Liscome Bay*, an escort aircraft carrier stationed in the Philippines. Grandpa's ship was torpedoed and sunk by a Japanese submarine on November 24, 1943. Grandpa, along with hundreds of survivors and frozen Thanksgiving turkeys, floated in the ocean for a day before being rescued by another ship. Grandma Taraba had no idea whether Grandpa was one of the 644 dead or one of the 272 survivors from the ship until he wrote home. On his return, Grandpa came back to his original neighborhood and his job as a dairy truck loader at Bowman Dairy.

On their return from WWII in the late 1940s, our soldiers and sailors found that many of Chicago's neighborhoods were beginning to transition from the quiet, older ethnic neighborhoods they had left, into what would become some of the roughest, toughest ghetto areas in the city of Chicago.

My first recollections of life begin in a three-flat tenement building located on South Throop Street in the Pilsen neighborhood. Pilsen was a Bohemian-Polish neighborhood located on Chicago's Southside. My Mom's parents, William and Ella Taraba owned the building. Mom, Dad and I lived in the middle flat of their building, which looked much like all the other boxy tenement buildings around it. Our building had little to offer in comfort but was one of the best kept in our neighborhood. Grandpa made constant repairs and, in great U.S. Navy tradition, repeatedly painted everything that didn't move. Our tenement had a brick front with a wide set of stairs leading up to a front door stoop, making it stand out from the dirty gray and brown dwellings around it. Grandpa had also added a wooden fence along the sidewalk in front of the basement flat. A narrow City alley ran behind our building's tiny, mostly bare dirt backyard.

None of the flats in our building had an inside bathroom. Each flat's toilet was in a tiny room in the unheated hallway outside the flat. When you had to use the toilet during the winter, this location tended to wake you right up. You considered yourself lucky if you did not get frostbite of the tush when sitting on the ice-cold toilet seat. Since there was no room for a tub in the bathroom, you had to take baths in a metal tub inside the flat. God, help you if, like me, you were a bit on the chubby side. You had to wash in sections, first, you'd wash the parts submerged in the water and then you'd wash the parts that didn't see any water because of overhang.

Each of the flats in the building had a single oil-fired heater to heat all the rooms. The heater in my grandparent's flat was located in the kitchen. They had three more rooms beyond the kitchen. The heater worked so poorly in the winter that two of these rooms had to be closed off until the spring. In addition, since one of these rooms was the living room, my grandparents never bothered to furnish it. With no heat, any living room furniture would have been ruined during the cold winter months. Thus, the center of all family activity was the kitchen. The kitchen was the dining room, living room, family room and den all rolled into one. It was a good thing that my grandparent's kitchen was large. During the winter, that allowed all of us to sit around the kitchen table right next to the heater.

During the hot Chicago summers, our building, like all the others around it, turned into a bake oven. We would try to escape that stifling heat by sitting out on the front stoop or in the cooler gangways between the tenement buildings. There were plenty of steps outside to sit on. Our flat had twenty-five steps leading up to it. Inside, there were twenty more steps leading up to Grandpa and Grandma's flat, then fifteen more steps leading up to the attic. The basement flat didn't have steps, its access was at ground level through a door facing the back alley.

There were few notable "natural" differences between the Seasons in our neighborhood. Spring announced itself when the few trees along the street grew leaves and there was no ice or snow to trudge through anymore. There were no flowers and very little grass in our neighborhood. My Grandpa labored for years trying to grow grass on the 10' x 10' section of dirt next to his alley located garage. He would manage to grow a few strands, which would quickly die from the fumes coming from H. Kramer and Co., a metal smelter located a few streets from our building.

Maybe those same fumes made Grandpa look older than he should have as a young grandfather. Grandpa always reminded me of Santa Claus, he was short and round with a bulbous red nose from drinking the beer he loved so much. His hands were always rough as steel wool from loading milk trucks most of his life. He had started at this job in his early teens out of family financial need. Grandpa always carried his lunch to work in a brown paper bag. When he finally had to get dentures, he would put them in his lunch bag and say, "My teeth can start without me if I'm late for lunch."

Besides the industrial factories in our neighborhood, the City alleys always made their own special contribution to neighborhood pollution. The trash cans in the alleys were always overflowing, so there was always a plentiful supply of flies and rats. When Grandpa took out the garbage, he had to make sure to take it before dark because it was very dangerous to go into an alley at night. You could never be sure that something wasn't lurking there, be it a big rodent or a human ready to leap out of the shadows on his unsuspecting victim.

During this time period, there were no major supermarkets or giant department stores in our neighborhood. Our neighborhood grocery was a small, family-owned store named Chester's. It catered to most of our regular food needs. If we wanted and could afford something more, we supplemented our food supply with items from the many neighborhood fruit stands, butcher shops and bakeries.

Bahensky Bakery was a special bakery we frequently visited. You simply could not walk past it without stopping in and buying something. The fragrance cloud floating in the air from the baking process was to the nose what a rare wine is to the tongue. Their bakery goods were made fresh in the back of the store. You always knew that anything bought there was the ultimate in freshness, baked using ingredients you could recognize and pronounce. They sold luscious cream puffs filled to overflowing with whipped cream. They had every kind of buchty (paczki or Bismark) you could ever dream of filled with almond, strawberry, raspberry, peach, blueberry, or cream cheese. As with all Bohemian bakeries, Bahensky's used a lot of apricot, poppy seed and prune in their baking, especially with a cookie called kolachy. Kolachy can be made in different shapes. It begins as a thinly rolled out sweet cookie dough with the fruit spread on top of or inside folded over dough. With such an early start on such bakery gems, it is not hard to understand why, to this day, I adore bakery goods. The incredible smells and tastes from Brahensky's turned me into a life-long pastryaholic!

It seemed that wherever you travelled in our neighborhood you would never starve, every block had its own venders selling popcorn, hot dogs, polish and Italian sausage, ice cream, or snow cones. There were also your friendly door-to-door venders who would come around in a horse drawn cart selling potential ptomaine at a bargain price.

Speaking of ptomaine, my story would not be complete without a few words about our many trips to the poor man's street bazaar, Maxwell Street. Today it would be called a colossal flea market. On Maxwell Street, you could find anything and everything you might ever want at a fraction of its price elsewhere. Even canned goods and other packaged foods were for sale at minimal prices, if you did not mind a few dents or tears. If you purchased any "street food," you had to be very careful or you might get something you weren't shopping for, ptomaine poisoning. The Maxwell Street Polish, the classic Chicago "street food" since 1939, consisted of a fried or grilled Polish sausage on a bun, topped with grilled onions, yellow mustard and sport peppers. It still is a classic Chicago sandwich that begs to be eaten, ptomaine be damned.

Most of the Maxwell Street vendors sold their merchandise from small wooden tables. After setup, all the sellers had to do was holler loud enough to draw a crowd, which they hoped would become their customers. The items sold on these folding tables were things like: ties, jewelry, shirts, socks, dresses and knick-knacks. The larger, more expensive items were sold from little shops located along both sides of the street. Dad bought shoes and some furniture for our flat there. All the merchandise was new and very cheap. You never knew where it came from and you never asked.

I once read a story in the *Chicago Tribune* about a man who bought a statue of Buddha for a few dollars on Maxwell Street. He learned later that it was solid jade and was worth over $5,000. That gives you an idea of the extent of the bargains that could be found there by a careful and shrewd buyer. People of any age or time period love a bargain. That's why Maxwell Street is still a bargain hunter's destination to this day. Some of the biggest merchants in Chicago owe their success to the selling they did on Maxwell Street. One of those early vendors, Morrie Mages Sports, grew to be one of the biggest sporting goods chains in the Chicago area.

Before I leave our neighborhood stores, I must tell you about a kind of store that is extinct today; the corner penny-candy store. These mom and pop stores sold everything a child would ever need to rot his or her teeth out in a matter of minutes. The name of our neighborhood penny-candy store was Mitzie's. They sold every sort of penny-candy plus anything and everything else kids "needed." In the fall, they supplemented the regular candy with red candied apples and Halloween masks. During the spring, they added kites, yo-yos, rubber balls, and blow bubbles.

I used to love to press my nose up against the penny-candy glass showcase and drool. I could buy a whole sack of candy for a quarter because it was either a penny a piece or two pieces for a penny! I could buy mouthwatering spearmint leaves and licorice records that unwound into long glossy black strips with a little piece of round candy in the middle. Long before marijuana was associated with the name Mary Jane, there was a chewy peanut butter candy with that name. Jawbreakers were available that did exactly what their name implied if you weren't careful. Then, there were watermelon slices, lemon drops, root beer barrels, and licorice babies. Mitzie's also sold ice-cold bottled soda and all types of ice cream products.

My personal favorite item at Mitzie's was bubble gum trading cards. Of these trading cards, I loved to collect *Movie Monsters* and *Funny Valentines* the most. I always made sure that, if we were anywhere within a two miles radius of Mitzie's, we stopped in to see what was new. Mitzie's might have just been just a "hole-in-the-wall" store but they managed to display every single item they had in stock. They had merchandise plastered on every wall and dangling on strings hung from the ceiling. With that much inventory in so small a space, you had to go in two at a time otherwise that tiny store might have burst at its seams.

As for recreation in our neighborhood, there wasn't much to keep a person amused. We had no park, no library and one movie theater. The hard-working blue-collar men of the neighborhood would heavily frequent the local taverns after work causing many a family problem. The women could go to Bunco parties (a dice game with 12 players) to win towels, pillowcases, and blankets. There were also "product demonstration" parties held in various people's homes. They were kind of like the Tupperware parties of the 1960s but sold dishes, pots, pans, and small appliances.

If all else failed, you could just sit out on your building's front stoop and watch what was going on with the neighbors next door or across the street. It was better than listening to the radio, everything was live, at least when it started. A kid could really get an education watching a mother nursing her baby out on the front stoop. You could watch the "fight of the week" between husbands and wives, brothers and sisters, neighbors or even cats and dogs. The kids were always playing stickball, riding their bikes or doing whatever they wanted on the sidewalk or in the street amid passing cars and trucks. Our neighborhood was just a typical late 40s big city neighborhood.

CHAPTER 2
THE GREAT SUBURBAN HOPE

The changing view that Chicago neighborhoods presented was fast becoming bleaker and bleaker. Young post WWII couples were becoming more critical of life in the City and the rising crime in the neighborhoods. My parents were among those couples who were searching for something better and safer for themselves and their children. As life would have it, my parents had to wait a few years before they could start to live their dreams.

As I said earlier, my parents were a handsome couple, both had slender figures that they covered with the latest fashions of the late 40s. Mom had long, bushy brown hair with a wavy pompadour and so did Dad, not the long hair, only the pompadour. Dad's hair had always been his pride and joy from teenage. He could have been described as a "macho man," even before the name existed. He had his name tattooed on his arm when he was in the Navy. He added Mom's name when they married and later each of his children's names. It's a good thing there were only three of us kids or Dad would have needed arms like an ape.

In 1946, when Dad returned from WWII, the country found itself in a period of growth and prosperity. Dad wanted some of that for himself and his family. Since he hadn't had much formal education (eighth grade), it was up to him to learn a trade that would help him survive and prosper in this world. He had always been adept at working with his hands and he loved cars, so he learned to be a tractor-trailer brake mechanic. In the early days, he made his money wherever and whenever he could. His favorite way was to repair cars in the alley behind our tenement. It apparently paid well as I remember him happily coming home with a fistful of money and taking us out for dinner and a movie.

I was born within the first year of my parent's marriage. They were originally going to name me Penny because they had paid the hospital bill with a cigar box full of pennies. In the end, they named me Bonnie because I was born close to Easter and Bonnie sounded like bunny.

Even though money was a scarce commodity, Mom and Dad found that they could still enjoy the finer things of life through Sears "installment buying." They bought a new sofa set, a console radio-phonograph, a bedroom set, and something totally crazy at the time, a Crosley television set. My grandparents thought my parents had gone totally nuts to waste money on a TV but it didn't take them long to get hooked on it, too. In no time, they were coming down to our flat every night to watch "the little box" showing tiny motion pictures. It got so we could hardly watch it ourselves because of all the people who "just happened" to drop by and stayed until WNBQ or WGN went off the air. In the early 50s, there wasn't much on TV. The programs that stick in my mind were: *The Howdy Doody Show*, *Rocky King-Private Eye*, and of course, live boxing and wrestling matches.

As the years passed, life in our flat became more and more impossible for us. Mom was feeling increasingly hampered in raising me because of constant interference from Grandma. The arguments between Dad and Grandma had also become more frequent and bitter. Since Mom had been an only child, Grandma was on the constant lookout to protect Mom and me from Dad. Mom was becoming afraid to let me go out to play, feeling the neighborhood just wasn't a safe place anymore. Living in Grandma's pocket had gotten to be too messy, so my parents decided to look for greener pastures. They began taking frequent drives "in the county." That's when they found their "little doll-house" in La Grange, Illinois.

La Grange was a Southwestern suburb of Chicago, about twenty miles from the Chicago Loop. My parents wanted to find a safe place that was far enough away from Grandma to reduce her interference but not too far for Dad to drive to work on Chicago's Southside. We looked for quite a while before we found our new home. It wasn't huge but they could afford to buy it with a G.I. loan. That was, if they could convince Grandma to help them with the cost of the down payment. Ah, what a tangled web we weave.

The previous owner didn't know how old the La Grange house was but local history had it being used as a motel for Chicago's 1933 *Century of Progress* World's Fair. It was a white, one story house with an attached garage, grass filled front and backyards and a large backyard shed. The way it looked made people think of a "dollhouse." It was small and cute. It became even cuter when

Dad repainted the white and trimmed it with green and dark yellow paint. He built wooden shutters for the front windows, each with a shamrock cut out of its center. Wow, did that improve the appearance of the exterior tremendously!

As for the inside of the house, there weren't many rooms but they were all we needed at that time. The living room was fairly large and completely paneled and trimmed in a dark mahogany wood. To the right of the living room was a small walk-through kitchen with an eating area covered with red and gold Chinese patterned wallpaper. Off the dining area, to the right, was a small sunroom with windows protected by striped canvas roll-up shades. To the left of the living room was a short hall to the single bedroom. The bedroom was large enough to fit our two beds and two dressers nicely. Off the hall to the right was our wonderful indoor, radiator heated bathroom. It included a sink, a toilet and a bath tub with a shower head!

That bath tub looked so inviting to Dad that he could hardly wait to take a bath in it. He didn't know at that point that the source of our water was 'hard' well water. When he took his first shower, he came out with his hair standing on end. He looked so funny! Dad didn't let that discourage him, this was suburban living and it was all ours. My parents were optimistic about handling any problems with the new house and confident that our lives would run more smoothly now that they were on their own.

When my parents first took me to see the house, I thought it was the most beautiful house I had ever seen. It had huge front and back yards full of green, green grass and giant maple trees and evergreen bushes on either side of the front door. I thought that the most beautiful part of the yards were the beautiful lilac bushes that surrounded the house on three sides. In the spring, it looked like an orchid colored wonderland with a fragrance that far exceeded any perfume ever made. I even thought the weeds looked pretty because they were growing things; not like in the City where nothing grew. Even the air in La Grange seemed so clean and crisp smelling. When we'd go back into the City to visit my grandparents during the summer, the difference was always very clear. About three quarters of the way home, Dad would tell us to stick our hands out of the car window to feel how cool the air had become compared to the stifling air of the City. In the winter, the snow in La Grange always looked sparkling white in the sun not like the black slush in the City.

In this new life, we were making for ourselves, every day seemed to bring something new and exciting. There was so much life all around, I wanted to see everything. There were so many kinds of birds to see. I had just to look out the window to see such exotic animals as rabbits running after each other and squirrels walking on the telephone wires. Even bugs took on a new meaning for me. The only bugs I was acquainted with in the City were cockroaches. Now I could have fun watching ants scrambling about carrying cargoes three times bigger than they were. I could see beautifully colored butterflies hovering over flowers. There were even garter snakes slithering around the yard. I would find their skins near our front yard drainage ditch. I considered myself super brave if I picked one up.

We had quite an experience with bugs on the first night after moving in. Dad hadn't had time to replace the storm windows with screens. It was a very hot night so Mom asked Dad to remove the storm windows so we could get some fresh air. No sooner had he removed them and opened the bedroom windows when a swarm of flying bugs came through the open window. They were big, armor covered bugs that made a loud banging noise when their bodies hit the bedroom walls. We suburban pioneers were terrified as this was our first night in "the country." Mom started batting them with a towel, while Dad hurriedly closed the bedroom windows. When we finally got to bed, we didn't mind the heat and stuffiness of the room anymore. In fact, I had my head under the blankets all night. The "attack" of those bugs really put our move from the City to the country into proper perspective. The following day, our neighbor told us that they were June Bugs and that they were totally harmless. That was nice to know now but we sure wished that we had known it the night before.

Another type of bug that was new to me was the Lightning Bug. It seemed a miracle to me how those little bugs could light themselves up like tiny flashlights without electricity. I spent many a night in the yard catching and putting them in a jar to watch them light up. I spent as much time as possible outside taking in nature and swinging on a swing that Dad hung from a backyard maple tree. I imagined myself as almost anything on that swing. Standing up and swinging I became a trapeze artist. When I sat sideways on it, I became a pirate on a ship. When swinging normally, I pretended that I was a movie star singing in a gorgeous voice, while my handsome boyfriend was pushing me. That swing was a very versatile and imaginative toy.

Another fond memory I have of our backyard is our trellis of tea roses. Each flower was tiny and perfect looking and they came back every year! The trellis was attached to the side of the shed at the back of our property. The previous owners had told my parents that people had rented the shed to live in during the Great Depression. It was possible, it had electricity and a wood stove in it. We always used it as a storage shed and it also held Dad's punching bag. We cleaned it out every ten years or when it had become an outdoor closet that would dump its contents on our heads every time we opened the door.

Our "doll house" was heated by a coal fed furnace and radiators. Every day, during the winter, Dad would get up early to fill the furnace with coal so it would be warm for Mom and me during the day. Not long after we moved there, Dad brought his parents, Edward and Catherine Rissky, over to see our new home. Dad's father was a real character. Every time he went anywhere, he would come prepared for anything. Their first visit was during the winter, so he came wearing five layers of clothing: multiple scarves, sweaters, shirts, a pair of rubber boots over his shoes and three pairs of socks. He took only the first layer off when he arrived but he was almost down to his underwear before the evening was over. As he took off the clothes piece by piece, he would throw them in a pile in the middle of the living room floor. When he had finally finished taking off all the clothes he intended to, there was a four-foot-high pile of clothes on the floor.

The reason for Grandpa Rissky's need to shed his clothes was simple. Dad, worried that the house wouldn't be warm enough for his parents, so he kept feeding more and more coal into the furnace. After a couple of hours, the temperature was hovering around 90 degrees! Grandpa Rissky suddenly jumped up and yelled at Dad, "What the hell are you trying to do, roast me alive?" After his outburst, he began putting his clothes back on to leave. The rest of the evening was called off because of heat. Grandpa Rissky went home saying that they wouldn't be back for a while. It was kind of different going to bed that night with all of the bedroom windows open in the middle of the winter.

Not long after the heat incident, we started to hear weird gnawing noises coming from the sunroom. No one could figure out what was making the noise and nobody was keen to investigate too closely. Dad talked to the next-door neighbors and they told him that it was probably just field mice. They said that when winter comes to "the country" the mice always create problems. They come into the house or garage looking for food and shelter. Dad agreed that that was probably what was causing the gnawing noise. One night, he went to the hardware store and bought a small mouse trap. He baited the trap with cheese and put it into the gap between our house's foundation and the front sidewalk. That was where he figured that the mice had to be getting into the house.

The next morning, we rushed to see what, if anything, had been caught in the trap. To our astonishment, not only was the cheese gone but so was the trap! That night Dad put out a new trap in the same place and went to bed confident that he would catch something this time. The next morning the new trap was gone too! Now Dad was super angry! He went out for another trap and really came back with a monster! It was so large it looked like it could catch a bear. We all hoped that whatever had carried the first two traps away wouldn't be as big as this trap suggested. The next morning, we were all much slower to go see what might be in the trap. We decided that Dad should go alone to look. This time the trap had caught something alright and it certainly wasn't a mouse.

Dad yelled for us to come see what was in the trap. It was filled with an animal about the size of a large house cat. It had grayish fur, a pink pointed snout, a hairless pink rat tail and hairless pink paws that looked like tiny human hands. None of us ever seen anything like it before! Dad carried the cage with its snarling occupant over to show it to our neighbor. Our neighbor, a son of the South, recognized it immediately as a possum. He told Dad that, "they make good eating when served with sweet potatoes." Dad stared at the possum and then at the neighbor in disgust. He, then, handed the cage to our neighbor saying, "Happy eating." Thus ending the caper of the "mystery midnight visitor."

Reading my story up to this point you might get the impression that moving to La Grange was a barrel of laughs, but life's bumps also had to be lived through. One of the least happy bumps was when our fresh water well went dry. Dad and Mom didn't have the money to repair it so we were forced to move back to Chicago. My grandparents had rented our old flat out so we had to move in with them. This made for very crowded living, plus, I was now old enough to have to start school. Instead of starting school in La Grange, as planned, I had to enter the first-grade at Komensky Elementary School in Chicago, across the street from my grandparent's building.

Komensky Elementary School was a big, old, boxy brick building. Even then, the walls were covered with graffiti; there were no doors on the bathroom stalls and many of the windows were permanently painted shut. It seemed unbelievable that anyone could learn anything in such an atmosphere. Not only that but I had the same teacher that Mom had had when she was in the first grade! Her name was Mrs. Welinsky. I don't remember her talking or moving much, just sitting behind her desk and looking imposing. She never exerted herself, any problems that occurred were ours to solve. She added very little vigor or enthusiasm to the already dismal classroom with its creaking floorboards and ancient, student marred desks.

We had the exact same work assigned to us each day and every day. Each child was given a cardboard shirt stiffener with his or her name printed on it. These were lined up along the blackboard ledge. When we finished our assigned work, we would paper clip it to our cardboard shirt stiffener. At the end of each day, we would unclip our papers and take them home. Our assigned work included writing the alphabet, practicing numbers and coloring blocks that we made by folding a sheet of paper into eight squares. To avoid the monotony, I would color the blocks lightly one day and heavily the next. We also learned a song about a robin in an apple tree and read the uproarious adventures of Dick, Jane and Spot the dog. For all I know, Mrs. Welinsky might still be "teaching" at Komensky Elementary School! To this day, every time I see a box of crayons, I think of how much business she must have given to the crayon manufacturers. Teachers like that never die; they just get honored in the school's trophy case for their long endurance.

After six long months of enduring Mrs. Welinsky and living with my grandparents, Mom and Dad saved enough money to re-drill our well. We quickly moved back to our "doll house" in La Grange. Mom and Dad decided that, after my Chicago public school system experience, they would send me to St. Cletus Catholic Grade School. This was a brand-new parochial school about a half mile from our house. On my first day, it was very hard for me to leave and go on a bus to school. To help a little, Dad walked me to the school bus stop, which was on another street.

That night he told Mom that it worried him that I would have to walk so far to get to the bus stop. There were no sidewalks and there would soon be snow. He said that he was going to take the next day off and follow the bus to see if he could get it to pick me up closer to home. Dad found that there were very few houses on the next street. I was the only one getting on at the bus stop. He went to the bus company and explained our situation. He told them that on our street we had several kids who would be taking the school bus. So, the next day the bus stopped in front of our driveway. It continued to stop there for the next 15 years to pick up me and my two younger brothers.

My first day at St. Cletus Catholic Grade School was very different from Komensky Elementary School, the entire school was sparkling clean and smelled new. The tiles on the floor shone like mirrors. My first-grade classroom was bright and cheery looking with colorful cutouts on actual bulletin boards. Our desks were turquoise in color with unmarred varnished tops that lifted for storage. All our books were brand new with no torn pages, crayon, or pencil scribbling in them. The bathrooms were tiled and there were doors on all the stalls, so you could have some privacy!

My teacher seemed very foreign looking to me, she was a traditionally dressed Catholic nun. She had on a long black dress, which I would learn was called a "habit." She wore a veiled black hat that covered her hair, ears, and neck. Around her neck was a white cardboard-like bib with a large cross hanging down over it. She was very unusual looking compared to Mrs. Welinsky. I liked her immediately. She was cheerful and willing to help with any problem a child in her class might have. She helped us on and off with our winter boots and saw to it that we got on the correct school bus to get home. I was very curious about her clothes. One day I asked her what she slept in. She laughed and said, "I sleep in pajamas like everyone else." I was really shocked by that answer. I hadn't imagined that a nun would wear anything so normal.

On the subject of dress, the nuns weren't the only ones who looked different. All of the girls were oddly dressed when compared to what was worn in my Chicago public school. The dress at Komensky had ranged from jeans to dresses and anything in between. At St. Cletus, all of the girls were dressed in identical clothing. In physical appearance, some of us were fat, some thin, some tall and others small, but they were all dressed in the same school uniform. This consisted of a gray jumper with a detachable bib that felt like you were wearing a full flour sack around your neck. Underneath that was a white blouse.

One of the most embarrassing things to have happen to a uniform was to spill milk down their front. This was a usual occurrence as we had to eat our lunch on our desktops. The desktops were tilted down towards you making it a sure bet that at least one milk carton would topple over before the lunch period was over. When the milk spilled in your lap the uniform fabric would immediately absorb it making it hard to even stand up. Try as you would, you could not wring all the milk out of the jumper or the bib. Once I tried to wash it out with hand soap, which only made the skirt look like it was growing fungus. Once the milk spilled on you, you had to sit for the rest of the day in a sopping wet mess waiting for it dry. As it did, the four pleats in front of the jumper would stick out straight and turn crusty hard. By the end of the day, a female "spiller" would march home looking like her body was encased in an inflated gray beach ball!

I only spent a month in St. Cletus' first grade. The principal had placed me in first grade because I had only gone to school for six months at Komensky Elementary School. My parents argued that I should really be in second grade. After a few tests, I was promoted to the second grade. Suddenly, I found myself in a new classroom with a new teacher and a new set of children to get acquainted with. Most of them were friendly but there were a few boys who couldn't help but make fun of my chubby poundage. That hurt me deeply. It caused me to develop a belief that I was inferior to everyone else because of my weight. The teasing just made me try harder to make new friends. I, also, tried not to show anger at the teasing because I figured that would just make the others dislike me even more. I had to laugh along with them and pretend that the fat jokes didn't hurt. How early our opinions of ourselves are formed by the thoughtless actions of those around us.

As the teasing continued, second grade became very traumatic for me. I didn't want to be in school with these strangers who didn't care for me. I wanted to be in the safety of my home. I'd stand against a school wall at recess and cry. As the year wore on, things did begin to improve as I and my new classmates got better acquainted. I also grew accustomed to the harder second grade work. My teacher, Sister Robert Marie, was always patient and understanding. When I was depressed over not understanding something, she would always pat me on the shoulder and give me words of encouragement.

Being in second grade meant making your first Holy Communion. It was exciting to be dressed up in a beautiful white dress and shoes with a bride's veil on my head. I guess the true meaning of the day took a back seat to its material trappings. It was an important religious day in my life but it was made far more memorable by the secular things that surrounded it.

Not all of the nuns and secular teachers that I had in St. Cletus are fondly remembered. My fourth-grade teacher was a tiny nun with coke bottle thick glasses. The only thing I remember about her is the sarcastic remark she made about the quantity of scotch tape I used to hold dried leaves on the cover of my Open House folder. I didn't want her to think it was ugly, so I took all the tape off and stuck it behind the leaves so you couldn't see it. When Open House Day rolled around and my parents and I came in the class room, all the folders were hanging up above the blackboard. There was one that stood out among the rest, it had no leaves on its cover. You guessed it, that folder was mine. This is an example of how I got hurt by doing something, so another person would accept me. I wonder if that nun realized the importance of what had happened. My guess is she didn't care one way or the other. She hadn't even attempted to put something on my cover to keep me from being embarrassed when my parents came to the Open House.

Thinking back to Catholic parochial education in the 50s, we were all so innocent, naive and protected from the "real" world outside the school. Even though we were pretty good kids, there were a few who helped break the monotony of our routine school days. There was a big ox of a kid named Michael Meyer, who depantsed one William Butz and flew his pants from the school flagpole. There was Donald Dumas, who took a window curtain rod, attached a string with a paper fish on it and went fishing out the window while the teacher was out of the room.

Of course, I can't forget those kids who earned themselves special nick-names. There was James "Booger" Buyens, whose nickname needs no clarification except to say that he had major nasal problems. Next on the list was Michael "Snot Rag" Zanta, named so because of his cocky attitude toward teachers and peers alike. These boys probably grew up to careers on life's higher plane. Oddly enough, my popularity increased considerably in seventh and eighth grades. I really do not know why because I was the same loveable chub nick as before.

During eighth grade, I was given a surprise birthday party and was voted by the class to carry the crown for the May crowning of the Blessed Virgin Mary. I was very excited to have such an honor bestowed upon me. When Sunday came, I dressed up in a new, blue party dress and my first pair of nylons and high heeled shoes. I had never worn makeup, so Mom put on a dab of rouge on my cheeks and some lipstick on my lips. I felt like a beautiful queen, until I arrived at school. When I walked into our classroom, my teacher came over to me and told me how very nice I looked. The other eighth-grade nun was also in the room. When she saw me, she immediately scolded me for having on too much makeup. Here it was my first time wearing make-up and she couldn't allow me to enjoy the moment. All of the rest of the girls had been wearing lipstick and eye makeup for years. I couldn't even get through my first time without being criticized. Maybe she saw me as a candidate for becoming a nun.

Most of our time at St. Cletus were happy, growing years during which we were imbued with values and principles that would last us the rest of our lives. By having our desks spilled out on the floor, we learned the importance of orderliness. By being punched in the back by a nun, we learned how to kneel straight in a pew. Finally, we learned that we should always raise our hands when asked by a priest, "Who is going to become a nun or priest when they grow up?"

I'm glad my parents wanted something better for me than they had had. I didn't appreciate it all that much while I was living through it. Today, I fully understand and gratefully appreciate their sacrifices. Along the way, I sometimes thought that they did things for the sheer pleasure of watching me squirm. Now I realize that the squirming was due to something we all go through, the pains of growing up.

CHAPTER 3
PICKLES AND ICE CREAM ANYONE?

At the same time we were having problems with our well in La Grange, a second complication popped up, the upcoming arrival of a new brother or sister. When Mom told me that she was expecting, I couldn't imagine why she would want another child. After all, I was a six-year-old spoiled, only child, who was as close to perfection as you could possibly get! I had no interest in sharing anything, especially Mom's attention.

As I told you earlier, we had been forced to move back to the City and into my grandparent's flat. About this time, Grandma began to get very involved in analyzing dreams and going to fortune tellers. Anytime she heard of a new fortune teller in the neighborhoods, she would immediately go to see what they had to tell her about the future. Grandma heard about a new fortune teller, Mrs. Shotz, who was supposed to be very good. She went to her a couple of times alone. She decided that she was so good, Mom should see her to find out what sex the baby would be. So, one day, Grandma, Mom and I found ourselves taking a long, hot ride across Chicago in an overcrowded bus. I figured Mrs. Shotz must really be something for us to travel so far. I was kind of disappointed when we got off the bus and walked up to a very old, poorly kept bungalow house.

With Grandma leading, the three of us went in and sat down in the front room waiting for someone to come out to greet us. The interior of the house matched the outside. The furniture was very old and a musty smell permeated the air. We had waited for about ten minutes, when a door opened and there stood a man who scared me out of my wits. To six-year-old me, it was a giant who shuffled his way into the room. He mumbled something which I didn't understand. His eyes were very strange looking, they bugged out and had a cloudy film over them. I learned later that he was blind and so was his mother, Mrs. Shotz. Since I was already a connoisseur of horror movies, courtesy of our

Crosley TV, I figured that he must be a version of the Frankenstein monster.

Boy, was I scared and did I want to get out of there! Suddenly, Mrs. Shotz walked into the room. Thank goodness, she was not as scary looking as her son! My fertile imagination had pictured her in many ways after I saw her son, Willie. She was in her eighties and looked a lot like the old gypsy woman in the *Wolfman* movies. I changed my mind about her son. He was obviously the Wolfman not the Frankenstein monster. I began to pray that we would leave before a full moon came out. I did not want to see what he would turn into, he looked bad enough already! To my horror, Mrs. Shotz took Mom behind a curtain leaving me with Grandma. There she was told that her baby would be a boy and that he would be "out of this world." To only receive that "fortune," didn't seem to me to be worth all the effort and fright! Even now I get goose pimples, when I think about it.

As the days went by, I became more and more curious to see what an "out of this world" baby would look like. About the time I felt I couldn't wait any longer, I found out I didn't have to. Mom told me that she had to go to the hospital to pick up the new baby. I would have to stay alone with my grandparents for a few days. It was very shocking to me that Mom would just up and leave me. She had never left me alone with anyone before and I knew that I was not going to like it. Mom was very fussy with me. She always made my meals at the same time every day and combed my hair in her own special way. The days I spent with Grandma gave me a taste of a life where nothing was on schedule. She tried awfully hard but she just couldn't do things the way Mom did.

From the first morning, my stay with Grandpa and Grandma went sour. I always had a three-minute soft-boiled egg for breakfast. It was done perfectly every morning, except for this morning. When Grandma made it, the inside of the egg looked and felt like a rubber ball. Next, she helped me comb my hair. When I had trouble with the part, she said that she would make it. When she was done, Grandpa said, "Why don't you put on your glasses, her part looks like a crooked road." She told him that, "If you can do better, you do it!" With that Grandpa grabbed the comb from her and tried his hand at making my part. He didn't do much better, but at least, per Grandpa, he got some of the "crooks out of the road."

Every night while Mom was in the hospital, I talked with her on the phone with her and tattled on Grandma. She loved hearing all the things that Grandma wasn't doing just right. One night, Mom called to tell Grandma not to take me out anywhere. The nurses had told her that there was a measles outbreak. Grandma told her that she wouldn't dare take me out, so Mom was relieved. The phone was hardly hung up, when Grandma told me to get dressed in my snowsuit and boots, we were going for a bus ride. When Grandma had it on her mind that she was going somewhere, she went, no matter if an epidemic was lurking just outside the door. It was a very cold, snowy night and we had to stand on windy street corners to transfer to different buses. We ended up riding down State Street, in the middle of the Chicago Loop. I was impressed by all the flashing and winking lights and the crowds of pushing, shoving people. As we rode along, I knew that I wasn't supposed to be here, but what could I do, I was just a kid. I smiled, sat back and enjoyed this exciting new adventure.

A major surprise for me that night was seeing my first black man. He was waiting at one of the bus stops. On seeing him, my eyes became glued to him. I had never heard that people came in colors, especially coal black. Grandma told me to stop staring, but I just couldn't take my eyes off him. She said that if I didn't stop staring, he would grab me, put me in a bag and throw me in Lake Michigan. It's was amazing how fast my eyes became unglued. Grandma warned me that I could never tell Mom about our trip. I didn't for the moment, but it did come out after we got back home. There wasn't much that Mom could do about it and I didn't get the measles. If I had, I'm sure Mom would have had many choice words for Grandma.

Finally, the day came when Mom was coming home and I could hardly wait. It seemed that I hadn't seen her in such a long time. When she walked into Grandpa and Grandma's home, I held back a little because she was not alone. She came in carrying a blue bundle which she introduced to me as my new brother, Bill. When Mom put Bill in his bassinet and took the blanket away, I looked in at him and wasn't the least bit impressed. He was long, skinny, bald, toothless and looked to have a terminal case of diaper rash. I thought for sure that Mom had better taste than this! I had figured that she would be given a choice of babies at the hospital, so why had she picked one that looked like a toad?

The other thing I didn't like about Bill was all the attention he was getting from everyone. He got to be held all the time and hand fed. I just couldn't take it! I told Mom that I wanted to eat the same things Bill ate. My wish was fulfilled and was I ever sorry! Mom gave me a bottle of Bill's formula and it tasted terrible. Then, she gave me some of his cereal and later some of his baby food.

Believe me, none of it tasted good! At that point, I decided to switch back to normal food. At least I would be getting something that tasted good, while they were giving Bill food that was, in my mind, questionable at best. I decided that they were giving him junky food, so he wouldn't like living with us and would go back to the hospital. It didn't work, he just kept hanging around. I think they should have tried more desperate measures, like raffling him off, the loser would have to keep him!

"My Life After Bill" went along pretty smoothly. We moved back to La Grange and tried to resume our past, quiet, country living. I was forced to learn to share Mom's attention with my new brother. As time moved on, I realized that my brother's arrival had dramatically changed our lives. For one thing, it was much noisier and for another, we didn't seem to go as many places as we had when it was just the three of us. Before Bill came along, we were always on the go to different places at weird hours. I had especially liked going to the drive-in movie. We used to stay until the wee small hours of the morning and then, on our way home, stop for a snack at the all-night hamburger joint, White Castle Hamburgers. This had all stopped. What I didn't realize then was that things always change no matter how much we want them to stay the way they are.

Bill's first year was uneventful, then shortly after his first birthday, life's road became bumpy again. Bill was sick with a mastoid ear and was in such pain that Mom had to walk with him night and day. I felt so sorry that someone so small had to suffer so much. I think that was the moment that I began to fully accept Bill as a permanent part of our family. I wanted him to get better. I no longer wanted him to go back to the hospital or be raffled off.

It seemed that the only thing that comforted him while he was sick was to look at our "fresh" Christmas tree. Mom told Dad to leave the tree up until Bill got better. That tree was up until April and it was a wonder that it didn't catch fire it was so dry and brittle. Dad looked awfully funny throwing out a Christmas tree in April but Mom never did care what the neighbors thought. She'd do what she had to do for her family no matter what. I remember her going outside once to pick up two slices of bread off the front lawn. After throwing out bread for the birds, she realized it was the only bread in the house and she needed it to make Dad a sandwich to take to work.

I figured that Mom needed my help with Bill, so I decided to start pitching in with his care. One way of helping Mom, I decided, would be to take care of

Bill myself and let Mom sleep in. So, one morning, I got up really early and waited by Bill's crib for him to wake up. When he finally did, I scooped him out of the crib before he woke Mom up. I felt that he was wet, so I decided to change his diaper. I figured it couldn't be too hard, I had watched Mom do it dozens of times. The thing was that Bill was not about to make things easy for me. He started kicking his legs at breakneck speed, so I had trouble getting the diaper between his legs. After about ten tries, I succeeded with the diaper, including putting a glob of baby cream on his rump, topped off with baby powder. The glob became a thick paste, so I felt that that should really protect him.

The next thing I had to do was get the sides of his diaper pinned. I lacked confidence there and started to perspire all over, fearing that I would puncture something vital. I finally pulled myself together, sat on Bill's legs, and fastened the two pins. I had done it! There wasn't anything a seven-year-old couldn't do! Then, Bill started to cry, the dummy! Mom woke up, jumped out of bed and panicked when she didn't find Bill in his crib. She ran into the living room and found him on the couch where I had changed him. I was just getting his bottle ready. I thought that she was going to faint when she saw what I had done. Mom told me that while she always appreciated my help, she did not in this case. She told me that she would take care of all his feeding and dressing. Well, from that day on, I never again attempted feeding or changing a baby, that is, until I had one of my own.

CHAPTER 4
THE TROUBLE!

Life moved along with reasonable normalcy until I was nine years old and Bill was three. That was when I noticed that things weren't going so smoothly between Mom and Dad. They were arguing regularly and the atmosphere continued to be tense when they weren't. What I didn't know was that this arguing would soon get out of hand and that we would have to go through many emotional problems before our lives could be pieced back together.

"The Trouble" started one night with Dad coming home from work very sick from an ulcer that he said he had developed while in the Navy. He told us that he couldn't stand the pain anymore, that he was moving out. Mom and I just stood there dumbfounded, not believing what we just had heard. Mom told him that she had had it up to here with him, that if that was the way he felt she wouldn't stand in his way. After saying that, Mom quickly packed his clothes into a couple of cardboard boxes and threw them into the garage.

Looking back on the situation, I think that what triggered Dad's action was just despair. He was now 36 years old and he realized that he would probably never be anything more than he was. He had had dreams and finally realized that they would probably never be fulfilled. All his life, he had wanted to run his own auto repair shop. He wanted to name it "Chuck's" and have a big sign on the front saying, "Don't Lift Up Your Hood and Cuss, Call Us!" It must have been extremely difficult for him to cope with the fact that he would probably never see that sign hanging up on his own business.

After Dad left us, he moved in with his sister Sylvia in Oak Lawn, Illinois. Sylvia called Mom to let her know that Dad had checked into the hospital to be operated on for his ulcer. Mom also learned that he had cashed in his life insurance policy and had quit his job at Mutual Trucking. Even after hearing this, Mom felt confident that Dad would come home after he recuperated and we would be a happy family again. So, we three stayed in our La Grange home until Dad was ready to come back. It was scary living there without Dad in the house. Some night's Mom and I could not sleep, our overactive imaginations playing tricks on us. We were suddenly afraid of the sounds of the wind and the shadows that the trees cast on the bedroom windows. Since Dad had taken the car, we had no transportation for shopping and had to walk everywhere to buy the essentials.

We were very grateful to Grandma, she bought us groceries and helped Mom pay the mortgage so we wouldn't lose the house. Mom, hoping to speed up the reconciliation, brought us to visit Dad at the hospital. Since we weren't old enough to be allowed to visit him in his room, we could only wave at him through his hospital window. Mom thought that seeing us would make him miss us and cause him to come home. What we didn't know was that the situation was more complicated than it appeared on the surface.

Being very worried about Dad's condition, Mom talked to Dad's doctor. He told her that the operation had been a success and that he would be good as new after a few weeks' recuperation. However, he hinted that there might be something wrong with Dad mentally. What led him to that conclusion were names Dad had mumbled while under anesthesia. They didn't seem to match ones he had heard before. The doctor wouldn't say more but Mom found out a few weeks later what the doctor had been hinting.

When Dad was released from the hospital, he went back to his sister's house and didn't want to talk to any of us. A few weeks later, Mom received a call from Dad's sister's husband, who told her that he couldn't allow this "deception" to go on. He told Mom that Dad was seeing another woman. The "other woman" was Gloria, the switchboard operator at Mutual Trucking where Dad had worked. Dad had been meeting her on and off on the sly for a while. Most of the men who worked with Dad knew all about the affair and took up a collection to buy us a box of groceries. They felt sorry that Dad had left us for "her." Aside from visiting Gloria at Mutual Trucking, Dad had been meeting her at his sister's house. I don't think that things would have gone this far if there hadn't been a convenient meeting place at his sister's. Dad evidently needed someone new to boost his sagging ego and Gloria became that boost.

Mom couldn't understand why he'd throw his whole family overboard for someone that he hardly knew. We had gone through so much as a family and now it seemed that everything was circling the drain. The only life we could look forward to now was moving back to the City with Grandma raising us while Mom worked. Mom just didn't want that kind of life for us, so she decided to fight for Dad, whether he was worth it or not.

The first ploy Mom tried was to make Dad believe that this situation had made me so nervous that my health was suffering. One day, she asked my aunt, next door, to bring me home from school at lunchtime. I was completely in the dark as to what was happening. My life was in such turmoil that I never knew what to expect anymore. Mom explained to me what she had planned. I was supposed to lie on the couch and pretend to be sick. She, then, put an iodine mark on my arm to mark where the doctor had given me a shot to calm me down. Dad was contacted through Sylvia. He was told that he should come over immediately as I was so sick that the doctor had to be called.

Dad soon showed up along with his sister. They walked right in and stood staring at me. I thought that the performance I gave was magnificent, for a nine-year-old. I had turned beet red, adding to the believability of my illness. Although, I was convincing at the start, my performance rapidly went downhill by my recovering too fast. My aunt, a huge roly-poly woman, started telling jokes. This made me laugh so hard that I forgot I was supposed to be sick. In the end, this elaborate charade did nothing to bring us back together. It also discouraged me from becoming an actress of stage or screen.

A meeting was setup with only my parents present. Mom wanted to talk the whole thing out without anyone else interfering. When Dad drove up, we could see that he had brought the boxes of his clothes along with him. It seemed that this time he would be coming home. Mom and Dad talked for hours but, in the end, he left once more with his boxes of clothes. He did leave us hopeful by saying that he had problems on his mind that he had to settle for himself before he could come home.

Shortly after this, another major player in this mess appeared on the scene. It was Gloria's husband, also named Chuck. He came over to our house looking for Dad and Gloria. He was a short, meek and mild looking man. He was partially bald and wore thick wire rimmed glasses. He told Mom that he was looking for Dad so he could shoot him! We could see that he was carrying a gun in his jacket pocket. Mom was terrified that he might go through with it so she had him sit down to try to talk him out of it. Fortunately, he wasn't totally out of control. After seeing Bill and me so scared, he said that he couldn't shoot our father no matter how much he wanted to. Believe me, we were all very relieved to hear that! We wanted Dad to come home and he never would if this man shot him!

Before Chuck left, he told Mom that Dad wasn't the first man that Gloria had run around with since they'd been married. He said that even though he still loved her, it would be awfully hard to forgive her this time. He just didn't know how he was going to handle it this time. After he left, we all felt sorry for him, he was so beat down and dejected. We were glad, though, that he had decided not to use that gun on Dad. We really didn't want to witness a reenactment of the St. Valentine's Day massacre in our driveway.

After a couple of hours, Mom called Dad to tell him that he had almost been shot over Gloria. This scared him enough that he told Mom he would think seriously of coming back to the safety of his own home. He said that he and his boxes of clothes were coming over to talk things over, once and for all. After Mom told me what he said, I was confident that all would end well. My confidence disappeared immediately when I saw Dad drive into the driveway with Gloria in his car! It was the first time that we had seen her and I couldn't believe that Dad had chosen her over Mom. She was tall, skinny, and had a big nose like the beak of an eagle. I had envisioned her as some kind of beautiful movie vamp to have been able to lure Dad away from us. I couldn't imagine how he could have fallen for "old eagle beak!" Right then and there, I felt absolutely certain that Dad had, at minimum, major vision problems.

Mom obviously felt the same way because, on seeing Gloria sitting in our car in our driveway with her husband, she literally went totally berserk. She ran into the kitchen, grabbed a bottle opener and ran madly out of the house toward the car. When Dad saw Mom charging towards the car with something in her hand, he locked the car doors. He knew that something bad would happen if she got a hold of them. Mom was only 5'2" tall and weighed a just a little over 100 pounds, but I think at that moment she had the strength to pull up a tree by its roots. My Uncle Jimmy, next door, seeing trouble on the way, ran over to pull Mom away from the car. Dad and Gloria screeched out of the driveway. So much for having a peaceful discussion. Now we were more depressed than ever. Time was running out for Dad's redemption. We couldn't keep living from day to day with so much uncertainty and no money.

After that episode, Mom stopped calling him. She told me that if Dad wanted to come back home, it was up to him now to make the first move. Every night we waited for him to call, but no calls came. Then, one day he did call! He said that he wanted Mom to come over to his sister's house to discuss the situation with Gloria and her husband. He was apparently getting tired of living with no purpose. Grandma came over to watch us, while Mom went to attend the big armistice conference. It seemed forever before I saw our car drive into the driveway. Uncle Jimmy had taken Mom there, but she had come home in our car. Dad and Mom came into the house together. Mom told us that Gloria was going back to her husband and that Dad was home for good.

When Grandma heard this, she became furious. She already had it in her mind that "The Trouble" would continue and that we would be living with her. During the "The Trouble," Grandma had burned special candles that were supposed to put a hex on Dad. I was happy that they hadn't worked. I didn't know what she had been trying to turn him into, but I was sure it was nothing good. She even had the candles burning during the peace meeting. When Grandma realized that Mom's mind was made up, she blew out her candles and stalked out of our house yelling, "You may forgive him but I never will." She held firm to this promise for many months. Thank God, we four were a family again and our lives could return to normal.

The next day, Mom called Mutual Trucking to ask Dad's boss if he could have his job back. His boss told her that he could, as he had always been a good worker. Things were really getting straightened out for us now. It was wonderful that the soap opera we had been living for the past few months had such a happy ending. Even Dad's clothes came back intact but with a few more miles on them. Even though he would never see, "Don't Lift Your Hood and Cuss, Call Us," on the front of his own service station, Dad finally realized that he had something far more important, his family! We would always forgive him, love him and help him with his problems. Whenever Dad lifted his hood and cussed, he knew that he could always count on his wife and children for help.

CHAPTER 5
THE SUBURBAN MENAGERIE BEGINS

One of the happier aspects of this earlier period of my life was the huge variety of unusual creatures, besides brother Bill, that came to live with us. The first such creature came into my life when I was three. It was a perky green parakeet. It wasn't all that unusual, only in the way it came to us. One day as Dad was working on a truck at Wagner Electric, he was surprised as a small, green object whizzed over his head. He looked around trying to see what it was, finally spying a small, green parakeet perched on a ceiling beam. He decided to catch it and bring it home. He told us that he had chased that bird nearly all day before it slowed enough for him to plop his hunting hat down on top of it. Mom and I were very excited that he had been able to bring the parakeet home. We named it Queenie and it became one of the first in a long line of pets who gave us so much happiness and love.

Around the time Dad caught Queenie, we bought a Cocker Spaniel, who we named Skipper. She was tan and white with a paint brush tail that was constantly on the move. She was a very lovable dog, but had her faults. The main one being that it took an eternity to housebreak her. When we moved to La Grange, Mom bought a beautiful red 9' x 12' oriental rug for the living room. Skipper especially liked it, squatting down every couple of inches to christen it. Mom was getting worried that Skipper would ruin it, so Dad put up a gate to keep her in the kitchen during the night. That didn't work very well, she squealed and kept us up all that night. Something had to be done soon, to keep the rug from getting moldy from her wetting. Mom thought and thought and came up with an ingenious plan to air the rug out during the day. She would crawl right under the rug, stand spoons up on end, then, she would open the front door to dry the rug out. It was always evident when Skipper had had an especially sloshy night. In the morning, there would be at least 25 spoons under the rug, each making its own little mountain. This made for very difficult walking. Thank goodness, Skipper was potty-trained before winter arrived.

Skipper was a very patient dog with children, but not overly so. A case in point took place while she was lying on my parents' bed. I decided to crawl on the floor beside their bed and scare Skipper. From time to time, I would poke my head up and make a face at her. After about the tenth such face, she got tired of the whole thing and grabbed me by the nose. I still carry a scar on my nose from that bite. When I see it in the mirror, I think of her and how stupid little kids can be. I should have been the one who got the swat from Mom, not her. Skipper loved to ride in our car and went everywhere with us. Skipper would always sit next to me in the car, her ears streaming behind her from the wind. If we had to leave her in the car, she would wait very patiently for our return.

When Skipper was four years old, she developed a rupture. She was operated on for it, but it just came back. It didn't seem to slow her down, she continued to be the champ of running upstairs. As Skipper got older, the rupture grew bigger, but it still didn't cramp her running or jumping style. One morning, shortly after she turned ten years old, we found her dead under the kitchen table. We were all heartbroken. We had lost our riding partner with the long shaggy ears and short wagging tail. A friend like that can't easily be replaced.

A month after Skipper's death, we decided that it was too quiet in the house without a four-legged friend. It was agreed that this time we would get a bigger dog than Skipper. After careful study, we concluded that the perfect sized dog for us would be a Collie. We pulled out the telephone book and began searching for a reputable kennel to buy our next dog from. The closest Collie kennel we could find was in Lisle, Illinois, about an hour's drive from our house. We decided to make the trip there the next Saturday.

It seemed that Saturday could not come fast enough for our family. We asked Grandma if she wanted to come with us and we all took off for the kennel. After getting lost for about an hour, Dad found the kennel. We were greeted by a very pleasant woman dressed in farmer's overalls. She asked us to sit down and said she would bring in the pups that were available for sale. She disappeared into a backroom for a moment then, six wiggling, furry little bodies came running into the room, flinging themselves on us. They were all so frisky and cute! We looked at each other, then at the pups and realized that it was going to be very hard picking just one puppy.

One did stand out among the rest, though. She was such a cute dog, with tan and white fur, perky ears, and a mischievous face. In our hearts, we all knew she was the one, but nobody wanted to speak up because she was the most expensive. We got in a huddle, the puppies included, and had a family conference. Grandma ended it by saying that she would pay the extra money if we all liked the "pretty one." We all said yes, so we had a new furry friend. It was a long ride home and we were not sure how the puppy would react to the car ride, so we let Grandma hold her. It was a good decision. The puppy's first car ride upset her stomach and she threw up on Grandma five times before we got home. As we pulled into the driveway, Grandma said, "That was quite a ride!" We all had to laugh because both the puppy and Grandma smelled terrible! We were all glad it was Grandma, not us.

The first order of business the next day was to name the pup. After at least fifty suggestions, we gave her the name, Lady. As the years went by, this proved to be a very accurate name. She grew into a very regal looking dog with long, silky, gold and white fur. This same beautiful fur became unreal when she shed. Every time Mom brushed her, she would get a three-foot-high pile of fur that looked like gold and white cotton balls. Mom said that it was a shame that she couldn't sell that beautiful hair to someone for wigs. It would have made a nice toupee for Dad, who had begun losing some hair, but it was the wrong color. If it had to have been black, I believe Mom would have thought seriously about making him a toupee. Lady did very little damage to our house's furnishings while growing up. She did, however, use an old wicker rocker for a teething ring. After all her puppy teeth fell out, we threw the rocker away, as there was nothing left of it but a pile of toothpicks.

About a year after we got Lady, another new animal was added to our family. This time it was a Bantam "Banty" Rooster. One Sunday, while we were at Grandmas for dinner, one of Grandpa's brothers came over with two roosters. He told Bill and me that we could have one, so we picked a reddish brown one. The other one was a dirty gray color and it really looked ferocious. Now that we had a rooster, we weren't quite sure what to do with him. Our section of La Grange was still mostly rural, with large open fields every couple of blocks, so a rooster didn't look out of place. Dad quickly got to work making him a nice cage. We installed the rooster and his cage in our little dining area and named him Pepper. He was quite a different pet, at daybreak every morning he would cock-a-doodle-doo, waking us all up. To start his day off right, he would eat a box of Sugar Corn Pops.

Anytime I think of Pepper, I remember his most amazing trick. Pepper learned his trick because Dad decided that he needed lots of fresh air during the warm weather. Just putting him outside would have been simple but we were living in a suburban neighborhood. Dad had to figure a way to put Pepper out while keeping him from running away. The solution he came up with was ingenious. I still can't believe it worked so well!

Dad made a small version of the corkscrew stake used to restrain a dog. The top of it pivoted so the animal attached to it could walk around without getting tangled up. Since a chain would be too of heavy for a Bantam rooster, Dad had to figure out a different way to attach Pepper to the stake. He solved this by using a band-aid and a piece of heavy, black thread. Whenever Dad wanted to put Pepper outside he would tie a long piece of heavy thread to a Band-Aid; take Pepper out of his cage; turn him upside down, and attach the band-aid around his leg. After doing this for a few times, Pepper caught on to the idea. Soon, when Dad took him out of his cage, Pepper would lay on his back and put his leg up in the air for the band-aid to be attached. Pepper loved his life with us. He had plenty of room to romp and many different varieties of flowers to eat. He stayed with us for five years before he died. I think that he finally died from living too rich a life for a rooster. Whenever I see a box of Sugar Corn Pops or Band-Aids, I think fondly of Pepper.

It seemed that every time we had a new pet addition to our family, they came to us in some bizarre way. Another such incident started when Bill broke his finger playing football in the field across the street from our house. Mom and Dad rushed him to the hospital emergency room. Bill came home with his finger in a cast and two frogs in a box. The hospital lab didn't know what to do with them so they gave them to Bill. Dad got busy building a cage for them and we named them Maggie and Jigs. The next morning, we discovered Jigs had disappeared. We never found him but Maggie managed to stay with us for over a year. Since Mom oversaw feeding all our pets, she had to get used to feeding Maggie live meal worms. She'd buy them in a little waxed container from the pet shop. To keep them alive, she had to keep them in the refrigerator. That was something different, having a supply of live meal worms always on hand in the refrigerator. It was a good thing that Mom was never faint of heart.

Around this same period, Dad got interested in tropical fish and decided to buy a fifteen-gallon tank from a friend at work. We all had fun filling the aquarium with many types of tropical fish. Dad bought the fish very indiscriminately, never worrying whether they would survive together. It was every fish for himself. Luck was evidently with him, the only fish that didn't survive in the tank were the Angel fish. They were too gentle to survive in a tank inhabited by our other "gangster" fish.

We decided Guppies would also be fun so we added a pair to the tank. When Mom saw that they were going to have babies, she bought a special trap to catch the babies before the mother could eat them. The first time that blessed event happened, she excitedly raced back and forth transferring the baby guppies from the big tank to little fishbowls. She didn't realize how often guppies gave birth! Only a few days went by before she was doing the same thing! Things were getting out of hand, there were little fishbowls all over the place chockfull of guppies. Something had to be done before we were overrun by fish bowls and guppies. Mom took care of the whole problem by removing the guppy trap and telling the mother fish, "Go to it and have a nice meal." That took care of our guppy population explosion.

Mom especially liked goldfish and was always after Dad to buy more goldfish for the aquarium. One day he came home with the ultimate in goldfish for her. It was the biggest goldfish any of us had ever seen, measuring in at over a foot long. We had an extra ten-gallon aquarium, so there was no problem where to put the fish. We named the fish Bubbles and she was sure a real conversation piece. Once a week, my parents would exercise her by filling our bathtub with water and letting her swim around in it for a few hours. It seemed that there was always room in our little house for anything. All we needed was a little imagination in finding the room.

After our first parakeet, Queenie, there was a long line of others but none quite like our little blue parakeet named Cookie. Besides being the longest lived, nine years, he was probably the most aggressive and intelligent of them all. To clean his cage, Dad had to wear a glove, without it Cookie would bite him so hard that he would draw blood. After being bit several times, Dad had gotten very leery about going anywhere near that bird without protection. Cookie was only like that with Dad. When Mom fed him, Cookie was always very gentle and polite.

Cookie knew every time a meal was coming because he had learned to recognize his food came from an orange Hartz Mountain box. As soon as Cookie spotted that box, he would holler and jump up and down until the food got to him. When Mom gave him fresh water, he would literally dive into the little cup to bathe himself. When he was finished, we'd always had to laugh at him because his feathers were totally drenched. Some of his head feathers would be plastered down while others would be sticking comically in the air. As he got older, Cookie lost all the feathers on top of his head and so began to look like a drenched, bald, little old man.

Another thing, that made Cookie unique among our parakeets was he enjoyed talking over the telephone. Whenever Grandma would call and keep talking too long, Mom would tell her that Cookie wanted to talk to her. When Mom would put the receiver by Cookie's cage, he would run over and start chattering at the top of his lungs, then, would be very quiet to listen for what Grandma had to say. As he listened to her, he would turn his little head from side to side to make sure that he didn't miss a single word. When I think about Cookie, it's hard to imagine how an animal that small could have become so like a human friend to us. I guess it was because Cookie had such a unique personality.

Along with being a home for all of the afore mentioned pets, our house served as a shelter for two stray cats. The first one that came to our door was a white and tan tomcat. He looked very weathered from his years of roaming free and easy. I took an immediate liking to him and pleaded with my parents to find room for him. They said he could stay for a few days in the backyard shed. I was happy that we weren't going to turn him away. We made a nice warm bed for him out of a cardboard box and blanket and settled him down for a comfortable night in the shed.

Next morning, we heard loud meowing at the front door. When Mom opened the door, there was our houseguest on the front step waiting for us to feed him. Dad examined the shed from floor to ceiling to make sure that he wouldn't get out and get run over by a car. The next morning the same thing happened again and continued to happen every morning for a week. Dad, finally figured out that the cat was crawling out through the chimney! We were impressed that he was smart enough to figure that out. Dad said that he was an older cat and had learned by experience how to survive. So, since luck also played a big part in his survival, we named him Lucky.

When winter came, we moved Lucky into our heated garage. Dad built a shelf under the garage window to enable Lucky to look out when he had to stay inside. I was always in the garage playing with Lucky and trying to make him into one of my dolls. He just wouldn't have any of it. He was a tough cat and wasn't about to be made into a sissy. He showed his disgust at what I was trying to do to him, by scratching and biting me. It wasn't done out of anger, only as a warning for me to leave him be. I tried so hard to make him into a lovable, friendly puppy dog but he would never have any of it.

After Lucky lived with us for a several years, he mellowed somewhat. Even so, I knew that he was always the boss. When we had trouble with mice in the house, Dad said that old Lucky would take care of them for us. One night we heard the banging and crashing of things falling in the garage and ran to see what was going on. As usual, we pushed Dad into the garage first. He came out gloating that Lucky was taking care of a mouse. With so much noise and scurrying around, we figured this must be a mouse of rare proportions. When the dust settled, we all went in to see how the battle had ended. There was Lucky in the corner of the garage standing on top of a live mouse. When he saw us, he let the mouse go and climbed up on his shelf. This left Dad to take care of the mouse with a broom. All Lucky had been doing was playing with the mouse, chasing it back and forth and batting it around with his paw. Lucky wasn't a mouse killer anymore. He had grown fat, use to having his food served to him and wasn't about to exert himself chasing after food anymore.

Dad always had one problem Lucky, he would do things in the garage that weren't nice. Lucky used his litter box most of the time, when he didn't, he'd squirt on Dad's tools or anything else that happened to be handy. Sometimes Dad didn't immediately notice where Lucky had done his business. It became evident where, when things started to rust. Dad said many times that he was going to tie a can to that cat's tail, but I knew he loved Lucky as much as I did. When Dad went in to the garage, I'd catch him playing with Lucky, trying to teach him a trick. Before we went to bed each night, Dad would tell Bill and I to look in the garage to see a circus. Dad had taught Lucky to jump on his shoulder and hold on for dear life as Dad ran back and forth in the garage with him. It looked so funny with Lucky bobbing up and down on Dad's back. That was the one and only trick Lucky learned while living with us.

Lucky had been with us for about seven years when we noticed that he was acting peculiar. He hadn't eaten and he seemed to be walking in slow motion. Mom called a vet and his answering service told her to bring Lucky in the next day. The service said they were sorry because, from what Mom told them, it sounded very serious. I was so worried about him I carried him around the house in a box all day. He was so lifeless, I prayed that he would last through the night. When we woke up the next morning, Lucky was dead. We had a lavish funeral for him when Dad came home from work. I mourned his passing for weeks. I've have never forgotten him, I still have a couple of small scars that bring his memory back to me.

Our other experience with a stray cat took place after Lucky had been with us for about three years. A beautiful gray and white Angora cat came to our door. She was so beautiful that we couldn't turn her away. She was pregnant and looked like she was going to have kittens in a couple of weeks. We decided to put her up in Lucky's old suite in the shed. With her long, thick fur, we named her Fluffy. She was much younger than Lucky, so she was a lot more playful and cute. She loved to roll in the grass in the backyard just as Lucky had. We were all looking forward to her becoming a mother. When her time came, Fluffy had only a single kitten and she refused to feed it. It was tiny, looking like a regular cat shrunk down to the size of a mouse. We just couldn't coax Fluffy to feed the kitten and knew it would die without nursing. Mom called a pet shop for advice. The owner told her that the kitten would live if we started to give it milk. I tried for hours to get that little guy to take milk but it didn't survive. From that time on, I didn't care much for Fluffy, she let her own baby die. Mom thought that maybe she was too young herself to give the kitten any care. We never knew what had caused her to turn her back on her baby. Fluffy lived out the next nine years of her life with us and had no more babies.

There were other parakeets, canaries, turtles, and chameleons around during my childhood, but for one or another reason they never made that much an impression on me. The reason is either that they lived their lives in a very ordinary fashion or they lived very short lives. Some of the chameleons and turtles didn't even live long enough for us to get them home.

CHAPTER 6
SOMETHING'S BURNING!

My life progressed in a normal manner after "The Trouble." Until I was eleven, nothing much happened that was noteworthy, then came June 1, 1958. What happened that day sent our family out down another of life's bumpy roads. It was at 5:45 a.m. when a whopper of a thunderstorm arose. I remember the exact time because the storm knocked out the electricity leaving our metal horse clock with its rotating number blocks immobilized at 5:45 a.m. The thunder was ear piercing and the lightning was blinding. We sat up in our beds waiting for things outside to calm down before trying to go back to sleep. At the time, we still had one bedroom with three beds in it. Grandma used to laugh and say, "It looks like the three bears live in here." I said everyone was awake but that wasn't true, Dad could and would sleep through almost anything. Instead of the storm subsiding, it grew more and more violent and we became more and more frightened.

The storm reached its peak with a final bolt of lightning so brilliant that it lit up our bedroom like a huge electric light. It wasn't just a quick flash, it stayed bright for several seconds. This was immediately followed by an intense, gut wrenching, explosion of thunder that shook the whole house down to its foundation. Mom, as always, was the only one of us brave enough to get out of bed to see what had happened outside. Dad, who had finally been shaken awake, told Mom not to bother looking. He believed the lightning had hit the pile of metal the next-door neighbor had put between the houses.

As always, Mom ignored him and went to look outside. She came rushing back to tell us that lightning had struck our front tree. She told us that a strip of bark about a foot-wide, running top to the bottom of the tree, had been stripped away by the lightning bolt. Dad, who just wanted to go back to sleep, insisted that there was nothing to worry about and told us to go back to bed. We kids took his suggestion, laying down to go back to sleep. Mom didn't feel as comfortable, deciding to sit on the couch in the living room until she was sure we were safe.

Thank goodness, she did. About five minutes later, she came rushing into the bedroom to tell us to get up quickly, that the house was on fire! I never saw Dad move so fast before in my entire life. He flew out of bed like Superman coming out of a phone booth. The only thing missing was his cape and his pants. Bill and I hurriedly got on some clothes and ran to sit in our car out in the driveway. Mom and Dad stayed behind to collect all our pets. The only pet to give them a problem was Pepper, the Banty rooster. He would not come out of his cage for anything. Dad's arm wasn't long enough to reach to the back of the cage where Pepper was plastered. As the kitchen began filling with more and more smoke, Dad told Pepper that if he didn't come to him immediately, he would end up being one roasted rooster. Apparently, Pepper, finally received Dad's message and ran to him to be rescued.

When Dad finally emerged from the house, we all breathed a sigh of relief, the house was really burning by then. Several of our neighbors had come over to tell us that they had called the fire department and to ask if they could help in any way. Dad thanked them, then moved our car over to Uncle Jimmy and Aunt Flo's house next door. They took us kids in out of the still pouring rain. Dad and Mom rushed back to help the neighborhood men try to keep the fire under control until the firemen arrived. My uncle told them that it would be better if the garage doors were open, so the smoke would be able to escape. Before anyone realized what was happening, Mom ran back into the house to open the garage doors. She took so long that everyone was afraid that she had been overcome by the smoke. Just as Dad was going in after her, the garage doors burst open and she rushed out coughing. She told Dad that the reason it had taken her so long was that she couldn't find the door lock in the thick smoke. God and luck were sure with her that day!

Unfortunately, there was a problem calling the fire department. We lived in an unincorporated area, so the regular La Grange Fire Department wouldn't service our area. After many calls, the neighbors finally got in touch with the Pleasantview Rural Fire Department located fifteen minutes away. We were glad when they came to put out the fire, their firemen were as considerate as possible with our belongings. They didn't use their axes to break every window in the house nor did they damage any furniture with water unless it was necessary. After the fire was out, they even carried our living room rug out into the driveway and washed it down. It had taken about two and a half hours to put the fire out. All this time I had been holding Pepper over in my aunt and uncle's house.

We were all frightened to go into our house and see the damage that had been done by the crackling flames and sooty smoke. To our relief, the outside of the house looked about the same as before the fire. I had expected to see a blackened, burnt out shell where our "doll house" once had stood. We were encouraged that the fire hadn't seemed to have done that much damage. That notion was quickly dispelled when we entered the house. A couple of months before, Mom and Dad had bought a new sofa set, end tables and lamps. They were excited that they had finally been able to afford some new furniture. Now they found that the new furniture was water logged, stained and smelled of smoke. When you looked up, you were greeted by big gaping holes in the ceilings all through the house. Seeing all of this, I just sat down and cried my eyes out. Mom told me, "Don't cry, we'll get other furniture and all this mess will be cleaned up eventually. Just be happy that all of us escaped safely and that no one was injured." Her saying that eased my pain for the moment. I decided to walk through the house and try to make some sense out of all this chaos.

After the firemen and neighbors left the scene and things had quieted down, Dad explained what the firemen thought had happened. The terrific explosion that we heard was lightning striking our front tree but it hadn't stopped there. The lightning went through the tree branches overhanging the house then jumped to the outside light located just above the front door. When the lightning hit the outside light, it blew it off the house and caught the electrical wires in the ceilings and attic on fire. It was a really freak accident of nature. The firemen told Dad that a fire like that happens only once in a million. Weren't we lucky that it had happened to us?

Mom called my grandparents to tell them what had happened. Grandma insisted that we come over to their house for supper and stay with them until the insurance agent could be contacted on Monday. We did go for supper but we didn't spend the night. We all wanted to go to bed in our own home, be it as it was. We hoped that it could be repaired quickly so we would not have to put up with the smoky stench for too long.

That first night was a long one as we were all very leery about sleeping in the house. The fear of the fire starting up again hung over us thicker than the smoky stench. To combat this fear, Mom said that we would all sleep together in the double bed. That was what the doctor ordered, Bill and I slept soundly through the night. We were confident that Mom and Dad wouldn't be sleeping much, that they would be our guardians through this long night.

Monday morning bright and early, Dad called the insurance company to report our fire. The secretary said that our agent would be out in the afternoon to inspect the damage. Dad assured her that we would be eagerly waiting for him. Meanwhile, Mom and Dad went up in the attic to assess the damage there for themselves. It was bad up there because that's where most of the fire had been concentrated. Everything up there was either burnt or water logged. There had been several old dolls up there and the fire's heat had molded all their bodies together. They decided that very little could be saved from that attic.

The agent, true to his secretary's promise, arrived in the afternoon. He proceeded to survey the house writing down the damages with a pad and pencil. After all his computations were finished, he told my parents to get in touch with some contractors and get three estimates for repairing the damage. That seemed simple enough, but as usual, it developed into one big Excedrin headache for my parents. It always seemed their destiny was controlled by Murphy's Law. If there was a minute chance that something could go wrong, it would always go wrong for them.

The first estimate came to us from the LeRoy Construction Company. My parents didn't even call them, they came to us. As my parents soon found, they came to give us the business, as well as, to get our business. The owner of the company, who apparently had a direct line to our insurance company, was there to make the first estimate. He was dressed to kill and had diamond rings all over his fingers. He also had a smooth line of talk that a desperate family like ours would be eager to listen to.

He said that he would estimate high and with the extra money, he would do marvelous things to the house. He would add an upstairs with two bedrooms, install new aluminum windows and awnings and would lay a new cement front walk. Wow, did that sound fantastic! He could tell he had impressed us. Our eyes were bugged out imagining what our house would look like with all those improvements. The final thing he threw into this bargain, making it a deal impossible to refuse, was to install new siding on the house. How could anyone resist such a deal! My poor parents couldn't, so when he pulled out multiple sheets of paper for my parents to sign, Mom and Dad signed them all, oblivious to the potential consequences.

When our insurance agent received their estimate, he nearly died from apoplexy. He rushed over to our house to tell us that the bid from the LeRoy Construction Company was totally unacceptable. First, he said that the bid was ambiguous as to what repairs would be made, and second, the final figure of $7,000 was a ridiculous amount for damage that had been done by the fire. He advised us to find a more reputable contractor to bid and stormed out of our house.

The next contractor was a little old man named Mr. Stark. He said his company was "small, but honest." Hearing this, Mom and Dad told him to send his estimate to their insurance agent. His bid came to $5,000, which was a lot lower than the LeRoy Construction Company, so my parents had confidence that it would be accepted. When our insurance agent received Mr. Stark's bid, he again rushed over to our house to let us know that he wouldn't accept this bid for the same reasons as the first bid.

Mom exploded all over our insurance agent. She told him that if his insurance company cared anything about our situation, they would put us up in a motel until the house could be repaired. If not, at least help us get an estimate that could be accepted as soon as possible. He said that the kind of estimate his company demanded was one that had everything that was going to be repaired written out; board for board, nail for nail and item by item. Mom countered with, "That's idiotic! Both contractors told us that they couldn't provide a detailed estimate until they know the true extent of the damage." The agent said, "Well, I'm sorry but that's the way it is. I will hold off paying you for as long as it takes you to get a bid that I consider suitable." With that said, he left in a rush. Mom had been steaming and looked ready to grab him by his shirt collar and throw him out the door.

We were all very depressed, the days were passing swiftly by and nothing was settled. Living every day in a home with holes in the ceiling, ruined furniture and naked light bulbs hanging from wires didn't do much to lighten that depression. On top of that, Mom and Dad received a letter from the LeRoy Construction Company's lawyer saying that, even though their bid hadn't been accepted, we had to pay a percentage of the bid to them. One of the papers my parents had signed guaranteed money for the LeRoy Construction Company in case their estimate was refused.

Mom and Dad didn't know where to turn, the amount that the lawyer was demanding was $2,500. It would be impossible for us to pay that kind of money, especially at a time like this. To be perfectly honest, it would have been an impossible amount for us to pay at any time. My parents decided to consult a lawyer to understand their rights, if any, in this matter. He told them that the case would probably have to go to court. He didn't believe that the construction company would like the bad publicity it would give them. He told them to sit tight and give him a couple of weeks to work on things.

In the meantime, two men came to our door offering to submit a bid. They told my parents that they did not work for a company but were freelance carpenters. My parents decided that, at this point, they had nothing more to lose, so they let them submit a bid. They were very odd men. The spokesman for the two was named Mel, he was short, thin and had a pencil moustache and a balding head. The other man, John, was a very tall, thin man with a bulbous red nose and thick salt and pepper colored hair. John's speech was difficult to understand as he had a speech impediment.

My parents told them about the situation with the insurance company and how nasty they had been treating us. Mel said that they would present a repair estimate that the insurance company couldn't refuse. He said that he knew a lot of people and places where construction supplies could be gotten very inexpensively. He also said that once the roof was torn off he and John could add a second story with two bedrooms for a very nominal price. That sounded all well and good but after the LeRoy Construction Company and Mr. Stark fiascos, my folks were not going to get too excited until his bid was accepted.

True to their word, Mel and John's estimate was $2,500 and it was quickly accepted by our insurance agent. With that acceptance, Mel and John became familiar figures around our house for the next five months! They never said that they were fast, just cheap. Dad said that he would help them all he could, so the repair time wouldn't be too lengthy. They never had a work schedule, every day they would arrive at a different time. Most of the time, they didn't start working before noon making sure that they would be there through dinner so they could eat with us.

It became apparent very quickly that the supplies they used were not top of the line or necessarily new. They got a "free" staircase from a condemned school building and most of the rest of the wood was second hand. It was obvious the wood was second hand, each piece was "pre-painted" a different color. Dad and Mom weren't particular where any of it came from. They were just happy that we were getting our home repaired along with two extra bedrooms thrown in the bargain.

Dad became angry with Mel and John mutiple times before they completed repairing our house. They were basically lazy men who were more than happy to hold off work until Dad could help them. Thus, most of the work was accomplished over the weekends. When Dad worked with them, he had no tolerance for "lazy" and would really make them move.

Several memorable incidents occurred while Mel and John were "working" on our house. When it came time to tear off the burnt roof, we were praying that they could complete it in record time. It was the summer and there was always a chance of a thunderstorm. With all three of them were working as quickly as possible, they got the walls and a temporary roof on without any problems. The next day the roofers put on the shingles, so we felt that we were safe from the rain. That night, what a surprise, it started to rain. Water began pouring into the house from at least twenty-five places. The living room looked like one big shower stall. What Dad, Mell and John had failed to do was to enclose the eaves. We all ran around like crazy people placing buckets and pots and sopping up water with towels and rags. We survived this flood only because the rain stopped before we ran out of containers to catch it in.

Several humorous incidents, all involving John, happened during construction. At one-point, Mel and John were in the new upstairs putting down a temporary floor. When Mel asked John to hand him something, John forgot that there wasn't a floor everywhere so crashed through the ceiling. Mom and I came running into the living room to find John's legs dangling through the new ceiling that had just been installed. Later, while they were installing the upstairs bedroom windows, Mel asked John to bring over the ladder. John put it through one of the windows. John was not an "adept" carpenter! It seemed that the two of them were forever doing things over because John would manage to ruin what little had been accomplished.

Another time, Mom was washing the dishes when two legs came down through the kitchen ceiling. The person on the other end of the legs told her to watch out, he was coming down. Mom stepped back just in time, as John's size 12 shoes, with John in them, came falling through the ceiling almost on top of her. John always did things differently. We never knew where he would be hanging from and we didn't want him landing on our heads. If we had been smart, we all would have worn helmets. Being around Mel and John was like watching Laurel and Hardy try to repair your house.

It was getting well into fall now and John and Mel were still very much with us, working at their leisurely pace. About this time, we heard from our lawyer who said that the LeRoy Construction Company wanted to settle out of court. They said that they would forget the whole thing for $200. By that point, my parents were more than happy to pay the $200 to be rid of them forever.

One of the last jobs that Mel and John did before they left was to re-side our house. Dad had to monitor them carefully because, if he hadn't, they would have fastened each piece of siding on with two nails. Dad told them to put at least six in each piece. With the high winds we often had, he did not want the siding blowing off the house. With the completion of that job, Mel and John got ready to pack up and leave. It was kind of a sad moment that caused Bill to cry. He thought that we were losing part of our family. Mel and John had lived with us from the end of June to the beginning of November, so it was very easy for Bill to have gotten used to their presence. If nothing else could be said for them, Mel and John had provided a lot of amusing memories of incidents which really weren't that funny at the time.

Everything was pretty much back to the way it had been before the fire. We settled down to our normal life and enjoyed our new addition. That lasted for about two years, then once again an event would occur that would bring new excitement to our lives.

PART II
THE CONFUSED YEARS

CHAPTER 7
SURPRISE, SURPRISE!

Even in times of trouble and despair, we had always made it through because we had each other. Our always sticking together made the good times even better and the bad times less traumatic. I guess it was this closeness and happiness that made me leery of growing up. As I noticed physical changes taking place to my body, I knew that other changes were imminent. I just wanted things to stay as they were, so I fought the changes any way I could. One thing I did was to refuse to wear a bra. I was very satisfied to wear an undershirt. I had no interest in being bound up in something that looked so weird. Another thing that seemed like a big pain was wearing nylons. They had to be held up by something, which again seemed too restricting. I was too used to letting it all hang out. I felt bobby socks should always be the socks of choice. As I approached my thirteenth birthday, I knew that I would never be "Miss Popularity" with the boys. I had always been a chubby child and now I was becoming a fat adolescent. My future as an adolescent looked kind of dreary and demanding. I wanted to delay it as long as long as possible by staying a child. Then, something very unexpected happened that forced me to act more my age.

It was mid-1959, Mom had turned 35 and Dad 39. Things were going along very smoothly, but Mom hadn't been feeling very well. She went to her doctor and found out, to her astonishment, that she was going to have another baby. She couldn't believe that it was true. At 35, she felt that she was too old to be having another baby. With the surprise also came fear. Mom had had a very hard delivery with Bill. The doctor had told her at the time that she shouldn't have more children. Now six years later, she had to think about delivering again and going through all that a new baby entails.

When Dad found out about it, he told Mom she would go to an obstetrician this time, not to the general practitioner who delivered Bill and me. Dad felt that by taking Mom to a specialist, she would have more confidence and be less afraid when the birth came. The obstetrician picked was considered very good but had a dour personality. Every time Mom went for a visit, he was curt and to the point, usually scolding Mom for gaining so much weight between visits. It wasn't her fault that, during her pregnancy, all she craved was pizza and spaghetti. Dad was more than happy to get her anything she craved.

The baby was supposed to be born towards the end of March, so Mom made sure that Bill and I were drilled in what to do while she was away. She had a new crib and her suitcase packed long before her due date. We had only one cardboard suitcase that, courtesy of the fire, now smelled of mildew. Mom needed to do a little modifying to it so it would be ready for a stink-free trip to the hospital. For six months, she filled it with cedar chips. By the time she was ready for the hospital, the suitcase was too. The mildew smell was gone, now traded for the smell of a home for wayward hamsters.

As the first week of March drew to a close, Mom was getting very nervous about the baby but also about the trouble Dad was having with our one and only car. He said that he would have to go to his friend's garage to fix it. At issue was the fact that his friend's garage was a two and a half hour drive away. On Friday, March 11, Dad took off for Lansing, Illinois, to fix the car. Unfortunately, that was the night that Mom started labor. Mom told Bill and I to go to bed, she wanted to be alone and do some last-minute things. Dad finally came home about 3:00 a.m. dead tired. Seeing his condition, Mom decided not tell him she was in labor until he got a few hours' sleep.

When she woke Dad up and told him, he said, "Why didn't you tell me earlier?" She told him that she didn't think it was necessary. Mom, then, called the doctor to ask him what she should do. He told her to get to his office as quickly as possible before the baby was born in the car! When Dad heard this, he grabbed Mom's suitcase, herded us all into the car and yelled at poor Mom to get moving. I looked at Mom and could see that she was now very frightened. It was an hour's drive to the doctor's office but the hospital was directly across the street from it.

We arrived at the doctor's office with Dad speeding and going through red lights all the way. The doctor's nurse rushed Mom to an examining room and a few minutes later, she was on her way across to the hospital. Mom was checked into the hospital about 11:00 a.m. The baby was born at 11:38 a.m., so she really cut it close! Bill and I waited in the car while they were in the hospital. Before long, Dad came racing to the car to tell us that we had a new baby brother and that Mom was doing fine. Dad told us that the doctor had a big smile when he came to congratulate Dad and tell him that his wife was fine. Sometime later, Mom confided in me that she had been terrified to have the baby. She had become convinced that either she or the baby would not survive the birth.

This time the birth of a new brother was a different kind of experience for me. There was no jealousy, only love and the anticipation of helping to take care of him. I realized I had changed emotionally, I didn't react like a spoiled little brat as I had in my "Life After Bill" period. Those ugly, selfish emotions had been replaced by a sense of maternity toward my new little brother. I was beginning to find it difficult to keep up with all the changes in me.

All of us waited eagerly for Mom and Mark to come home. We all tried to keep things the way Mom had left them. Grandma and Grandpa were now living just a few blocks away from us. They had been the last white family, courtesy of racial "Blockbusting," to move out of a Pilsen neighborhood that had become too dangerous for them. Mom and Dad had helped them find a nice brick, two-bedroom house in Countryside, Illinois, so they were just settled in when Mark was born. Their new location allowed Grandma to make dinner for us while Mom was in the hospital.

The night before Mom and Mark were set to come home, a surprise snowstorm moved in. By morning, there was about twelve inches of snow and Dad didn't have snow tires for our car. Since Grandpa did, he let Dad borrow his car to get through the snow to the hospital. Bill, Grandma and I went along with Dad. It was terrible driving but we made it fine. The hospital nurse had told Mom that she might have to stay another day in the hospital because of the weather. Mom told her that she didn't know her husband, he'd make it to pick her up no matter what the weather.

My first glimpse of Mark was shocking. He looked nothing like I expected compared to Bill's birth! He was a beautiful baby with chubby, rosy cheeks, light brown hair and large brown eyes. He weighed 8 pounds 1 ounce, the biggest baby born to Mom. His weight was probably due to all the pizza and spaghetti she had consumed during the nine months before he was born. We were all so happy that Mark's birth had turned out so well. Little did we know that his healthy appearance didn't mean that he would be a healthy baby. Mark had gone through so much illness by the time he was five, that it was unbelievable that such a little guy had suffered so much. There were many times when we weren't sure that he would survive to adulthood.

The first six weeks of Mark's life were golden. He was the picture of health until he suddenly developed a high fever with vomiting. We all thought that he had caught the flu and that he would get over it like anyone else. After two weeks, he did seem to be getting over it but he had lost a lot of weight. Mom was confident that she could get the weight back on him now that he was well again. Unfortunately, she didn't have the time, two weeks later he was sick again in the same way as before.

I vividly remember rocking Mark in his buggy to help him get to sleep and Mom feeding him repeatedly until he could keep something down. Mom and I would take turns sleeping in the mornings because Mark rarely slept and was constantly crying. I felt so sorry for him, he always seemed to be burning up with fever. After Mark had been sick in the same way three times, his doctor told us that he had been born with a virus and would probably continue to get these fevers until he was a teenager. That was not the news that my parents wanted to hear. It surely wasn't something for us to look forward to, especially Mark. For the first time, I was now very glad that I was older, allowing me to lend a hand in caring for Mark. My ability to help care for Mark made our personal relationship very close and dear to both of us.

I was forced to cut down my help with Mark considerably the year that I started at Nazareth Academy. Nazareth Academy was an all-girls Catholic high school, established in the early 1900s. It was founded to provide girls with a higher quality of education than in public schools. Also, to provide girls, whose parents weren't sure how to help them, get back on the right track. Nazareth's main building was a mixture of new and ancient. The ancient part of the school had a few classrooms, but most of the rooms were used as bedrooms for aged and sickly nuns. Some of the rooms still had the wood-burning fireplaces that had been used as the primary source of heating in earlier times. The school was run by the Sisters of St. Joseph with the help of many lay teachers. The tuition cost of Nazareth was not cheap but Nazareth's educational reputation was sterling.

While I was in the eighth grade at St. Cletus, I decided that Nazareth Academy was the high school for me. My parents and I knew that I would receive a very good education there and, as for me, I knew that there would be no boys, so I wouldn't have to feel any boy's rejection. I was content to concentrate on my studies and hide my social life away in a corner. I felt that, if I didn't show interest in doing things other kids were doing, like dating, they'd be less likely to pity me. Let's face it, it doesn't matter how nice or smart a girl you are, if you don't have an appealing exterior, you start with a strike against you. Most people won't take the time to delve through the fat to get to your personality. Being overweight, I believed that I didn't stand a chance of enjoying a high school life competing with thin, prettier girls. Nazareth was the perfect corner for me to hide my body away, and that's what I did.

My first year at Nazareth Academy was one of learning how to survive the rules and the mounds of homework that they dished out every day. It wasn't a super strict school, you just had to remember rules such as, no crossing in the middle of a hall or at class changings. Everyone had to walk to their next class in single file, even though it could take forever if you had a class in the old building. If you broke any of the rules, you were issued a pink detention (DT) slip. Getting one meant that you had to stay after school and do some cleanup work. When I got my one and only DT during the second week of school, I felt like a social outcast and a menace to society. Somebody had left behind some garbage on our lunch table, so, the four of us who had used the table, got "pink" DT slips. Getting a DT was shattering to me, I took things very seriously and anything negative became an immediate crisis. My parents' unconditional love helped me survive such traumas during this period.

The Nazareth dress code for our freshman class turned out super. We got to be the first class to wear the new school uniform. During the first two years, previous classes were required to wear a navy-blue skirt, a white blouse and a navy-blue jacket. In their second two years, they were required to wear a similar outfit but with a gray tweed skirt and jacket. For footwear, everyone wore the ever-popular white bobby socks and black and white leather saddle shoes.

The new uniforms my class were required to wear were very modern looking. They consisted of the same white bobby socks and black and white leather saddle shoes and white blouse, but exchanged the jacket for a navy-blue wool blazer with a pocket and the skirt for a plaid wool skirt. For our next two years, we wore a brown wool blazer with a brown plaid skirt. If you won special award medals, you pinned them to the blazer's pocket. There were two other dress codes; you could not wear any makeup other than lipstick and, you could not roll up the waist of your skirt to make it shorter than it was supposed to be.

There were many fine teachers at Nazareth but there were also some clunkers. During my freshman year, all my teachers were excellent, except my gym teacher. She was a short, stocky woman with bulging leg muscles and a very short haircut almost like a man's crew cut. She was a loudmouth bully, who thought nothing of roundly ridiculing girls who couldn't do what she expected of them in gym. Of course, I was one of those ridiculed girls. I had gym twice a week and loathed it every time it rolled around. I was poor at everything in gym, so I always left gym class with my inferiority complex flag flying high. This teacher's treatment made me decide to try harder than ever to excel in my academic subjects. I studied so hard that I was on the Honor Roll for each of my four years at Nazareth! I wasn't the kind of pupil who could just sit in their seat and absorb the knowledge. It took long, hard hours of study to achieve my goals. At least, if I could excel in my studies, I would have something to be proud of myself about.

In my sophomore year, I had a couple of teachers who, to this day, stick in my mind as simply fabulous. My biology teacher, Sister Evangelista, seemed very strange to us at first. She wore very thick glasses that magnified her eyes to four times their normal size, making her look like a movie's mad scientist. She was an excellent teacher, if you made an effort to follow what she was saying. She'd go off on so many tangents during a lecture that your head would be spinning when you left her class. Most of the time she was very patient with us. When she had had enough of our nonsense, she knew how to dish out extra work to compensate for her aggravation. One of the things she, and we, enjoyed was taking us outside the school on field trips. During some of these walking journeys, she would stop to talk very fervently to trees. I began to think that she must have been leaning over a microscope so much her brain wasn't on an even keel at times.

Also, in my sophomore year, I had a Latin homeroom class with Mrs. Patzke, who had the reputation of being a scourge to her students. We all shook in our shoes on the first day in her room. She was a very firm lady but, to her homeroom class, she was like a second mother. We did all kinds of interesting things while in her class. One day, we held a classroom "white elephant" sale to help raise money for the Catholic missions around the world. For the Ides of March, the class decided that we would "bury Caesar." All of Mrs. Patzke's homeroom students hid in the vacant classroom next to ours when the bell rang to start class. Before Mrs. Patzke could figure out where we were, the entire class marched into the room wearing mourning arm bands. The last six girls carried a casket with the remains of Caesar in it. Some of the girls put on a play with the "Ides of March" theme and afterwards we had refreshments. It was a nutty idea but we all had fun doing it. Mrs. Patzke, good sport that she was, let us dress her in a toga and put a laurel wreath on her head. She was so impressed with how she looked that she wore the toga and laurel wreath for the rest of the day.

Finally, in my Sophomore year, believe it or not, gym class became bearable for me. My new gym teacher, Sister Lawrence, understood that not everybody is built to be an Olympic star. She was a very petite and vivacious lady. The first time I saw her, I thought it was funny to see a nun dressed in full habit, wearing tennis shoes and dribbling a basketball. Sister Lawrence knew that I was trying to do the best I could in her class, so she gave me, and others like me, credit, not ridicule, for doing that.

My sophomore year also included a living nightmare; Mark was sick with fever and vomiting again and he wasn't getting better this time. Every day he was weaker and weaker. One evening, when Dad came home from work, he found Mom really upset. Mark was acting in a strange, almost delirious way. When Dad took his temperature, it was 107 degrees! Mom and Dad quickly wrapped Mark in a blanket and rushed him to the hospital's emergency room.

When Dad told the emergency room nurse Mark's temperature, she said that our thermometer must be broken or Dad must have read it wrong. She took Mark's temperature and found it was, indeed, 107 degrees. She ran as fast as she could to get an ice bath tub ready for Mark. The nurse undressed him, laid him in the tub and began to pack ice around him. My parents watching her do this, were afraid that Mark would develop pneumonia from the ice. The nurse told them that her main objective was to get Mark's fever down so he would survive. Mom and Dad told Bill and me everything that had happened to Mark, when they finally came home at 3:00 a.m. They said that the ice melted as soon as the nurses put it on Mark because he was so hot. The ice had brought down his fever very quickly keeping him from going into convulsions.

Mom and Dad told us that what the doctor was the most concerned about now that the fever had subsided, was finding a vein to get intravenous fluids started. With Mark so dehydrated, the doctor couldn't find a vein that hadn't collapsed. The doctor and interns tried for hours to get an intravenous line going, sticking the needle everywhere in Mark with the hope of finding an non-collapsed vein. My parents said that Mark's body was now full of needle pricks. The doctors had even tried to find a vein in his forehead. After hours of failures, an intern found a vein in Mark's ankle. He had to cut into his foot to get at it but he saved Mark's life by doing so.

The intern was so happy, he was almost crying when he told Mom and Dad that Mark was out of danger. Mark now had intravenous fluids flowing through him like an expressway. The look of intense relief on parent's faces as they told us about what Mark had gone through and how happy they were that he would be okay, reflected how bad things had been. Suddenly Dad collapsed on the bed and cried his heart out. That tore all of us up, we hadn't seen him cry many times before. He just had to release the tension and emotion that was bottled up in him from all those hours at the hospital.

Mark had to stay in the hospital for five days, making our house kind of a joyless place without him. He had only been with us three years but he had planted an indelible mark on each of our hearts. The day he came home, I just couldn't wait to see him. When Mom carried him through the front door, I was shocked at how thin and weak he looked. His crib was in the living room and after being placed in it, he just lay very quietly in it. When he looked over and saw me, he got a big smile and tried to pull himself up. Even though he was thin and weak, he could still smile after all he'd been through. Mark was some tough little guy. I picked him up and hugged him tightly. I was so grateful that he was back home with us again.

Mark suffered long-term effects from that fever that caused him to be very slow to learn to talk. At three years old, what few words he did say were very unclear. Most of the time he used his own sign language to tell us what he wanted. Even when he started first grade, Mark was very difficult to understand. His teacher told us that Mark was such a wonderful little boy that the rest of the children in his class didn't make fun of his speech. Instead, they tried to understand what he was trying to tell them. Mark eventually went to a speech therapist who helped him tremendously in speaking correctly. To this day, Mark speech still carries traces of the damage that 107 degree fever inflicted on his two-year-old body.

CHAPTER 8

JUNIOR AND SENIOR POTPOURRI

I was now entering my junior year at Nazareth and nothing much had changed from the previous two years. The prospect of long hours of homework and endless hours of studying for tests seemed a permanent part of my life. I decided to take some general classes and drop some of the college preparatory classes. I had great grades and I knew that I could get into college if I wanted to. I just didn't feel that was what I wanted to do. The work at Nazareth had been so difficult for me that I figured college would be nearly impossible. I just couldn't imagine enduring another four years of such stress! I believed that, if I continued to do well at Nazareth, I could get a good job when I graduated. That job would allow me to pay my parents back for all the sacrifices they had made to send me to Nazareth.

The two general classes that I chose were Shorthand I and Business Typing I. I dropped Latin III and Algebra II. From the first day in Shorthand I, I knew that I loved it and would do well. My two years of Latin had trained my mind well for translation. I loved to transcribe shorthand, it was like translating code. Where Latin had been a 'dead' language; shorthand seemed a very contemporary and valuable language. Since I'm left handed, my shorthand never quite looked like anyone else's. My teacher, Mrs. Clime, was a terrific teacher and cheerleader. She told me that, if I could transcribe my shorthand, that was all that really mattered. Since I was always able to read what I had written, I had no problem throughout the school year.

Business Typing I was a completely different story. Thank goodness, I had Mrs. Clime for typing as well! It was with her unending encouragement that I finally got my fingers unfrozen and moving at 60 words per minute. Since beginning typing concentrates on learning which keys hold which letters, numbers and punctuation marks, then using them quickly, there were a lot of timed exercises. Every time we had a timed exercise, my fingers would freeze up and I would average about one word per minute. Another problem I had was positioning my fingers on the wrong keys to start with! When I'd look up after a timed exercise, thinking that I had finally gotten a good score, I would end up with a page of gibberish!

There were two other girls in the class with similar problems to mine, so we consoled each other. After one timing exercise, I looked back at my friend Pat. I saw her staring at ten typewriter keys all jammed together and not a single word typed on the page! When she saw me looking at her, we both broke down into a fit of laughter. We understood that these evil typewriters were our worst enemies! Mrs. Clime refused to let us give up. She kept telling us that all we needed was more confidence and less fear of the typewriter. She told us emphatically that, contrary to what we had heard, the typewriter would not eat our fingers off! With her strong encouragement, we all made it through her class with Bs and Cs.

When I was doing my shorthand homework, Mark thought it looked like great fun. Mom bought him a stenographer's notebook of his own and he would practice his own version of shorthand with me every night. He would sit for hours filling page after page with little chicken scratching's that only he could translate. He got so immersed into writing his shorthand that his chicken scratching began to appear everywhere. He would sneak it into my textbooks along the bottom of the pages. When I opened a textbook in class, I always knew Mark had been there because of his marks.

We added another unusual houseguest to our family menagerie about this time, Corky, a female raccoon. How we ended up with her was strange. My parents used to go to a drive-in named The Beacon for ice cream. Dad got friendly with the owners. One night they told Mom and Dad that they had a pet raccoon named Thelma. My parents were fascinated by the stories the couple told about Thelma. When the couple saw my parents interest, the owner said that he could get them a raccoon for a nominal fee. He would even build them a cage like their raccoon had. My parents decided that we really did need a raccoon to be able to enjoy a completely fulfilled life, so a deal was quickly struck.

When the drive-in owner talked about a cage, he really meant a cage! It was about 5 feet high, 3 feet wide and 6 feet long, which made it a major addition to our small house. My parents wrangled the cage into our dinette area and Corky joined our family. At the first she wasn't very sociable. Downright mean, would be much better words to describe her. The drive-in owner had told us that when she got used to us, she would let us pick him up. Apparently, Corky had never read that memo. We all had numerous bites applied to us when we did anything not to her liking. Even with her bad temperament, she was a beautiful animal and very interesting to watch, especially at dinner time. She'd wash anything Mom gave her in her water bowl before eating it. Her favorite food was fried chicken even though the breading would get very soggy underwater. Her favorite treat, by far, was vanilla wafers. It was hilarious watching her wash the wafers in her water bowl. Her paws would get all sticky and the water would turn to vanilla mush. Whatever she managed to get into her mouth she really enjoyed.

Corky loved to play with Mark's hair. Mom would push Mark's high chair near the cage then Mark would put his head down on the tray. Corky would reach her humanlike paws through the wire of the cage and try to touch Mark's hair. It looked like Corky was shampooing Mark's hair, especially when she had the remains of vanilla wafers on her paws. It was tough getting a comb through Mark's hair after one of Cory's vanilla "shampoos."

We only had Corky for a year. I guess she didn't get the exercise she needed to keep her body in shape. She would always sleep in a barrel that was built into the back of her cage. One morning, when we checked on her, she wouldn't come out of her barrel. On closer inspection, we found that she had died during the night. Even though Corky had lived with us a short time, we had accumulated a year's worth of happy memories of her.

My junior year at Nazareth included two major events that anyone living through them would never forget. I was in shorthand class, when the P.A. system came on. The principal announced that the President of the United States, John F. Kennedy, had been shot while riding in a motorcade in Dallas, Texas! This shocked every one of us to our roots. We all prayed that the President had only been wounded. It just seemed to us that a person as young and vital as President Kennedy should be invincible and nothing should hurt him. About a half an hour later, the P.A. came on again, this time the principal announced in a shaken voice that President John F. Kennedy had died in Dallas from an assassin's bullets. The entire class went silent, we were all numb and shaken after hearing this dreadful news. Several girls had their heads down and were crying. That day in La Grange, Illinois, was windy, dark and rainy, it seemed that even the day was mourning the President's death.

Over the years many stories have been reported about President Kennedy suggesting that he was far from a saint and had hidden health problems. That never mattered to me, during his presidency, he brought a new surge of patriotism and love of country to everyone. The American people, as a whole, had fallen in love with all the doings of this young first family who lived in the *New Camelot*. Many of us felt that John F. Kennedy's tragic assassination swept away a source of vigor and enthusiasm that our country truly needed

The worldwide music phenomenon that started just months after this tragedy was something that helped lift our spirits. It was a "mania" that swept over people of all ages all over the world. It wasn't just a passing fad, it was a movement that would influence our lives and music for years to come. That "mania" was the British Music Invasion, and the chief purveyors of it were The Beatles. They sure infused a new excitement into my life. Since I had always felt an "outsider" to other things teen, I could now be an "insider" by becoming involved in Beatles Fever. And involved I became, collecting everything about my new loves that I could get my hot little hands on. I bought Beatles trading cards, dolls, magazines, records, posters, and I made a scrapbook of articles covering my four mop tops. I felt like I was a part of something historic and legendary. By keeping up with every aspect of their lives, I shared the excitement of their exploding careers. My fondest dream, like thousands of other girls, was to marry one of the Beatles and become the envy of every girl worldwide. That would have been a sweeping change in my life since no one ever envied me for anything other than my good grades. The Beatles made me feel good about myself, that I was a normal teenager, who could "go bananas" over somebody just as easily as anyone else my age.

As I entered Senior year, I became less tense and worried over homework and tests. The quantity of homework had gone down and most of my teachers weren't to be taken seriously anyway. I had a sociology homeroom where the nun, Sister Carol, taught with a two-track mind. The first track covered condemnation of Communists and Communism. The second track covered the plight of black persons in America. The two subjects were, in themselves, very worthwhile to study, however, they got kind of boring after enduring her repeated rather shallow coverage for nine months. We knew that other things had to be encompassed in sociology, unfortunately, we never got to learn what they were.

The other nun who I would have given a one-point rating to that year was Sister Julianna, who I had for both Shorthand II and Typing II. She had it in for me from my first day. She didn't care for the way I wrote my shorthand, no matter what Mrs. Clime thought, so she gave me tons of extra homework to "cure" my left-handed problem. She told me that it didn't matter how well I could transcribe, she would never give me an A in shorthand unless I did it her way. I was extremely frustrated after having such a wonderful teacher for the first year of my clerical classes. I knew that I would have to go with the tide, do the best I could and maybe she would soften, nope. No matter how fast I took shorthand or how accurately I could transcribe it, she always gave me a B. On the last day of school, when she gave me my 120 words per minute certificate, she told me that my shorthand hadn't improved one iota since my first day of her class. That hurt but I knew that Mrs. Clime would have been proud of me and I was proud of myself.

It's very difficult for a child to go through class everyday knowing that her teacher has no appreciation or respect for her. I firmly believe that many teachers have no idea how much their attitude towards a child can influence his or her ability to learn and to fit comfortably into society. If children have teachers who treat them poorly it is easy to see why other children might contribute to it, making the child's life painful and their self-esteem very low. I was fortunate that I only had one teacher like that to contend with for two hours a day, five days a week for nine months of school.

As I approached my eighteenth birthday with high school graduation looming over me, my parents finally realized that they were getting older right along with me. Dad had gone to the dentist and had lost a couple teeth that affected his smile. Mom had to have an abscessed eyetooth pulled so her smile was not the same as before either. Dad decided that they needed to find a place that could make them replacement teeth either inexpensively or just down right cheap. A man who Dad worked with recommended a Japanese dentist's name and told Dad to try him. Dad called him, the price was right, so we piled into our car one Saturday and headed into Chicago. We drove around for a while (did I fail to mention Dad wasn't so hot with directions?) until Dad finally located the dentist's office. When we entered, the office resembled a large closet with tooth enamel dust piled deep on everything. The dentist was very short and had an accent as thick as his glasses. Dad wasn't so sure this was the guy he wanted to fix his teeth, so he sent Mom to the chair first to have a mold made for her new tooth.

Everything went smoothly for Mom and within minutes he had made a mold of her tooth and had matched her tooth color. When Dad saw this, he developed renewed courage and marched right over to the chair that Mom had vacated. Dad needed a bridge with four teeth so his work was a bit more involved than Mom's. The dentist mixed up a new batch of molding plaster and put it in Dad's mouth. When the plaster dried, he tried to remove it and found it wouldn't budge. Dad's eyes widened as he began to get panicky. The dentist pulled and tugged with all his might but the mold still would not come out. The dentist, all 4'-6" and 110 pounds of him, then climbed on Dad's lap and began to tug frantically on the cast while saying it was just a little stuck. Since the office was also the waiting room, we could see all the goings on. We began to have difficulty breathing and seeing, we were laughing and crying so hard. It was like a scene out of a *Three Stooges* short! Suddenly, the mold, with the dentist attached, came flying out of Dad's mouth. Dad's eyes were streaming tears too, just not from laughter. After he calmed down, Dad blustered that he had never been worried. Right! We all knew that that was one big whopper! The dentist had their teeth ready in a couple of weeks and they were very well made for the price. After that, every time I saw Dad's new toothy smile, I would grin remembering what he had gone through to get it.

During this time, Mark's health held pretty well. He continued to have fevers and vomiting, but nothing like what had hospitalized him before. There was, however, someone else whose health we had to be concerned. This time it was Mom, she was having terrible stomach pains. She got some temporary relief from taking Alka-Seltzer but then the pains would return as severe as before. Finally, Dad insisted that she see a doctor. The x-rays the doctor ordered showed that she had a stomach ulcer.

Mom always seemed to have little resistance to any germ or virus, perhaps because of the pneumonia she had when she was sixteen years old. Grandma had told me that her doctor didn't think she would survive it. She did because of the doctor's use of a new drug, Penicillin. After that illness, Grandma told me that Mom had never been the same physically. She couldn't gain weight and she always tired easily. When I was very young, Mom had had to go into the hospital for a bladder infection. Relatives on Dad's side began gossiping that she had cancer, but, it was a bladder infection and nothing more. Every time she would catch a cold from us kids, it would go directly to her lungs, causing them to fill up with phlegm, making it difficult for her to breathe. Every time she got these terrible colds, we were all feared that she might not have the strength to fight it off this time.

Mom had also suffered through a very difficult delivery with Bill. He was turned the wrong way and the doctor had a very difficult time maneuvering him into the right position for delivery. Dad and her doctor had been afraid that they were going to lose both of them. Mom had also suffered over the years from infected fingers, infected eyes, a broken toe, and abscessed teeth. When she went to a dentist to have teeth removed, he administered gas that made her sick for a while. She never seemed to win at the health game, now a stomach ulcer was the newest health issue to hit her.

Her doctor put her on a special diet, so we decided that we would all go on it to make it easier on her. For the first week, all she could have was a poached egg, pudding, Jell-O, and milk. After a few of days on that diet, it was beginning to become mighty hard for us to look a poached egg in the eye. It was worth it though because Mom was feeling so much better. Mom was still sick as my high school graduation approached. We didn't go out to dinner to celebrate but came home and had, you guessed it, poached eggs, pudding, Jell-O, and milk. This selection of food for my graduation celebration made the day even more memorable for my entire family.

All of the suffering that Mom had endured, with as much dignity as possible, made me admire her that much more. She had had a hard life, both physically and emotionally, but she managed to survive whatever came along and not lose her sense of humor. She was never afraid to do something new that might help us. She reminded me of an octopus with far reaching tentacles. Even though you could always find her at home, she had the skill to reach out to us far beyond the house. Dad was the doer but she always provided the strength that pushed him along. It seemed that she could convince anyone to do anything even if they didn't want to. I just couldn't argue with her logic. She seemed always able to come up with solutions to our problems, even when I didn't think she understood them. I could always come to her with my problems, and I was always better for having talked with her about them. Sometimes, thinking of all that she went through in her life, I feel ashamed of myself for complaining about anything.

Now that I was a high school graduate, I was looking forward to getting a job. However, before going job hunting, there was something else I wanted to do even more. Bill and I had purchased $5 grandstand tickets to see my Beatles "Live in Concert" at Comiskey Park, Chicago, Illinois, on August 20, 1964! You cannot imagine how excited I was to be able to see my idols in person! When the big day finally arrived, Dad drove Bill and me to Comiskey Park, dropping us off in one of the parking lots. It's hard to describe the feeling of raw electricity that crackled in the air over the park. I swelled with pride when I saw the vast number of people that were jammed into this place to hear "my" Beatles sing. I had made sure to bring my trusty camera (with film, phew), so I could record, what was surely going to be "the most thrilling day of my life." Bill and I weren't exactly sure where our seats would be, but we were hoping they would be good. Our hopes were dashed as an usher led us up flight after flight of stairs. When we were finally shown our seats, we were so high that it was hard not to get a nosebleed from the altitude! It was almost impossible to see what was happening out on the field, and the music playing from the stage P.A. was unintelligible with all the yelling and screaming from the waiting audience.

Since we had arrived almost two and a half hours before the concert, Bill and I had a long, tiresome wait sitting on hard wooden bleachers. It was terrible what sacrifices one had to make to see the ones you love. With each passing minute, the excitement and screaming grew as fast as the incoming hordes of people. When some "nut" started a rumor that the Beatles were in the helicopters that were circling the field, everyone in the stands began screaming louder and waving insanely. I guess the "nut" reasoned that they couldn't get the Beatles into the park any other way. No one knew if it was true or not, but just in case, I waved frantically along with everyone else in the waiting horde.

It seemed like an eternity before someone came out on the stage to the start the show. First, a group of go-go dancers came out to dance to the music of the King Curtis Band. They were good, but not the reason we all came. They were on for thirty long minutes and then, an instrumental group from England, the Sounds Inc., mounted the stage. It was getting more exciting, at least, they were from the same country as the Beatles, but again not what everyone was waiting. This was torture, pure and simple torture!

Then, the moment I had been waiting for arrived, four ant-sized, human beings, and their escorts, scurried across the field to the stage waving to the crowd. Even though I couldn't tell for sure, I knew it was "them." No other persons on earth have ever gotten a standing ovation like they got from the start of their act to the end. The park was in total chaos. Berserk girls ran onto the field only to be caught by security guards, who bodily carried them away. With the constant screaming of thousands of girls, you could only catch a couple of words from a song before the Beatles voices were completely drowned out. It wasn't important for me to hear them sing, I had listened to their songs thousands of times. I was sent to heaven just hearing a few words in their actual live voices.

When the concert ended, it left me with a feeling like a balloon emptied of air. We fans had given our all to our idols, there wasn't any more we could give. We started to slowly move towards the exits with hoarse voices and aching ears, it was wonderful. It took us about an hour and a half to finally immerge from the bleachers and another hour to locate my parents and get the car moving. We saw license plates from all over the country, and loads of buses, station wagons, and trucks with signs in their windows saying "Beatles or Bust." This concert would be a part of each attendee's life that would never be forgotten. Believe me, I never will! I still love you, my Beatles.

CHAPTER 9
FAT AIN'T WHERE IT'S AT!

Now that I had met with my Beatles, I was ready to go out and conquer the business world. I knew I wouldn't have any problem getting a job, I had been on the Honor Roll for four years, I had four years of perfect attendance and I had superb Typing and Shorthand proficiency certificates. I marched out into the world with my head held high in utmost confidence, only to quickly return feeling confused and rejected.

A few weeks before graduation, the senior class took numerous tests for job placement. One of these was for Civil Service jobs. Since everyone was talking about how great a Civil Service job was, I was really hoping that I would get a call for an interview. After a couple of weeks, the Personnel Department at Hines Veterans Hospital in Maywood, Illinois, did call asking me to come in for an interview upon graduation. I was ecstatic, I was an avid fan of Ben Casey and Dr. Kildare. To work in a hospital would be exciting and rewarding, even if I only got to work in the office. At least I would be close to each day's life and death dramas. I was sure that I would get the job, if I could overcome one slight problem, how to get there for the interview. Our family only had Dad's go-to-work car, and, since Nazareth didn't have a driver's education class, I had never been taught how to drive. I was going crazy trying to figure out how I would find a way to get to Hines. The personnel manager told me that once I started I could probably join a car pool to and from work, but that didn't solve how to get there for the interview.

As always, when faced with such a dilemma, I did the only rational thing possible, I dumped the whole problem in Dad's lap. Dad said that there must be a bus to Hines, so he would find the one I should take. One night after supper he set out to forge a trail to Hines Hospital for me. He said that he would leave his car at home and try to get to Hines using only the bus system. He left about 5:00 p.m. saying that he would be back soon. Boy, was he ever wrong!

Hours had passed and he still hadn't returned home. We were beginning to worry about him when, at about 11:00 p.m., he came through the front door. He looked totally wiped out but was carrying a dozen bus schedules. He told us that he had begun to fear that he would never get home. He went on to say that there was just no way to get to Hines by bus from La Grange. He had learned that you had to take three buses whose conflicted schedules made it nearly impossible to make connections. The second bus arrived five minutes "before" the first bus arrived, so you had to wait for the next bus. That bus would arrive ten minutes "after" the third bus had left, so you had to wait for the next bus. In winter, it would be nearly impossible to stand in the cold waiting to make all the connections. I was disappointed. I had figured that Dad would fix the bus schedules for me just as he had done at St. Cletus years before. I was learning that my parents could not make the impossible happen. They tried to make it okay by telling me that there would be many jobs that I could interview for closer to home. I felt sure that they were right because I had worked so hard in high school to be able to get a good job afterwards.

The next tactic I employed in looking for a job was to scan the neighborhood newspapers for jobs available in the local area. I must have gone to around twenty-five businesses asking to interview for jobs they had advertised. The excuse they used for not interviewing or hiring me was that I didn't have work experience. How could I get work experience if they wouldn't even give me a chance to get some! No one would even offer to give me a chance to work for one day to gain experience. What I still didn't realize was that my personal appearance wasn't conducive to what employers were looking for. After so many near immediate rejections it became obvious to me that they would have hired a girl with half my office skills if she was thin and pretty. My weight was the thing that made my appearance less than pleasing to them. My parents tried to boost my morale, but that was getting harder to do. Dad kept saying that he could get me a job in the office at Mutual Trucking where he worked if I wanted him to. At that moment that was the last thing that I wanted. For once, I wanted to do something on my own and be independent. I wanted to get my own job, but I certainly wasn't getting anywhere. I had a long way to go to learn how to fit into the "real" world outside of high school and home.

After a couple months looking for a job on my own to no avail, I decided to go to an employment agency. The one I picked was in an office above the La Grange movie theatre. It was named Aldridge Personnel. I talked with a woman on the phone who sounded very nice and encouraging, she told me to come right in. When I arrived, I was surprised to see that she was a large woman with bleached blonde hair who weighed around 300 pounds. She was friendly to me and right now in my life, I really needed some friendliness. She told me that her name was Kay, that she and her brother operated the agency. She told me that she would find me a job and it would be close to home. I left her office on top of the world! I went home all pumped up, expecting a short wait before job interview offers would come rolling in. After not hearing from Kay for two weeks, I called her. She said that she still working on it but didn't have anything for me right now. She told me to be patient that something would turn up soon.

Three long months crawled by, during which not one thing ever turned up for me. When I called Kay again, she said that she did have one job available as counter help for Ma and Pa's Old-Fashioned Candies. I almost flipped out, was this the type of job that I had been preparing myself for during my four, long, hard years at Nazareth? Being as desperate as I was, I went to the store to fill out an application only to find that, unbelievably, I couldn't even get a job like that.

That night I went back the paper and found an ad for help wanted at the local nursing home. What caught my eye was that it said "NO EXPERIENCE REQUIRED." I knew that I had plenty of that, so I decided to try for an interview and I got one! I was impressed, they gave me an actual interview with salary even discussed. This was something very new for me, I had never gotten this far in any interview. Previously, after taking one look at me, everyone told me that the job had already been filled, that it had never existed or that I didn't have the experience to do it. At the end of this interview, the woman told me that I was hired! I almost fell out of my chair! She explained to me about the uniforms I would need and handed me a questionnaire with 25 questions pertaining to medical subjects. She told me that she needed to understand how much basic medical knowledge I had. The first question was, "What is a normal temperature?" I knew that right off, so I was confident that I would continue to do well. When I got to question #20, "How would you prepare a body for embalming?" I froze up. I hadn't thought about death being a large part of such a job. I had been solely thinking that the job would encompass my untiring nursing devotion to the patients who lived there. Seeing my perplexed look, the woman made it clear to me that, since nursing home patients were usually very old, death was a near everyday occurrence and I must be prepared to deal with it calmly and rationally.

I thought about question #20 all the way home. By the time I arrived there, I had decided that this just was not the job for me. I was not ready to prepare a body for embalming in any way, shape or form! It was not a subject studied in a Catholic girls high school (or public ones as far as I knew) and I was glad that it wasn't. All that night I tossed and turned from recurring nightmares involving bodies covered with white sheets lying on tables, each waiting patiently in line for me to make them ready for embalming. Even to a seasoned horror movie fan, it sounded awful! The effect of this interview was to focus my job search to typing and shorthand jobs only, leaving the nursing of people, alive or dead, to those who could handle it.

Time had passed so quickly during my searching that I suddenly realized I had been looking for employment for eight months! I had had such confidence in Kay Aldridge, I couldn't believe she had let me down. One day a policeman friend of Dad's told him that Kay and her brother had left La Grange because they couldn't pay the rent on their office. After hearing this, I felt that I had no luck in picking anything. Out of all the employment agencies, I picked the one that was a fraud.

I decided to try to find a more reputable agency. The one I picked was located above the La Grange Federal Bank. I figured that being located over a bank made it more reputable than one located over a movie theater. This agency was run by a woman and her female assistant. The assistant gave me typing and shorthand tests before I could speak to the boss, on her return from lunch. Upon the bosses' return her assistant told her that I had done exceptionally well on the tests. The boss asked me to come into her office where she began to rip me apart. She told me that she was pleased with my skills but not with my appearance. She said that before she could send me on a job interview, I would have to wear better fitting clothes and have my hair done. Next, she made a call to Kemper Life Insurance in Chicago, told them about my skills and, also, that I was overweight. When she finished the call, she said they wanted to meet me, despite my weight. If they decided to hire me, they would work with me to help me lose weight.

Leaving her office after all of that, I felt the lowest that I had ever felt. She ended my interview by telling me, in no uncertain terms, what she thought was wrong with me. She said that they didn't normally handle "riffraff," but my skills were excellent and she didn't want to pass up a potential job placement commission. All the way home on the bus, I cried. I was in the pit of despair.

When I arrived home, I told Mom what had been said to me. She got extremely angry saying to forget about Kemper, if they didn't want me the way I was then they could go hire a model with no skills.

Mom called Dad to tell him what had happened and he was just as angry. He told Mom that he would talk to the boss of the business across the street from where he worked and call right back. His return call came very quickly saying that they had an immediate opening for a secretary. If I wanted to interview for the job, he would bring me in the next day. The boss told Dad that he would give me a one-day trial and then decide if he wanted me to stay. When Dad came home that night and told me, I felt depressed and uncomfortable that I needed his intervention to get even a trial job, but I just had to get a job.

Mom said that at least I wouldn't have to worry about transportation. If I got the job, I could ride to and from work with Dad every day. She said it was great that they were giving me a trial day. At least, it offered me a chance to gain one day's work experience. After all her attempts to convince me, I decided to go with Dad. I still wasn't at all happy about it, I had had my hopes up so many times before and nothing had come true. I decided that I would be very nonchalant about the whole thing and maybe things would turn out different this time. At 6:00 a.m. on a Thursday morning in February, I woke to go to my first day of real work. I was very nervous and anxious and the weather didn't help to ease my fears. It was a typical Chicago February day, dreary with a light drizzle falling and a cold clamminess that penetrated to your very bones. With the morning so dark, it seemed that I was getting up in the middle of the night. I didn't really care about any of that, I just wanted this job to work out for me.

I dressed carefully and met Dad at the front door. Mom kissed us both goodbye and we were on our way. It was something different for Dad to have a passenger riding with him to and from work. I think that he expected that I would give him some company during the long ride into the City, he was wrong. I just sat next to him like a mannequin. It was way too early in the morning for me to manage much of a conversation, so the ride was very quiet. Instead we both just listened to the car radio, which was enough to put me back to sleep. Dad had always listened to a radio station playing soft '40s and '50s music for years. It was very quiet and soothing, but hardly the type of fare to wake you up in the morning. I started thinking to myself that if I ended up riding with him every day, he would have to change his listening habits and get some life into his music.

About 45 minutes later, we arrived on South Wabash Avenue in Chicago. Dad told me that a friend's daughter had just started working at Bosler Supply Company, where I was going to put in my trial day. He said that she would show me the ropes there. She also drove in with her father, who, along with my Dad, started work at Mutual Truck Parts at 7:30 a.m. I wasn't scheduled to start until 8:00 a.m., so I had a lot of time to kill. When we parked at Mutual, a young woman walked over to our car and introduced herself as Mary. I wasn't quite sure about her. Mary's hair was disheveled and she was wearing about ten pounds of makeup. However, she was very friendly and seemed to have a good sense of humor. She sat with me in Dad's car, while we were waiting for 8:00 a.m. to roll around, pointing out Bosler Supply Company across the street from us.

Mary told me that Bosler was a hardware and mill supply jobber that distributed products for the biggest names in hardware, tools, and paints. Bosler looked like all of the other buildings in this industrial section of South Side Chicago, old and decrepit. Mixed among the many companies along South Wabash Avenue were several condemned buildings and a mammoth low-income housing high rise. It was not the best of neighborhoods. I was hoping that the interior of Bosler would be much nicer than its exterior.

Mary told me that it was time to go in, that Frank, the head of accounting, had just opened the front door. I looked at the building with mixed emotions, swallowed my fears and followed Mary through the front door. From the foyer, there was a long staircase leading to the office area. I was told by Marie, the switchboard operator, to have a seat until the personnel manager arrived. That gave me a chance to take in my surroundings and the people already there. The main office looked just as old as the buildings on South Wabash Avenue. The wooden desks were antiques with knobs and handles missing, drawers that had been stuck for years, and thousands of scratches to show their years of use. The mechanical typewriters looked like they were of World War II vintage. Down a short hallway on the right were three offices. The first office was the president's, the second the personnel manager's and the third was shared by the company's two vice-presidents. Reading the names on the doors, I noticed that three out of the four carried the same last name, "Hecktman."

At last the personnel manager arrived and asked me to come with him. His name was Mr. Neidorf. He was in his early fifties and had a head of solid gray hair. He scared me a little, he seemed so stern and abrupt. He asked me where I went to high school and the speeds on my typing and shorthand. He told me that I would work for one day. Another applicant was coming in the next day for the same one-day trial. He dictated a letter to me and sent me to an empty desk to type it. The ancient mechanical typewriter I had to use was unbelievable. I couldn't set the margins and the keys were all out of alignment. After ruining five sheets of paper, I finally typed a letter that looked halfway decent and gave it to Mr. Neidorf. I had typed everything correctly except his name, which didn't add to my confidence (or his). Next, he gave me about 5,000 pink order copies to sort into numerical order. I was kind of disappointed, I thought that a secretary's job would be a bit more glamorous than this.

Before long, Mary came to my desk to let me know that it was time for our morning break. During that break, I got to meet some of Bosler's employees and to learn the company's history. Two Jewish men, Abe Belsky and Nathan Hecktman, had founded Bosler in the early 1900s, to make and sell leather goods such as horse collars. When horse collars became obsolete, Bosler expanded its line to include industrial and mill supplies. When Abe Belsky died, the entire company moved into the hands of Hecktman family. Nathan (Nate) Hecktman, the surviving partner, was now the full owner and Mr. Neidorf, the personnel manager, was his brother-in-law. The two vice-presidents were Jordon Hecktman (Nate's son) and Mac Hecktman (Nate's brother). Bosler was a Jewish family-owned and run business. When first meeting other Bosler employees, the first thing they asked me was who in the family I was related to, believing I must be Jewish.

Although most of the bosses were Jewish, most the employees were not. Frank Abbot, a short, thin, 50-year-old man with bushy hair, was the head of the accounting department. Margaret, who worked for Frank in accounting, was a very thin, blonde about the same age as Frank but with the nervous energy of a twenty-year-old. She and Frank had both worked at Bosler for over twenty years. Dave, Merle, and Gerry were all newcomers to the accounting department. Dave was a married man in his 30s. Merle was a single man in his 20s, who was working on a new data-phone system for Bosler. Gerry was a young woman in her early 20s, who was getting married in a couple months. Gerry had gotten her job at Bosler because her mother was Mr. Neidorf's housekeeper.

In the office area where I was working, there were several other people. Kathy was a short, chubby girl in her 20s who had a very short temper and a big mouth that was constantly spewing gripes. Ida and Etta were Jewish women in their 50s. Ida had only been with Bosler for a few months, joining after her husband passed away. I liked Ida immediately, she was very friendly and helpful to me. Etta worked part-time. She would come in when the filing piled up too high. Marie had been Bosler's switchboard operator for twenty years, so she knew everything there was to know about Bosler and its employees. She lived in a south suburb not far from La Grange, so we hit it off right away. Marty was a young man of 18 going on 35, who worked in the billing department for Bill Lasky. Marty was a good person but had had so many problems as a child, that he had a bleeding ulcer by 16. Emil was an older man who worked with Marty and did more complaining than work.

Bill Lasky seemed like a very strict and uncompromising person but, if you did your work, you got no grief from Bill! If you did not, there was a good chance that you would be seeing the door very quickly. Bill had been with Bosler for twenty years and he had lots of pull with the bosses. That first day I almost committed a major lunchtime faux pas, which someone saved me from, I sat down in Bill Lasky's chair at the lunch table! That would have really gotten me off to a good start with Bill!

Bosler's lunchroom was just OK. It included a big table with chairs and candy and soda machines. If you pulled up the room's brittle, yellow window shades to look through the grimy windows, you were treated to a view of trash strewn South Wabash Avenue with all its bums and derelicts. The office coffee was provided from a rented, drip coffee maker that was also in the lunchroom. Employees could buy a cup of joe for a nickel. Of course, the women were assigned to oversee making the coffee. Sometimes, the men who worked downstairs, would sneak up to the lunchroom mid-morning and make more coffee. This was not kosher, so to speak, so a sign had been placed by the coffee maker declaring that "Only authorized personnel," namely the women, could make the coffee.

My first day of work dragged on as I continued to sort the pink purchase orders. When 5:00 p.m. rolled around, Mr. Neidorf came to tell me that I could come in again the next day. I thanked him and told him that I liked it at Bosler. As it turned out, I stayed there far longer than those two days. When I finally left Bosler, I had worked there for over three years. Dad would periodically remind me that I should have asked him for job finding help from the start. He would smile and say, "Don't lift your hood and cuss, call us!!"

As time passed at Bosler, I also got to meet most of the men working downstairs, the "inside salesmen." They worked with our "outside salesmen" and customers. They were a friendly bunch with good senses of humor. Since it would take many pages to cover all of them, I will just tell you about the more interesting ones.

Bosler had an order counter downstairs where customers could walk in off-the-street and buy hardware or paint. Leo was the nutty guy who oversaw the counter. Dad had known him for many years, as he did most of the old timers at Bosler. When Dad and Leo got together, the squirrels would come out to gather the nuts. Leo was in his 40s and very small in stature. He had combed back black hair, an "always" tan, a big nose and was a major practical joker. If one of the guys downstairs found a screwdriver in his sandwich, he knew exactly who had put it there.

Another person who brought laughs to Bosler was "Flash," named so because he dashed around so much. He always had a bunch of papers in his hand, so you never knew if he was working or just fooling around. He was bald and looked exactly like the old-time comedian, Ben Blue. Flash oversaw the inside salesmen, the shipping room and all kinds of catalogs and price lists. If a good customer wanted to buy a TV, he could come to Flash. Flash would give him a contact at a company where he would receive the cheapest price. Flash was a ladies' man. Where there was a group of women, Flash was always in their midst.

A few weeks after I started fulltime, Bosler had a mystery to deal with. Someone had thrown Dykem steel blue dye all over the inside salesmen's wash-room. The bosses were very worried. Since very few people would work in this kind of neighborhood, they had to hire who they could and most of the time they weren't very good. Many of the men working in the shipping room had been in jail at least once. Mr. Neidorf had always tried to observe new employees until he was sure they could be trusted, so this incident made him very nervous. He felt that things could only get worse, the person doing this might be a "nutcase." The bosses decided that a lie detector should be brought in to attempt to catch the culprit before something more terrible happened. So, one morning the lie detector was brought in and all the inside salesmen had to take the test. After an entire day of testing, they found that the man responsible for throwing the dye was a recently hired black man. He was immediately fired and so ended the case of the "Blue Phantom." It was kind of exciting, like being involved in a Perry Mason case.

After a short time at Bosler, I became VP Jordon Hecktman's personal sec-retary. Jordan was 36, tall, prematurely bald and very good looking. He was the firm hand at Bosler, so much of the managing duties had moved to him. With his rise to prominence came the rejuvenation of Bosler. He had originally considered moving Bosler to a "better" location, but most of the employees said they wouldn't move with the company. Further, a move away from the South Wabash Avenue location would mean the potential loss of the Bosler's Chicago Loop customers, who took advantage of Bosler's close proximity to purchase from them. With all of this in mind, Jordon decided that he would do better for the Bosler by just updating the business in its present location. He started by having the office area paneled and bringing in new desks and typewriters. I got a new Selectric typewriter, which made typing beautiful. Next, he ordered changes to the downstairs, breaking through walls to enlarge the warehouse area. Also, with the introduction of the data-phone department, more and more customers wanted to use the system because it made their paperwork and ordering much easier.

The Bosler building contained many little rooms that were used for storage, especially the third floor, which was filled with junk and old files. When one of the office women had to visit the third floor to look something up, someone else had to go along for protection. Mary and I usually went together, not staying too long, because it was spooky. Morrie told me that in the early days, Bosler's third floor was mostly rental apartments. Now the only tenant left was Joe "the Janitor" and his wife. Joe was in his 80s and could barely walk, so he wasn't much of a janitor. He would come down to the office once a week to argue with Mr. Neidorf over some minute repair. Mr. Neidorf would always give him time no matter how busy he was. On his return trip to his apartment, Joe would always stop to talk to me. He said that I reminded him of his first wife, who was fat like me. It didn't sound like a compliment to me, but to Joe it was. He told me that his first wife had been the greatest person in the world and he missed her very much. He told me that his current, third wife, was "no good!" I guess he was right, whenever I saw them together, they did nothing but argue. The arguing mostly was because Joe's wife was jealous of Marie, believing that she was trying to take Joe away from her. She must have been senile, because none of us ladies saw much to be jealous about in Joe.

As I got to know Mr. Neidorf, I got to like and respect him more and more. His abruptness was just his manner, he really cared for those who worked for him. He was a constant "nibbler" and his doctor was always yelling at him to stop eating so much. Bosler had several customers who manufactured candy, so he always had the drawers of his desk filled with bubble gum and chocolate bars. He always ate well until it was time for his doctor's appointment, then he would fast all that day. When he returned from the doctor, he would immediately start nibbling again. Once he came to my desk and asked me if I had anything to eat because he was starving. I took the cookies out of my lunch bag and gave them to him. He loved them. From then on, he gave me money to keep a supply of the cookies on hand, but I wasn't supposed to tell him where they were. I was only to give him two a day and that was all. He was so funny about the cookies. If he noticed where I had them hidden, he would tell me to find a new place to hide them. He had absolutely no willpower when it came to eating. He was always under a lot of stress, didn't smoke, so he had to do something with his nervous energy.

Speaking of eating and weight, after four months of working at Bosler, I had lost ten pounds from all the running up and down the stairs that I had done. I wondered what would happen if I cut down on some of my food. I told Mom to pack a lunch for me with only dessert. It was always easy to give dessert away and I had to take something in a bag for lunch or I would never hear the end of it from Dad. He never cared how I looked as long as I wasn't hungry. I never ate breakfast and now I was eliminating lunch, so I was anxious to see what the result would be. It could be the beginning of a whole new life for me. I never knew how it felt to weigh less than 200 pounds or wear a dress smaller than a size 20.

As the weeks passed, I became more and more a part of the Bosler "family." When I started, many people had been standoffish towards me. As I worked at Bosler longer and longer, I began to understand why they were. They didn't want to spend time getting to know you until they knew that you weren't an employee who was just passing through. Bosler, like other companies, had a pretty high employee turnover, many employees only worked there for a day or a week and then were gone. As everyone got to know me, I got to know much more about them. My growing relationships with others was made much easier when it became known that I was Chuck Rissky's daughter. Dad was an institution on South Wabash Avenue, it seemed that everyone knew him and liked him. He had been coming over to Bosler for many years to purchase tools for Mutual Trucking, so the "old timers" at Bosler had known him for years.

With my wider acceptance came more and more responsibility. I had started as Jordan's secretary, but since I was the only one in the office who could take dictation, I became secretary to anyone who needed one. Thank goodness everyone didn't need one at the same time. Besides my secretarial duties, Mr. Neidorf asked me to learn how to operate the switchboard, so I could relieve Marie for breaks and lunch. That unnerved me a bit because I was just getting used to answering the phone on my own desk without stuttering. Now they wanted me to take care of calls that could result in business for the company. I had grown very friendly with Marie, so she was happy to teach me the board and told me not to be nervous. She knew by now that I would be staying at Bosler for a while, so teaching me would not be in vain, as it had been so many times before.

It didn't take me long to realize that, if I kept my head while on the board, everything would be all right. I gradually became more and more confident. I learned to recognize the voices of callers from various companies and to route them to the appropriate salesman downstairs. While most callers were generally the same people, Marie taught me who were VIPs and who should not be kept waiting. At this point, I still had not yet met Mac Hecktman, Bosler's key salesman. He was currently on vacation but rarely came in to the office when he was working anyway. I just knew second-hand of his demand for perfection. When he did come into the office, everything switched to fast forward. When I wrote up his telephone messages, I had to make sure that I wrote down the return telephone number, he always dialed his return calls himself. He was a wonderful salesman and vice-president for the company. He was kind and friendly, if, things were done the way he wanted them done. I got along well with Mac during the time I worked at Bosler, I always tried to please and he recognized my effort.

My big test at Bosler came when Marie went on vacation, I was to be on the board fulltime. I made up my mind that I would do the job flawlessly. The days flew by because the board was constantly active. I was drained by the end of each day from the constant concentration and pressure to get callers through or to get their messages written down. I grew more positive that I would make it for the two weeks, then the office air conditioning broke down. I had to sit all day in a small corner with the switchboard, feeling like I would die from heat prostration. It was over 100 degrees in the office and any windows that could be opened didn't get air to me. I was beginning to wonder if I would survive. Obviously, I did survive but after a day like that, I was glad to hand the board back into Marie's keeping. I had proven that I could do it but I had no interest in handling the board full time. Marie's job was safe!

From my first day at Bosler, I learned that there were two groups of women in the office; the older ladies in one group and the younger ladies in another. Mary, Gerry, Kathy, and I comprised the younger group, me being the youngest. We would go on breaks together and generally eat lunch together.

Mary never brought a decent lunch, but would buy expensive junk food from a "roach coach" or a nearby greasy spoon. It was a wonder that she never died from ptomaine. She came from a large family where she received little of anything except criticism. Mary was good hearted and kind but felt unhappy that so few people cared about her. When I told Mom what Mary was eating, she began making Mary a lunch along with mine. All the while I worked at Bosler, Mary was guaranteed a lunch from Mom.

Gerry, as I said earlier, had been at Bosler the longest of our young group. She got married a couple of months after I had started. If I had any questions about the various aspects of marriage, all I had to do was ask her. Attending an all girl's high school put me behind in such knowledge. She seemed so worldly that I asked her whenever I had questions that only a married woman could answer.

Kathy had many issues. She wasn't pretty, didn't have a nice figure and so took whatever she could get in the way of boyfriends. She was currently going out with a Hispanic musician named Marty. Every Friday she would bring a suitcase to work saying she was going to spend the weekend with Marty. I was so ignorant of such things I never realized what she was doing until Gerry enlightened me. Kathy told us that she got nothing but static from her relatives about her relationship with Marty. This situation made her nasty towards the older ladies. She was forever yelling and complaining when Shirley asked her to do something. She kept it up until Mr. Neidorf finally called her into his office and let her go. As I said earlier, Mr. Neidorf really cared about his employees, so he arranged an appointment for her at an employment agency. He couldn't just toss Kathy out into the cold, he knew she was living with her widowed mother and needed the money. On her final day, Kathy gave everyone in the office the cold shoulder, put on her coat and walked out the door. We heard through the grape vine that she did marry Marty.

With Kathy's departure, the office duty roster had to be reorganized. I was assigned the new duty of handling the incoming and outgoing mail. Each morning, I would sort out the mail for the four bosses then open and sort all of the invoices in alphabetical order. That took at least an hour depending on the amount of mail. Next, I placed the downstairs mail in an ancient dumbwaiter box that could be pulled between the first and second floor with a rope. The dumb-waiter had a bell so I could alert somebody downstairs to pick up their mail. Most of the time it just sat there until I'd yell down the chute to "pick up." If that didn't work I kept my finger on the bell until someone couldn't stand the noise.

I was also assigned the duty of hand folding all outgoing invoices, placing them in envelopes, and making sure they were mailed out at the end of each business day. When Margaret, in accounting, began complaining that she couldn't keep up with the filing, I was also assigned that new duty. I was fast becoming a "Jill of all trades" in the office. It made me really feel that I was becoming an "integral part" of Bosler. With all this work, running around and not eating much, my weight began melting off and I was thrilled.

Many unusual people passed through Bosler while I was there. One of the most colorful was an Arabic man who they hired to work in accounting. He seemed very strange to everyone and on his first day he didn't do one stitch of work. He just talked constantly of his adventures in the Royal Air Force (RAF). When he sat with us for lunch, he told us that he had the power to tell fortunes. When lunch was over he said that he "had to take his leave of us" then kissed each of the ladies on the hand. He was handsome, very neatly dressed, but a weird duck even for Bosler. After two days, he disappeared never having told any fortunes.

An interesting part-time employee was a tall, muscular Hispanic woman with four children. One day she became so fed up with one of the downstairs guys hitting on her that she went to Mr. Neidorf. She told him that if he didn't do something about the person, she would bodily pick him up and throw him through a window. Apparently, Mr. Neidorf believed she could and would do it because, the next day, the man in question's desk was vacant and he never returned.

We also had our share of weird people come up to the office supposedly looking for the walk-in counter. One day a bedraggled looking black man came staggering up the stairs and shoved his head through the reception desk window. He had bandages wrapped all over his head and wore torn and tattered clothing. He asked Marie for some money to buy something to eat. Marie tried to ignore him but when he didn't leave, she gave him some money hoping he would. He just kept standing at the window blabbering and it became plain from his smell that he was drunk. Marie was becoming quite unnerved by him, so she called down to Leo at the walk-in counter. After a few minutes, little five-foot-tall Leo came upstairs and went out to talk to the man. Within a few seconds, the guy was running down the stairs and out the front door. Everybody asked Leo what he had said to him? Leo told us that he hadn't said much, he just showed him the four-pound hammer he had in his hand. What Leo lacked in height he made up for in brains.

Earlier I mentioned that the data-phone department at Bosler was really taking off. Since Merle was leaving for the Navy, Mr. Neidorf had to find someone to take his place. He hired Max then added Maria, a Puerto Rican woman. Maria was in her mid-thirties and spoke somewhat broken English. We used to love to listen to her speak, she had her own way of saying things. Right from the start, she did not get along with Max. Actually, neither did the rest of us. Max was a proverbial "know-it-all," who sweated a lot but never used deodorant. Maria had to work in a small room with him and she said his stench turned her stomach. She got so fed up with his smell that she put a can of Right Guard deodorant in his desk drawer, but he didn't take the hint.

Maria was a temperamental employee from the start. She would only show up two or three times a week saying she was always sick. We started taking bets on as to whether she would appear from day to day. If the weather was bad, we knew we would never see her that day. The managers put up with her because, when she did come in, she really worked hard. They considered that she was better than nothing. Maria stayed at Bosler for about one year before she returned to Puerto Rico.

Shortly after Kathy was laid off, Mary began to change drastically. She did not seem very well. Before, when a salesman would say something like, "you look like a zebra your stockings have so many runs in them," she would laugh. Now she had become withdrawn and didn't seem to see much humor in anything. It seemed that she had a lot on her mind that needed help straightening out. Gerry and I kept asking what was wrong and if we could help but she would always change the subject. Mary finally she confided that she was pregnant out-of-wedlock, that her parents had gone berserk when they found out, and that they had never liked, Carmie, the boy she was dating. They had warned her that this guy would get her "in trouble." Now that she was "in trouble," they wiped their hands of her. The boy's parents had told Carmie that he didn't have to marry Mary. Carmie finally told Mary that they should get married as soon as possible. He was all heart! Mary admired him for his going against his parents' wishes and agreeing to marry her before the baby came. When everyone at Bosler got wind of Mary's plight, things weren't made any easier. She had to put up with a lot of nasty comments when she announced her upcoming wedding. Some told her that she had better hurry and get it done before the baby was born.

Mary's wedding preparations were made very quickly with little thought of anything but expediency. No one was helping her with anything, which meant that she had to do everything herself. Since her parents were boycotting the wedding, she had no one who could help her pick a dress. One day she announced that she was going shopping for her wedding dress after work, all by herself. Ida, who was always a very caring woman, asked Mary if she would like her to go shopping with her. Mary said that she appreciated her asking, but that she would go by herself.

The wedding took place over a weekend and Mary was back to work on Monday morning. She brought in the couple of out-of-focus Polaroid pictures that comprised her wedding album. The reception had been held at a table in a neighborhood restaurant. I really felt bad for her, it had, obviously, not been the kind of wedding that a girl dreams of. The most heartbreaking thing was that Mary loved Carmie so much that she was blind to his failings. She was only one month pregnant when they got married, so had a long time to go before the baby came. Carmie made sure that she worked every minute she could. Mary grew fatter and fatter until it became almost impossible for her to do her filing. She said she always felt hungry so she would sneak food into her desk drawers, then put her head down in the drawer to snack. As the months passed, she did less and less work while eating more and more. Since her desk faced Bill Lasky's, he could see what work wasn't getting done. When things got dicey between them, we knew it wouldn't be long before Mary was unemployed.

About two months before Mary's delivery date, Mr. Neidorf called her into his office to tell her that it was time for her to 'retire'. He told her that it was for her own good, she was too far along to be bending over the files. We were all glad that, at least, Mr. Neidorf seemed to care for her well-being. I always felt that if Bosler hadn't let her go that she would have had the baby in a file drawer.

We didn't see Mary again until after her baby was born. She brought her new son to Bosler to show him off to us. The baby was clean and neat and Mary wasn't her usual sloppy self. It seemed that she was doing much better than before. I talked with her once, after her visit, and things didn't sound like they were going very smoothly. She told me that her brother-in-law had moved in with them, that he expected her to wait on him the same as her own husband.

She told me that the brother was driving her crazy, but she couldn't complain to Carmie because he always took his brother's side. I never heard from Mary ever again. I wonder if she is still giving and not getting anything back.

After Mary was gone, Gerry and I became super friends, we were the only two young women left. Gerry had had a beautiful wedding with everything planned and executed just so, quite the opposite of Mary's. Gerry married a man who made her happy in every way. Gerry wanted to work at Bosler until she got pregnant, but the pregnancy never materialized. Jim and Gerry tried everything to find out what the trouble was. Early in their marriage, the doctor found a tumor on one of Gerry's ovaries and believed that was the problem. Jerry soon went through the surgery to find that the tumor was benign and both ovaries were intact. Her doctor told them that the chances were excellent that she could conceive. Since Gerry had always been underweight and frail, she tried fattening herself up in the hope that a baby would be forthcoming, but nothing worked. It was a shame, she was the type of person who had everything in control at all times and most things turned out like she wanted them. This situation had proved to be out her control.

I had envied her so when she was married. Gerry and her husband had the thrill of sharing a life together, having children, a home, and memories that would last them all their lives. I wanted that for myself and with my losing weight, I thought that that might help me to get there. My coworkers began noticing my weight loss, so that did wonders for my ego. However, even with my weight gone, there still wasn't anyone around who I was interested in impressing.

Merle was a very nice guy and I liked him but the feeling was one sided. When he went into the Navy, I tried carrying on a correspondence with him, but it ended after a couple of letters. I was constantly hoping that a man would start working at Bosler who was young, unmarried and who would become interested in me. However, as the months passed, I grew to think that my hopes and dreams were in the category of science fiction. With my life as it was, there wasn't any place, other than Bosler, where I could meet a young man. I found this very depressing. I was nearly 20 years old and I had never even been on a date! My youth was rapidly slipping away and I had yet to enjoy the things that girls my age had been enjoying for years. I realized that I was becoming used to the idea that there might not be any more in my life than my immediate family and Bosler. Still, in my heart, I knew that what I really wanted was to meet and marry a man who would care about me and love me. I had so much love I wanted to give to the right man. Unless I wanted to continue to live my status quo, I had to do something else to find him other than just working at Bosler. Bosler was not conducive to finding the person I wanted in my life. I needed to do something to change this situation, but at the time I didn't know what.

CHAPTER 10
SHOVELS, WE GOT!

As 1966 ended, the mild December weather we had been enjoying lulled everyone into thinking that we might have a snowless winter. It seemed that Chicago was going through a perpetual fall and that was kind of nice. Usually January was the worst month for Mr. Winter to show his wrath. Now, as we moved into the last week of January, it still hadn't snowed. We Midwesterners began to feel smug about the mild weather, bragging that Illinois was getting weather more like Florida.

Then, just as everybody was putting his or her winter underwear in storage, Mother Nature decided to show us once again how much she was still in charge. Around noon, Thursday, January 20, 1967, it started to snow. Nobody was greatly alarmed, we were long overdue for snow. It started with normal flurries, but as the day passed, the wind came up viciously and turned the flurries into a raging blizzard. As the radio became abuzz with severe blizzard warnings, everyone at Bosler became quite uneasy. The switchboard became jammed with calls asking if Bosler had shovels available. Leo finally posted a sign in the business's window saying, "Shovels, we got!"

Dad called me to tell me that we were not staying on Wabash Avenue until 5:00 p.m. He said we would leave for home at 3:30 p.m., which was okay with me. When I walked out of Bosler's building to meet Dad, I couldn't believe how eerie it looked. The sky was so overcast and black that it I felt I could reach up and touch it. The force of the blowing snow against my skin felt like tiny pebbles were bombarding me. I was glad to get into our station wagon and be on our way home. As we pulled out, we realized that everyone in Chicago must have had the same idea of an early exit to beat the worsening weather. The traffic was crawling along at about two feet every hour, a near standstill. As we sat locked in the traffic, the snow began coming down even heavier. With the blistering wind, the snow began to form into huge drifts that made it nearly impossible for cars to navigate and for snowplows to have any impact.

As things worsened, cars were being abandoned, causing an even bigger traffic jam. For cars still on the road, the lane markings disappeared under blowing snow. Cars were going wherever the drifting snow permitted. After about four hours, we were still only ten minutes from Wabash Avenue. We had on an AM radio station and I remember hearing Sonny and Cher's "The Beat Goes On," and Tom Jones' "Green, Green Grass of Home," being played repeatedly. It made me wonder how the beat would go on after a snowstorm like this and if we would ever see the green grass of our home instead of snow.

As we were going nowhere very slowly, Dad began to worry about running out of gas. All of a sudden, he pulled off the main street deciding to try the side streets. We quickly noticed that there was no traffic to contend with on them! It seemed we were about the only car travelling on them, which made it very scary. The traffic lights had all failed and the wind blowing the snow against the windshield was causing a blinding, dizzying effect. In spite of all this, Dad plowed on, not stopping for stop signs fearing that if stopped, we would have never have gotten moving again. As long as Dad drove the car at a slow, constant speed there was less chance of it getting stuck. Even so, about half the car's motion consisted of sliding from one side of the street to the other. That was the last thing we wanted, if we got stuck on these nearly empty side streets, we probably wouldn't be found until spring.

As the hours passed and the snow grew even heavier, the radio reported that most Chicago streets and expressways were closed leaving thousands of people stranded in their cars or at work for the night. Dad said confidently, "We will make it home," but as more time passed, I wasn't quite as confident as he was. Finally, around 10:00 p.m., six and a half hours after we had started for home, Dad turned onto our La Grange street and a huge feeling of relief washed over us. We were home! Well, almost, the car became stuck in the snow just one block from our house! Thankfully, several people were out on the street trying to help those whose cars were stuck. They gave us a big push and the car slid into its cozy garage for a night of rest. Dad and I dragged our tired bodies into the house, told of our adventures, ate our long overdue dinner and I wearily made my way upstairs. That night as I slept, my mind kept repeating Dad's phrase, "Don't lift up your hood and cuss, call us." I was very thankful that we had not been on the cussing end that day!

By the time morning had arrived, the snow had slowed to a light flurry, but the fury of the previous night wasn't easily forgotten. We watched the TV news as it showed downtown Chicago paralyzed in the grip of a record-breaking storm. It was the strangest sight I had ever seen! There didn't seem to be a soul anywhere around! The TV cameraman made it look even stranger, there were no cars moving on downtown streets either! Chicago looked like a city in a science fiction movie after a nuclear war, empty. Evidently, most of the cars had made it out of the Chicago Loop, then became stuck in the snow on every street and expressway. Everyone was thankful for any shelter they had found and weren't crazy enough to leave it, after spending hours to find it. No one bothered to head for work that Friday morning, they had no interest in reliving the travails of the night before. Many hundreds of cars were stuck so far into snowdrifts that there was no hope to get them out without a thaw. When the snow had finally stopped, the official average snow total for the Chicago area was nearly two feet with three to four-foot snow drifts. What made the situation even worse was that the city of Chicago had been completely unprepared for it, it had already put most of its snowplows in storage. Old Man Winter had finally made his grand entrance and we were not prepared to fight back. It's amazing how much mankind has learned and achieved, yet can be thrown for a loop by a snowstorm. There are some things that we will probably never be able to control no matter how hard we try.

After this record-breaking, whopper of a snowstorm, we still had to contend with several minor snowstorms, which added insult to injury. For the rest of the winter, we were repeatedly reminded that when Mother Nature's fury is unleashed there is very little you can do but grin and bear it. For the rest of the winter we were all in constant fear that we would receive another major zap, maybe even harsher the next time. With new snow being constantly shoveled over the existing snow, we began to feel like moles going through burrows to get where we wanted to go. It became natural for us to see seven-foot piles of snow on street curbs and along walkways.

As March ended, the snowdrifts finally began to shrink and the ground snow became thinner and thinner. As the melting continued, we began to see patches of sprouting grass, like green whiskers growing out of a man's chin. These few beautiful green blades offered hope that we would soon see spring again and that there were other colors to the landscape than white and dirty white.

My life at Bosler was going very well as I became more and more a part of the Bosler family. It seemed that I, now, had a finger in every department. My responsibilities had grown again, I was assigned the job of the monthly filing in accounting. I had also been assigned to fold customer invoices and learning how to operate the postage meter. Once I had the postage meter down, I was assigned to get out all the mail for the entire company each day. The more I learned, the more my responsibilities grew. I was getting experience in every aspect of our office.

I began to enjoy running the switchboard more and more. As I began to recognize each customer's voice, they started to acknowledge me and ask me how I was. Every once in while I would be thrown for a loop when a person with a thick accent would call in and I couldn't understand what they wanted. However, I always had a couple of people downstairs who I could give these calls to and who wouldn't get too mad. Ronnie was one of those people, so it was to him that I usually gave such calls. After one such call, Ronnie called me to ask what the heck kind of calls I was giving him. I said that I couldn't understand what the man wanted so I was hoping that he could. Ronnie said that the man who had just called wanted him to pick up a load of dirty towels. I burst out laughing, it sounded so funny. The man had apparently reversed the phone number and thought he was talking to the Chicago Towel Company. After that incident, I became a bit warier of the calls I passed along as Ronnie hadn't seen much humor in the towel situation. I did, so every time I saw him after that I would ask him when my towels would be ready.

My weight was getting to be less of a problem for me. By spring of 1967, I had lost 35 pounds, so I became really gung-ho about losing more. I decided that I would go on the Ayds diet plan. Ayds were a diet candy that, when eaten with a hot drink, were supposed to suppress your appetite. That diet sounded so easy that I decided to try it. I bought myself a box and ate the suggested two candies. I couldn't believe how good they tasted, I hadn't eaten candy for many months. I decided that if two were good then four would help me lose weight even faster. I just couldn't stop at four. I continued eating them until the entire box was gone. That was a super-fast diet plan. These things were far too good for my own good. Not wanting to get hooked on diet candy (or its expense), I decided that I would continue with the eating habits I had before the Ayds diet.

Sadly, things at home weren't as perfect at this point. Lady, our collie, was nearing ten years old and began having bladder control problems. Mom just couldn't understand why Lady was having so many accidents. She had always been an extremely sensitive dog, who never made a mess anywhere in the house. Something was radically wrong, so Mom decided to keep a close eye on her. One-day, Lady had a very difficult time getting up after lying down for a while. Mom called the vet telling him that Lady was urinating freely and could hardly walk. The vet told her to bring Lady in as soon as possible. So, as soon as Dad came home from work, we all went to the vet. Upon examining Lady, the vet told us that she had had a stroke from which she would never recover. The vet could tell that we didn't want to put her to sleep, so he told us that we should make her last days as comfortable as possible. He told us Lady would probably feel much better if she was left with him for a bath, she had gotten very raw from the urine. Mom and Dad told him that they wanted him to do everything he could for her, she was a very integral part of our family.

When Lady came home the next day, she seemed much better, but she still couldn't walk well enough to go outside to do her business. Dad, as always, got busy building something to help her. After a couple hours in the garage, he built a contraption that could hold Lady up while she did her business. It was a framework of wooden rails with two wide lengths of cloth strung between the rails. Lady was laid on the cloth so she could be supported to relieve herself on newspapers placed under her. It worked well but the drawback was that during the day, my 107-pound mother had to carry Lady down the steps into the garage and then lift her unto the platform. Lady weighed about 80 pounds with her back half dead weight from the stroke.

Day after day as we watched Lady, she became worse and worse. It tore the hearts out of us to see this and we prayed that God would relieve her of her suffering soon. About ten days after her initial stroke, she stopped eating and we all knew that we were close to losing her. It was hard losing someone who we had given so much love to and who had more than reciprocated that love for ten years. The only solace we had was that Lady had had a good life with us and the memories of all the good times we had with her could never be erased.

On Sunday afternoon, we were eating an early dinner, while Lady was laying in the living room with her head on a pillow. Mom stopped picking at her food, began to cry and said that Lady had died. We all ran into the front room and found that it was true. Mom had been so close to Lady that she knew when she breathed her last breath. Shortly after Lady died, a storm arose with torrential rain and high winds. It seemed an appropriate kind of weather to mourn the loss of a loyal friend.

After the storm had subsided, Dad dug a hole in the back of the yard and buried Lady in the place she loved so much. All of us knew that Mom would miss Lady the most and that something would have to be done to help alleviate some of her grief. The solution was to bring a new little puppy into her life as soon as possible. With a puppy around Mom would have very little time to grieve for Lady. Dad and I had to wait until Monday to do research to find a new furry companion for Mom and all the rest of us, truth be told.

When Monday came, Dad and I began phoning various kennels to see what breeds they had in stock. He and I decided that we would stop at Archer Kennels after work, which was located a short way from our house. I called Mom to let her know that we would be late coming home. She sounded so depressed that I hoped even more that Archer had a puppy who would steal Mom's heart the minute she saw it. From what the kennel owner told me, I had the impression that Archer was a huge kennel with every conceivable breed of dog to choose from. After driving past several times, Dad and I finally found the kennel. The reason we kept missing it was because it was a tiny building. Upon entering, we were greeted by a slow moving, sour old man who told us to look around, which didn't take long to do. It was just one small room with cages built along three of the walls. As we looked in the cages there seemed to be a lot of puppies that looked alike and whose breed was listed as Rat Terrier. They were cute, but not distinctive enough to mend Mom's heart. In a couple of cages there were some older pedigree dogs, giving the impression that they were still there because they didn't have the greatest personalities. Finally, Dad found a Border Collie puppy that he thought Mom would like. I didn't agree, I thought it would remind her too much of Lady.

We were just about to leave when I noticed a very tiny Beagle puppy. There was something about her that tugged at my heart. When I picked her up she fit nicely in the palm of my hand. She had a round little belly, long floppy ears and a white star in the middle of her forehead. She had large sorrowful eyes that made her look desperate to find a loving home. I told Dad that this was the puppy for Mom. He said that we would bring her over after dinner and let her pick which dog she liked best. I knew in my heart which one it would be.

When we arrived home, I tried my best to hurry dinner along as much as possible. When everyone was finished, I quickly cleaned up. In a matter of minutes, Dad and I had pulled Mom out the door and into the car. She told us that if this had anything to do with a puppy that she wasn't interested. We told her that all we wanted her to do was to look and that was all. She finally agreed to "only go look." It only took us a few minutes to get to the kennel this time. We escorted Mom in and let her browse. Dad pointed out the Border Collie that he had favored, but Mom wasn't impressed. Next, I tried my sales pitch. I have to admit that it didn't take much of a pitch once she saw this little one. What really won Mom over was when she picked the puppy up and asked her if she wanted to come home with us. The puppy immediately began to lick Mom's nose with her little flapping pink tongue. That was it for Mom, we were now the proud owners of a Beagle puppy that we named Mickey.

When Mickey was introduced to her new home, she seemed right at home. She was a very mischievous little lady, who we had to carefully watch to keep her out of trouble. After five days, Mom noticed that there was blood in her stool. She called the vet and he advised her to bring in a stool sample to be analyzed. His analysis showed that Mickey was sick with worms that were feeding off her blood. That accounted for her fat belly. He said that he would try to save her with transfusions, but couldn't guarantee anything. We couldn't believe that we were going through another life and death crisis so soon after losing Lady.

During those five days, we had all come to love Mickey as though we had her for years. Dad was so mad that he called the kennel to tell the owner what was happening to the puppy he had sold us. He told Dad to bring the puppy back that he would give him another one. Dad blew his corks. He told the man that we loved this puppy and that we weren't going to bring her back to be put to sleep. Dad told the man that the kennel was dealing with living things and not some piece of inanimate furniture that could be returned if it was defective. The longer he talked, the angrier Dad got, until he told the owner that he ought to come over and punch him out for selling sickly puppies. That really put some fear in the old coot's heart. He told Dad that he would call the police if he saw him around. Dad hung up with the satisfaction of knowing that there was one scared guy who would think twice before selling sickly puppies again.

With the phone call over, there was still the worry about Mickey surviving. Mom and Dad took Mickey back to the vet, where she was given three blood transfusions. The vet now felt that Mickey's chance for survival was much better. We were all so relieved, we wanted Mickey to have a long life in our home. Once her illness was over, Mickey's personality really began to immerge. She was a very energetic, friendly and loving dog, with a stubborn streak that just wouldn't quit. While a small puppy, we kept Mickey in the kitchen behind a wooden gate. She chewed it up so thoroughly that there was nothing left but toothpick sized pieces of wood. Dad, then, built a thicker replacement gate but the same thing happened. Dad's next gate was heavy wood covered with sheet metal and that worked fine. Mickey had to be confined to the kitchen because she refused to be housebroken. When she had access to the whole house, she would go berserk. She would run around the living room at about fifty miles an hour. If there was furniture in her way, she would just run right over it. It took her almost three years to calm down, but when she did, she became a dog more sensitive and clever than many humans.

In August of 1967, Mom decided that the entire family was going on an out-of-state vacation. Growing up, we had never had a vacation away from home for more than a day. Since I was now 20, Bill 14, and Mark 7, Mom said there weren't many years left for us to go on a family vacation. I couldn't understand why she was worried, after all, there wasn't anyone around who wanted to marry me and snatch me away from my family. I felt that I would be with them for many years to come.

Since Disneyland was financially out of the question, we decided that we would go to the Midwest's premiere family vacation destination, Wisconsin Dells. Since we wanted to take Mickey with us, we rented a light housekeeping cottage at White Pines Cottages, "a place, not fancy, just clean, comfortable, and friendly," per their brochure. We packed our suitcases and Mickey and we were off for a wonderful Wisconsin vacation. When we arrived at White Pines, we found the cottage to be as advertised. It was a homey place where Dad could cook us a fine breakfast of his own "Wisconsin eggs" (toad-in-the-hole) and Mickey could gaze out of the screened windows while we enjoyed the Dells.

We stayed in the cottage for five days while taking in every activity and amusement we could afford in the Dells. The Dells Boat Tour was spectacular with the Wisconsin River winding through beautiful, multi-colored rock formations and forested areas. Along the way we watched a reenactment of the famous Stand Rock dog jump.

The WWII-era amphibious Duck Boat ride was thrilling as we went from land to water to land at high speed, with water flying in all directions around the boat. They even allowed us kids to drive the boat a little to receive an "official" duck boat pilot's license.

We took a more sedate ride in a horse-drawn carriage through Lost Canyon. This trip took us along a tortuously twisted, narrow and deep canyon cut through the Dell's beautiful, multi-colored rocks. A trip so difficult that, "the horses have to be talked through each trip by their driver," lest you get stuck in there.

For the meek, timid and us, we made the trip through the Enchanted Forest with its giant mushrooms and Prehistoric Land where you could ride on a dinosaur.

After dark, we went to see the Stand Rock Indian Ceremonial. This American Indian dance ceremony was performed in a bonfire lit, natural rock amphitheater by Pueblo and Winnebago Indians dressed in beautifully colored headdresses and clothing. It was spectacular!

Our final must see was the Tommy Bartlett Water Ski Show and Dancing Waters. There, we saw teams of people pulled by speedboats doing things on water skis that no one would think about doing on snow skis. The show ended with a display of multi-colored, dancing water fountains, choreographed to music; a precursor to Las Vegas's Bellagio water display.

After all of this excitement a family of five could get really hungry. We visited Bonanza Steakhouse a number of times during our stay. In 1967, $1.59 got you a complete dinner there: a salad, Texas toast, a baked potato, and a sirloin steak!

After four days, we were pretty much thrilled out and were looking forward to going home. Dad, in his own inimitable way, said that his finances were growing small after paying for five people's food and admissions, that, "while he wasn't broke, he was badly bent." Mickey, now five months old, had only eaten our cottage's screen door. In retrospect, I am so glad we got this family vacation in because, unknown to me at the time, I would be married the following year and leave home for Florida with my new husband.

Shortly after our return, my cousin Judy from next door, asked me to be a bridesmaid for her wedding. I told her that I would be glad to, but in my heart, it made me feel more unloved than ever. Everyone around me seemed to be getting married and I, at 20, had yet to go on my first date. Mom tried to console me by telling me that, the first boy I would go out with would be the one, so why waste time on the rest. I thought that she was really piling it on but we all know that mothers are like that. Even if their kids are social duds, they never seem to notice. To them all of their kids are beautiful, smart and graceful.

They seem to look at us through different kind of eyes than everyone else. It's awfully nice having a mom around like that, they make life more tolerable in troubled times.

Judy's wedding preparations progressed with all the frenzy and confusion of any wedding. I grew to be excited as I had never stood up for a wedding. Any girl would get excited over a reason to buy an elegant long dress. Since the wedding was scheduled for November, the bridesmaid's dresses were red velvet with a mini jacket fastening in back that concealed the basic sleeveless dress. However, I thought that the matching red velvet hats resembled something that Maid Marion of Robin Hood fame might wear.

When rehearsal day arrived, Judy kept telling me what a nice guy I was paired up with for the wedding. She said he was a quiet and a perfect gentleman. She intimated that with my experience with men, I wasn't ready for anything more. What she failed to mention was that he was also a lush. I had built visions that this might be the man of my dreams, but when I met him, I knew that he wasn't. We went through the ceremonies without a word between us of anything personal. He didn't know how to dance, so we just sat through the evening while he drank and drank. It was really one dull evening! I absolutely knew then and there, if I wanted to find my "someone", I would have to do it myself. No one knew who I needed or wanted better than me.

After the Judy's wedding, things calmed down to their usual routine. I continued to lose weight and gained more and more confidence in myself. I no longer felt that I had to apologize to other people for being fat. I was finally becoming my own person. I still tried to get along with everyone, but, it didn't bother me anymore if I couldn't. I had learned that a person can't be liked by every other person, it was a losing battle to try to change that. At Bosler, desirable single, young men were still sparse. I just couldn't figure out where I was going to meet some young men, so I'd know "Mr. Right" when he came along.

Before long, Christmas was approaching and we all were all busy with our preparations. With Christmas came Christmas cards, one that came to me that year was destined to change my entire life. It was from Ann, one of my best friends in high school. She wrote a short note telling me about what she had been doing since graduation. She mentioned that on Saturdays, she was a hostess at the Chicago YWCA USO. She told me that I could be her guest, if I wanted to come with her. Her offer intrigued me, so I phoned her and we made plans to meet up and go to the USO the following Saturday.

CHAPTER II
AND THEN CAME CAMELOT

All that week, I eagerly awaited Saturday. I kept telling myself that my purpose for going to the USO wasn't merely to find an eligible male, but that was pretty close. I didn't quite had marriage on my mind, I just wanted to find someone who would be interested enough in "me" to ask me for a date. It was getting ridiculous already. I would be 21 in three months and had yet to see what a date with a male was like. Someone asking me out would really give my ego a major boost and it sure was in need of that! I was willing to settle for one date and I didn't even care if he asked me out again. I just wanted to find out what made a date so special that it made it the ultimate thing to brag about during adolescence.

When my plans for Saturday were made, they naturally involved Dad. He would take Ann and me to the Chicago YWCA at Wabash and Monroe streets. Every Saturday it was opened as a USO, and only "fine, upright young ladies," were allowed to become hostesses. I thought that if I enjoyed it, I would apply to become a hostess. I considered myself as fine and upright as a lady could get. To put it another way, I was boringly good, which I figured would be an excellent qualification.

It was near the end of January and very mild, so we didn't have much trouble getting downtown. As Ann and I entered the YWCA elevator, I found it hard to hide my anticipation. Ann signed us in at the reception desk and I received my "guest" badge. Ann gave me a tour to show me where everything was. She told me that the protocol was that girls could ask the boys to dance, as we were their hostesses. I thought that that was kind of bold, but I was game for anything. After Ann's tour, we stationed ourselves along the dance floor and we waited for the music to begin. Apparently, the protocol also included all of the girls sitting on one side of the room and all of the guys sitting on the other. When the disc jockey started the music, everyone just sat. Ann and I sat for almost an hour twiddling our thumbs before I told her that I was getting up and going to ask someone to dance. It had become obvious that if I didn't make a move, I would be sitting there all evening with Ann. I knew it wasn't just me, there were only three couples dancing. I said farewell to Ann and made my way to the guy's side of the room. Most of them seemed to be very self-conscious about dancing, so they literally had to be pulled up out of their seat. A couple of guys graciously accepted my invitation, but after our dance they sped quickly back to their chairs.

As I made my way back to my chair on the girl's side, I was very disappointed. These guys seemed to be acting more like junior high boys than men in the military. None of them seemed able to dance or even carry on a conversation. I suppose part of it was that I was almost 21 and they were 18 or 19 and shorter than I was. I decided that maybe an older crop would show up if I came often enough, so I applied to become a hostess. I received the application a few days later. It required me to supply three character references. I knew that I could count on a good reference from my boss, Mr. Neidorf, so I approached him first. He was all smiles when I asked him and he gave me a good reference, so I was on my way to being an USO hostess.

As soon as I was accepted for USO hostess, I called Ann and told her that I thought going every other Saturday was more than enough. She agreed, so in early February we returned to the USO. As I scanned the crowd, I recognized a couple of guys who had been there the first time. Nicky was a farm boy from Mississippi with an accent so thick that I only understood half of what he was saying. I liked him, he was polite and easy going. He was sort of a younger brother type guy. We danced several dances together and passed the time congenially. This was much better than going around begging strangers to dance with me. Dennis was another guy who I spent a Saturday with. He was from Chanute AFB in Rantoul, Illinois. He was shy and quiet, but, at least, danced closer than the rest. He said that it took a big effort for him to get to Chicago, so I knew that I probably wouldn't see him again. He promised that he would try to come again, if I was going to be there. When Saturday rolled around, neither Dennis or Nicky were there, so I had to peruse the area for new acquaintances.

This Saturday was special, the USO was sponsoring a Sadie Hawkins dance for the leap year. Sadie Hawkins was a character in *Li'l Abner*, who chased and captured her males during leap year. In *Dog Patch*, it was a tradition for the women to chase the men and lure them into marriage on February 29. It was

March 2, but no one cared because the spirit was there. The girls were more than ready for some romance to celebrate leap year; unfortunately, the feeling was only confined to them. On this particular Saturday, the guys were exceptionally true to the principle of non-participation, plunking down on their side of the room. Many of the girls just held down their chairs for most the evening. After an hour, I decided that I had enough of this foolishness. I had come from too far to have a wasted evening. So, with every ounce of courage I could muster, I set out to confront the enemy. As I looked them over, they made me think of a line of birds sitting on a telephone wire. In all my weeks as a hostess I had never encountered such an unenthusiastic bunch.

I walked down the guy's row of hard held chairs asking if anyone wanted to dance. There were five in the group I was speaking to. They all sort of leaned together to confer on who would be the sacrificed one. I noticed a guy in the group who I had danced with once before. I figured, if no one else wanted to dance with me, he would accept my offer. Tom was short, blonde, wore glasses and had danced with me as if I had leprosy. He was no prize, but I figured I would take him over no one. When their conference finally ended, a guy stood up and said that he would like to dance. After a quick once over, I decided that he held promise.

I liked how he danced. When he held me, he had a nice, friendly firm hold which I liked. As we danced, I found out that his name was Patrick Harrington. He told me he was stationed at Naval Station Great Lakes, was from Bellingham, Washington, in the Pacific Northwest, was 22, and had graduated from college. As the dance ended, we parted, he thanked me for the dance and turned to go back to sit down. I just stood there hoping that he would ask me for another dance. Giving up that hope, I turned to go back to my chair when to my surprise, he turned back and asked me if I wanted to dance again. Not wanting to seem too anxious, I ran into his arms.

As the evening wore on, we danced every dance and shared a soda. I learned that he had come to the USO because he was on a blind date with the older sister of a friend of his. He was supposed to run defense with the older sister, to allow his friend to enjoy the company of the younger sister. Pat and the older sister hadn't hit it off at all, so they parted after an hour. I was very happy that his blind date hadn't worked out, because I was having one of the best evenings of my life. The rest of the evening just flew by and it was soon time to leave. I told Pat that I had had a wonderful time and he said that he did, as well. He asked if he could meet me again next week. I told him that I would be here, but in my heart, I was reluctant to believe he would be. I would just wait until next week to see how sincere he really was. I wouldn't get carried away with myself at this early a stage in our relationship, especially since we hardly had a relationship yet.

All during the following week, I had very little on my mind but Pat. I couldn't wait to see if he'd be there on Saturday. When the day I was longing for arrived, I was anxious, and a little fearful, that Pat wouldn't show. As Ann and I rode the USO elevator, I knew that if Pat wasn't there I would have a very disappointing evening. As the elevator stopped at our floor, we walked out and I planted myself by the reception desk so I could get a good look at who was arriving. While my eyes were firmly fixed on the elevator door, I felt a tap on my shoulder. When I turned around there was Pat. I was thrilled and elated that he had kept our date and from his expression, I knew that he was feeling the same. I couldn't believe that he thought so much of me that he had come all the way from Great Lakes again. From that moment, I began to look at him in a completely different way than other men.

Pat was close to six feet tall, so he towered over me (did I tell you that I am 5' 2" tall?). He looked a little thin, but I supposed that that was from eating great Navy food at Great Lakes. His hair was dark brown, parted to the left side, having grown out of his boot camp buzzcut. He had a wide smile and a square jaw. Already hooked, I thought he was the most handsome man I had ever met. He wore a dark green shirt with an auburn V-neck sweater over it, dark green pants, black Navy shoes, and gray plastic Navy-issue glasses.

As we danced the evening away, I noticed that he was pulling me closer to him for the slow dances. That made me slightly uneasy, because the USO did not allow close dancing. I didn't want the supervisors to think that I was a girl of loose morals, but in my heart, I loved the warmth of him. We again shared a soda, for which he borrowed the money, and we talked about our families and anything else that came into our minds. With the chiming of twelve on the USO clock, my magic evening came to an end.

Pat asked if I would be here next week and I said that I would. He asked for my address and said that he would drop me a line during the week. After we said good night, Ann and I waited for her father but I felt like I could float home on a cloud of ecstasy. There's no describing what a person feels when they first fall in love. It was a feeling of everything being right for me and the rest of the world. It's was a feeling that all the awkwardness of a lifetime was gone. I had emerged from my cocoon as a woman capable of attracting a person of the opposite sex. At that moment, I had finally attained what every girl craves. Even though I was older than most, the thrill of having my first boyfriend was just as wonderful. As a matter of fact, I think it was even more wonderful, because I had waited such a long time for him to come along.

All that following week, I waited impatiently for Saturday to come. Then, on Thursday, I received a letter from Pat, and I cherished it as though it were a letter from the President. It was a very short letter but it contained all the words that I wanted to hear and conveyed all the feelings that I, myself, felt. Pat wrote that he was eagerly looking forward to seeing me on Saturday at the USO. It was very concise and to the point, but I read it over and over again like some treasured piece of classic literature.

The previous Saturday, Pat had mentioned that his birthday was March 18. Since the upcoming Saturday was March 16, I decided that I would remember his birthday with a some small, but meaningful gift. After dinner, I put on my coat and started out the door in search of a gift for my very special friend. When Dad saw me going out the door, he asked where I was going in the dark. I told him that I had some shopping to do. He said that if I waited for a minute, he would drive me. This was one time that I didn't want him around asking me a lot of questions. It was something very personal to me and I didn't want him involved just now. I told Mom where I was going and what I wanted to buy. I think she understood how I felt and told Dad to "cool it."

As I entered the store, I was excited to be looking for a gift for a young man, who wasn't my brother. I didn't have the foggiest idea of what to buy, but I would know it when I saw it. After about twenty times around the store, I saw a display case containing St. Christopher medals. That seemed exactly what I was looking for. Their prices ranged from very cheap to very expensive. Since my cash "on hand" wasn't great, I decided on cheap. When I arrived home with it, I felt horrible that I had gone cheap on the gift. It bothered me all the next day until I decided to return it and use my reserve funds to purchase a better medal. I didn't want to give Pat a medal that would turn his neck green after 37 seconds of wear. I was delighted with my new purchase, it was quality sterling silver. I couldn't wait until Saturday.

When I found myself in the USO elevator again, it seemed hard to believe that my long-awaited Saturday had finally come. When I came off the elevator, there was Pat waiting for me. After I shed my coat, we were off to the dance floor. We both enjoyed music and dancing very much, it was a perfect way to start our date. After dancing to every sort of modern music and moldy oldie, we stopped to share our "regular" soda in the cafeteria. I decided that this was the perfect time to spring my surprise on him. From the way Pat had been talking, I knew that he was a little homesick for his family, so I hoped that my birthday gift for him would make him feel better.

When I presented him with my birthday gift and card, he was so happy and appreciative that I knew spending the extra money on it had been well worth it. He told me that he hadn't expected a surprise like this. He immediately took the medal his sister had given him off and put mine on. The remainder of the evening was spent talking about everything under the sun. When the 12:00 p.m. curfew drew near, Pat said that he would really like to take me out to dinner and a movie the next Saturday. He said he would try to come in on an earlier train so we could have more time together. I told him that I would try to work something out on my end, so I would be downtown to meet him.

For two days, I pondered over how I would get downtown early. Dad was working half days on Saturdays, so I couldn't ask him. Then, I came up with a brilliant idea, I would convince Mr. Neidorf that I needed to work on Saturday to catch up. That way I could drive in with Dad and have one of the men downstairs drop me off downtown. I immediately wrote Pat and asked him to call me at Bosler when his train arrived in Chicago. This was really going to be a super Saturday, I was going on an actual date outside of the YWCA USO. It seemed to me that our relationship was progressing perfectly. Being with Pat for just those few hours on Saturdays had brought me a joy unknown to me before. With every passing hour, we seemed to become closer and closer. We didn't have the luxury of being able to see each other every day or even a couple times a week. Both of us had to work hard and come long distances for the privilege of being together for a few hours on a Saturday! Neither of us had the luxury to waste time, we had to get acquainted at breakneck speed.

Working that Saturday morning at Bosler was a real drag, I didn't really have anything to do and so the time just crawled by. When noon rolled around, I was very eager to hear from Pat. When the call finally did come in, Pat told me that he was in Chicago and would meet me at the USO in an hour. We had hardly hung up when I was running downstairs. I found Flash and asked him if I could ride downtown with Leonard the deliveryman. He said sure and would set up the whole thing. Flash was always one to take charge in times of emergencies. Before long, I was deposited in front of the YWCA USO on Wabash and Monroe. Since there was a March chill in the air, I decided to wait in the lobby.

After a half hour, I began to worry why Pat hadn't shown up. I knew he wouldn't stand me up after all both of us had gone through to meet. I went outside, waiting there until I was turning a pale shade of blue. I went upstairs to see if he was there, he wasn't. I described Pat to the woman at the desk but she hadn't seen him. She said, "You do know this isn't the regular USO, the YWCA is only used on Saturdays. Maybe your boyfriend is waiting for you at the USO on LaSalle." That seemed a very plausible explanation, so I raced for LaSalle. Since I had not idea where I was going, I had to stop a few people along the way to ask if I was going in the right direction.

After what seemed an eternity, I found the USO. I walked up the stairs and asked the hostess if she knew if a Navy man named Pat Harrington had been there. She said that she had no way of knowing, so I was back where I had started. It was getting on to 4:00 p.m. and I was cold, tired, and very disappointed. I decided that I had better start thinking of finding a way back home. Just as I turned to go down the stairs, I felt a tap on my shoulder and there was Pat standing there with beet red, windblown ears and a running nose. He told me that he come to wait at the USO on LaSalle but, when I didn't show, he figured that I was waiting at the other USO. When he arrived there, I had already gone. We must have inadvertently passed each other in the flow of pedestrian traffic. It was all so confusing, but we were both glad that we had gotten together. It was a big day that neither of us wanted to miss. It would have been a waste if we had missed it because of miscommunication.

We had lost a good part of the day, so we had to hurry and make up for it. Pat took me to a little restaurant for something warm to thaw us both out. Since it was located next to the Woods Theater, we decided to go see the movie, *Wait Until Dark,* that was playing there. A very good movie was made even better with Pat's arm around my shoulders. I was so intent on watching the movie that I even put on my glasses so I could see it.

After the movie, Pat said that he had gotten tickets from the USO to see Liza Minnelli and the Sandpipers at the Auditorium Theater. This was really going to be a night to remember. When we arrived at the Auditorium Theater, it took us about fifteen minutes to climb up to where the seats were. We kept asking the ushers, "Are we there yet?" and they just kept pointing up. Our seats were located "just below heaven" and right next to the spotlights on a metal platform that shook whenever anybody stood up or sat down. I didn't mind, it was nice going someplace different with my Pat. When the show began, we had a hard time distinguishing Liza Minnelli from the Sandpipers. On stage, just like when I saw the Beatles, they all looked like tiny finger puppets. However, what they lacked in size was made up for in great sound. It was a good show with the best songs from both acts being performed. After the show was over, we rounded out our evening with a few dances at the YMCA USO.

That Saturday's memories had to last me through the following two weeks. Pat had duty watch the next Saturday. The week after, he called me on Friday to tell me that all leaves had been cancelled because of the race riots taking place all over Chicago since Martin Luther King's assassination. Pat told me that some people from the Base had been beaten up on the street. In response, Pat and other petty officers had been put in charge of armed recruits to protect the Base. Dad and I had come home from Chicago with our headlights on to show sympathy for Dr. King. I was worried for Pat's safety, he had become very important in my life.

With everything pretty much at peace in Chicago, normal living resumed and so did the leaves at Great Lakes. On this Saturday, I rode the Burlington train into Chicago, so I could meet Pat's Northwestern train a half hour later. My riding the train allowed us to spend more time together. I was sitting patiently in the Northwestern station's waiting area, when hordes of sailors emerged from the train. It was like looking for a needle in a haystack, all of the sailors looked the same. It seemed that they all had the same haircut, wore the same glasses and were all tall. Since I hadn't worn my glasses, I just waited for Pat to find me. I didn't have to wait long, in no time I saw him rushing toward me. He grabbed my arm in his and we were off to conquer Chicago.

This Saturday we went to the Prudential Building for a breathtaking aerial view of Chicago. After that, we walked around in the Field Museum and then Pat took me for a steak dinner at the Michelob Lounge on State Street. It was very good and inexpensive. I knew Pat didn't have that much money so whenever we could keep it simple and inexpensive it made me feel better. I knew he was the type of person who wouldn't let me pay for anything, so I didn't want to embarrass him by offering.

We topped off a very enjoyable evening by going to see the movie *Camelot* with Vanessa Redgrave, Richard Harris, and Franco Nero. I don't think I ever enjoyed a movie more. It was a very romantic movie but with a sad ending of love lost by them all. When we walked out of the Bismark Theater, we both were very misty eyed. As we were crossing the street, I grabbed Pat's arm, looked up at him and told him that I wanted to thank him for such a wonderful evening. Then, I stood on my tiptoes and planted the first kiss that I had ever given to any guy right on his lips. After pulling me onto the sidewalk so we wouldn't be run over, Pat told me that he had equally as good a time. We walked arm in arm to the Northwestern Station where I sent him back to Great Lakes. I would get home by means of good old Dad, who never really realized how much of his little girl's heart was already lost to another man.

That first kiss lingered on my lips through the entire week! However, since he did not give me one back, I feared that he might not feel the same way emotionally about me that I felt about him. I just had to wait for him make the first move. When Saturday arrived again, I found myself at the train station waiting to enjoy another day with the person who was fast becoming the most important person in my life. We spent the day wandering in the Museum of Science and Industry, went to the Holloway House Restaurant for dinner and ended up dancing the night away at the YWCA USO. As I walked him to his train, he bent down and gave me a quick kiss on the lips. Now I knew that things were getting serious with him too. I didn't have marriage in mind when I first met Pat, I was just thankful for his excellent company. Our relationship was changing into something other than companionship for both of us.

Saturday, April 27, was the day after my 21st birthday and I was wondering if Pat would remember my birthday. When he got off the train, he was carrying a present that turned out to be the soundtrack album from *Camelot*. Evidently, that movie had as great an impact on him as it had with me. Along with it, he gave me a necklace that held a pinkish aurora borealis medallion. It was beautiful and it was only much later that he confessed it had been very inexpensive. He never knew how much pleasure I got from his presents. I wore that necklace until it turned my neck and everything I wore green and the chain rotted away. We strolled around the Art Institute and Grant Park. I guess I had really started something with my first kiss because, after that, it was Pat who offered me the kisses. I guess it had broken through the wall of shyness that had still been between us. It was amazing how fast Pat moved with a little encouragement.

That day we were caught up in an anti-war demonstration at the Picasso plaza. Some Chicago TV News people saw Pat's military haircut and Navy glasses and pounced on him for an on-camera statement of his view of the Vietnam War. All Pat said to them was, "It's not my war and it never will be," then we pushed through the crowd. Everyone stationed at Great Lakes had been warned never to make public statements about the War. Also, Pat was in the Naval Security Group and they didn't want anything said that might be confidential. After the shouts of the demonstration were out of range, we went for a steak dinner and to see *Gone With The Wind*. Afterwards, as we were walking to the Palmer House to meet Dad, I remembered that I had left a present I bought for Mark on the theater floor under my seat. We raced back to the theater where Pat talked the janitor into letting us back in. It was very difficult to find the same seats we had in the pitch-blackness. I was literally crawling up the stairs on my hands and knees. Pat, having a good sense of direction, found the present and we were on our way to the Palmer House again.

Dad always came to pick me up a half hour before the last train to Great Lakes. We waited and waited for him, but this time he didn't seem to be coming at all. I got worried that he had been in an accident so I called Mom. She told me that she had gone to bed early, but assumed that Dad and Bill left at the usual time. So, all we could do was wait. About an hour later, Dad pulled up in front of the Palmer House. Upon seeing the car, we rushed out through the revolving door, and since Pat was carrying all of the packages we had accumulated, he got stuck in the door. Some of the packages had really weird shapes to them after Pat got through the door. Dad said that he and Bill had fallen asleep and had only awakened an hour before. He and Bill left not waking Mom to tell her they were leaving very late.

We were both glad that nothing had happened to them, but now Pat had a problem, the last train for Great Lakes had already left. We couldn't take him to La Grange because Dad was remodeling, the house was a mess and I didn't want his first look at our house to be like that. Dad's solution was to drive Pat to Great Lakes. I was very skeptical to say the least. Dad had never been good at finding places that were close to home, now he was going to drive to Great Lakes in the dark. This was surely a 21st birthday that I would always remember.

While Dad was filling up his gas tank, he asked the attendant for directions to the Naval Station Great Lakes in North Chicago. The attendant told Dad that had no idea how to get to that Great Lakes place or what it was! Dad decided it had to be north of us so he got on Lake Shore Drive and we were off to somewhere north. We drove for hours, literally! I believe, many times, driving through the same area two or three times. We found North Chicago and eventually Great Lakes at around 4:00 a.m. Pat conveyed his goodbyes and appreciation for the ride then went through the gate. He was the lucky one. He got to go to bed, while we still had to find our way back to La Grange. Our truly long journey finally ended when we arrived in La Grange at 7:00 a.m.

At work on Monday, everybody asked how I enjoyed my birthday with Pat. I told them with a big smile, that I had had a wonderful birthday but that I didn't get to sleep until 7:00 a.m. That comment really raised a lot of eyebrows. Good old moral Bonnie had stayed out all night with a sailor, tsk, tsk. I was slow to tell them that Dad had been with us for the last six hours. It was fun to make believe, at least for a few minutes, that I had had a risqué birthday date.

Our next Saturday, May 4, was planned to be a completely different date. Ann and I were going to ride the Northwestern train to Great Lakes and meet Pat and his friend Tom there. We were setting Ann and Tom up on a blind date hoping that they might find what Pat and I had found together. All of us had a tremendous evening and Ann and Tom seemed to hit it off quite well. We went to see some old movies at the Base theater, had a lunch of hamburgers at the Base's Rathskeller, then pizza at the Non-Commissioned Officer's (NCO) Club for dinner. When I warmly kissed Pat goodnight, to our surprise, so did Ann and Tom. Things had sure progressed rapidly with them. It was only their first date and already they were on kissing terms.

Ann and I boarded the last train bound for Chicago, finding it a bit unnerving riding the train so late at night. A large group of women got on with us but seemed quite different than us. They looked and acted like 'ladies of the night' who got their amusement (and maybe money) from spending time with the sailors at Great Lakes. Ann and I simply scrunched down in our seats and looked intently out the window until our Chicago stop was called. Dad was right there waiting at the Northwestern station to take us home.

The following Saturday was really special, Pat was going to come to La Grange for Mark's First Communion. I was very nervous. Pat hadn't met Mom or Mark yet and hadn't seen the house that I grew up in. We were to pick him up at the Northwestern station in the early afternoon after Mark's Communion mass. We waited for him, but he wasn't on the train he had said he would be on, making me even more nervous. Knowing him as well as I did now, I couldn't figure out what could have happened to him. I had wanted things to go perfectly. The next train would come in an hour later, so Dad said we would wait for it and see if he was on that one. To my great relief, I spotted him among the wave of sailors who had come into Chicago for the weekend. He looked like he had run alongside the train the whole way. He had missed the first train due to a surprise inspection and no one could leave the Base until it was completed. The Navy couldn't care less what was going on in personal lives.

Anyway, I was just glad that he had arrived safely. It had already been an off and on celebration. The previous week, Mark had come down with German measles and we didn't know if he would be able to make his First Communion. Luckily Mark's spots faded away before Saturday and he felt fine. When Pat was among the missing, I had become resigned that the whole day would be tragedy. Instead, we all went out to dinner and then to a movie. After Dad and I returned from seeing Pat off on the train, I had a talk with Mom. She said that she liked Pat, he was soft spoken and had such nice manners. That put me in Seventh Heaven, Mom had the same opinion of him that I did. Now I knew that my eyes hadn't been completely blinded by love. I always valued Mom's opinion, especially when it coincided with my own.

The following four Saturdays were spent in much the same way with Pat and I meeting early in the morning, touring downtown Chicago, having dinner, and going to a movie. We walked through Lincoln Park Zoo, went on a boat ride on Lake Michigan and viewed most of the movies that were around at the time: *The Odd Couple, The Planet of the Apes, Half a Sixpence, Rosemary's Baby, The Prime of Miss Jean Brody* and *Yours, Mine, and Ours.*

One Saturday we had to see two movies, it rained all day and we couldn't walk around and see the sights. When we weren't in a theater, we spent time sitting in the Greyhound Station waiting for the rain to stop. We even had a good time doing that, though that does seem hard to believe. We found that when two people are in love, every minute they spend together takes on new meaning. It isn't so much what you're doing, it's that you're doing it together.

Word had gotten around Bosler that Bonnie had a boyfriend. When Mac Hecktman heard about it, he told me that he would like to treat us to a nice dinner downtown. I immediately wrote Pat to tell him that he'd be having extra money left over this week, we were being treated to a dinner at Maurice's. We both thought that it was super for Mac to do that for us. This Saturday was June 22, and it started out like every other Saturday had for the past few months. Instead of staying in the waiting-area for Pat's train, I decided to wait right by the tracks where his trains came in. That way I would be right there when he got off the train and not have to wait an extra minute to see him. After our greetings, he said that since it was such a beautiful day we should take a leisurely walk along the lake front. I agreed and we headed there. After a kind of short walk along the shore, Pat headed us to a vacant bench. As we sat down Pat turned to me saying that he had a little present for me, but I would have to decide if I wanted to accept it. I was so naïve, I thought it would be perfume or something, but why would I have to decide if I wanted to accept it. Pat bent down and pulled a small box from his camera case. My brain finally began to register that no perfume came in a small box like that. I opened it and there was a set of rings, an engagement ring and a wedding ring. I was shocked, but hadn't lost my reason, so I told him that I wanted it more than anything else in this world. As Pat slipped the engagement ring on my finger, I knew that we were both as seriously in love as two people could possibly be.

With my engagement ring came an immediate urge to spread the word to my parents. I called home and Mom answered. She didn't seem as surprised as I thought she'd be. I guess she knew that more was going on than met my naive eye. Dad came on next. When I told him, there was complete silence on the line. Finally, he said that I should have taken a coat downtown, it was going to get cold. I truly believe that this was the first time in his life that he was truly at a loss for words.

After I hung up, I asked Pat if he had told his parents about us yet. He said he had only told them that he had met a beautiful Bohemian girl, who had kept him from being so lonely. Pat's Mom had been appalled that her son would be going out with some "bohemian beatnik." Apparently, the West Coast wasn't that clued in to the ethnic diversity of the Midwest. The West Coast bohemian life-style of the 1950s had revolved around coffeehouses, dressing in black, not wearing shoes, having straight, ironed hair, playing a guitar, and reciting poetry. Pat's Mom didn't grasp that Bohemia was a part of Czechoslovakia and a nationality like German or Irish. Pat's Mom had major worries about who her naïve son might get involved with. She had warned Pat when he left for Great Lakes that he should be wary of those "Chicago Girls." Now that Pat and I were engaged, I figured I had better write to her and tell her a little about myself to correct any wrong impressions.

I couldn't believe what a mind reader Mac Hecktman had been for giving us an upscale dinner on this particular Saturday. It was a meal fit to celebrate our special day with thick rib eye steaks and champagne. We ended the day by going on a boat ride on Lake Michigan with Pat taking pictures of me and the beautiful sunset. He did get a little too exuberant with his picture taking. He leaned over me, nearly strangling me with the camera strap, to get the pictures he wanted. That wasn't a very nice way to treat your future bride. I guess after a couple gets engaged some of the formalities slip.

When I returned to work on Monday, I got busy mailing out invoices. I didn't want to say anything about our engagement until someone noticed my ring, which didn't take long. As soon as Ida came to help me, she grabbed my hand, gave me a big hug and kiss to congratulate me. If this went on all day, I was sure I wouldn't get much work done. With Ida's congratulations, the word spread like wild fire and everyone came to look at my ring. When Mr. Neidorf saw all the people milling around, he asked Shirley what was going on. After she told him, he went back into his office grumbling that, "nobody tells me anything." Later, he called me into his office to congratulate me and find out what our plans were. I said that they were very tentative, but I thought I would be leaving Bosler sometime in December. He told me that he didn't even know that I had a boyfriend, but he gave himself credit for it since he had given me a reference for the USO hostess application and I had met Pat there. He, then, waited impatiently for Jordan to come in so he could be the first to tell him about me. It was a fantastic day, I received heartfelt congratulations from everyone. With all this happiness came the realization that I would soon be starting a new life away from my family, home, and friends. I felt kind of sad about that, but in my heart, I knew that it was time for a change in my life. I couldn't think of a better life change than to trade my job for being a wife and mother.

As I told Mr. Neidorf, our plans were tentative. Pat's electronics school at Great Lakes would finish at the end of August and he wasn't sure where the Navy would send him from there. It was rumored that his most probable duty station would be the Naval Communication Station, Cheltenham, Maryland. I had to get things in order so I could go travel to Cheltenham after our December wedding. Pat's leaving meant that I would have to do all of the wedding planning by myself. As long as both of us could write and phone, I figured that we could keep things straight that way. It was going to be a hectic and very lonely three-month time for me. I merely had to handle my time like I had before I met Pat. It was remarkable how much he had added to my life since meeting him in March. I could take solace in the fact, though, that we would be spending our whole lives together.

Our following Saturdays were spent much as before, but with something new added, planning our future together. Pat told me that our life was not going to be easy, he was earning very little money as a petty officer third-class. I reassured him that I wasn't used to living in the lap of luxury. He said that we wouldn't even be near luxury's feet as he was only paid $76 every two weeks. I told him not to worry until the time came, we could work everything out together.

For now, our major worry was about getting as much wedding planning in before Pat left. After all, he was going to be a rather integral part of the ceremony. Since Pat's parents couldn't participate in the planning from 2,500 miles away, we had to plan our wedding centric to my meager family. We both decided that we'd have only a best man and a maid of honor. Bill would be the best man and his girlfriend, Mary Ann, would be the maid of honor. Mary Ann's parents were very nice and were just as excited about the wedding as my parents. They even took Pat, me and my family out for a lobster dinner to celebrate our engagement. It was there that Mary Ann's mother tried to persuade us to get married before Pat graduated from his Navy school. We were both very much in love, but we didn't want to rush things that much. Mom was very relieved when we said that we would keep things the way we had already decided.

As the weeks dwindled to Pat's leaving date, we both knew that our very wonderful courtship was coming to an end. We would become a married couple soon and would be with each other all the time and not just once a week. We decided to play his last weeks in Chicago as two single people going out with each to have fun with no responsibilities or commitments to each other. Our marriage meant that we promised to love and take care of each other no matter what. We would soon lose our carefree attitudes and set our minds to making each other the happiest possible. We went to see *Camelot* again, that had been the start of our future commitment. I went on the train to Great Lakes a couple more times for picnics on the beach with Pat.

Just after our engagement, there were weird things going around the "doll house" in La Grange. Something was up and I wasn't supposed to know about it. Mark and I were never left alone together, so I knew that something was being kept a secret and that Mark knew all the details. In my mind, it was definite that Mark was the one that I had to work on, and for me that was very easy work. Mark at the age of eight was the biggest blabber mouth around, so if you wanted to know anything, all you had to do was pump young Mark.

A couple of weeks passed and things were getting really strange. Mom and Dad were going out at night to who knows where, and then there were questions of where different people that I knew lived. I was dying to know what was going on, so when my chance came, I immediately took Mark into a dark corner. Without any physical torture, he spilled every bean there was. It was as I had expected; a bridal shower was being planned. Mom and Dad were out having the decorations made, the restaurant reserved, and the meal planned. I knew that my poor Mom must have been going crazy, she had never been involved in a shower before, much less planning the whole thing.

I couldn't keep on with the charade of the "three monkeys," so I told her that I knew what was going on, and to her relief, she said, "Thank God, now you can help me out before I go completely nuts." Everything was pretty much done already except for getting the invitations out, which had to be pretty soon since Pat was leaving at the end of August. It is a Bohemian-Polish custom that the husband-to-be would be present at the bridal shower, so it had to be planned for the early part of August. I sat down and made a list of all my relatives and the women at Bosler. Mary Ann's mother wrote all the invitations. Soon after they were mailed out, Mom was in a frenzy that she hadn't received any responses. I told her that people don't respond as fast as you want, probably most of the responses would come the week before the shower. I was right but poor Mom was about to have a breakdown before we heard from everyone. With all the responses in, there were going to be almost 50 women there, quite a number with our small family.

When August 4, rolled around, everyone was glad that shower day had finally arrived. It had been awfully hard for me at work to keep pretending that I didn't suspect a thing, and for Mom to pretend that she didn't know that I knew. Today the whole charade would finally be over. The day itself was sunny and humid with temperatures in the 90s. When Pat was deposited at the restaurant, he was a bundle of nerves. He had never been to a shower before and he knew virtually no one at the shower. He didn't grumble about having to be at the shower or that he'd be the only man there. Pat just chalked it up to the idea that things were done differently in Chicago, especially in a Bohemian family. He knew that he was joining a family that was different from everyone he had known. We were a sort of conformist, non-conformist family, who did things not according to what was proper, but by what would make the most family members happy.

The wedding shower was being held at a Bohemian restaurant, The Blue Bonnet, in Brookfield, Illinois. The food consisted of a family style meal of pork tenderloin and sliced beef with side orders of sauerkraut, dumplings, mashed potatoes, corn, green beans, rolls, relish tray and Bohemian pastry. It was a nice spread and everyone ate until they were ready to burst. What the guests couldn't finish, as per custom, they stuffed in their purses for later. Mom had also brought a monstrous shower cake baked by, you guessed it, her favorite Bohemian bakery. The decorations on the ceiling were compliments of Dad, Pat, and Bill.

Besides the actual wedding day, I think the day a girl remembers most is her wedding shower. It's a congratulatory sendoff from all your friends and family into your new life. The presents they give can help make your transition into married life easier, and, hopefully, save the newlyweds some money. We got some very nice gifts, but we did receive some good candidates to be stuck up in the attic or a closet. Neither Pat or I were coffee drinkers at the time, but we got four coffee percolators, including a 30 cup version! Since we didn't see too many parties of 30 people in our future, we knew it would find a place in a future attic.

A present that was worthy of remembering was the gift that Pat gave me. Mom bought a slinky nightgown that was supposed to be from Pat, but she forgot to tell him about it. When I opened the package and held it up, Pat was very surprised and kind of red. He recovered rapidly when the women began clapping and oohing, pretending that he had picked it out. One of my aunts began doing sort of a strip tease with her clothes on. She stuck discarded present bows all over herself, then ribbon tassels on her chest. All the while doing a dance. She was the hit of the party. Another aunt began yelling out risqué comments about some of the presents. I received four peignoirs sets and each time I held one up she would yell out, "There'll be a hot time in the old town tonight," or, "She'll never use that, because it'll mostly be under the pillow." Everyone laughed every time.

As the last of the presents were loaded into Dad's station wagon and the last thank you and goodbye were said, our next issue was to get Pat back in time for the last train to the Great Lakes. Since it was Sunday, the last train would leave Chicago at 5:45 p.m. and it was getting onto five o'clock already. We all raced back to the house and unloaded our gifts. There was still half of shower cake left, so Mom handed Pat the cake and told him to take it back to the Base. Pat said that he couldn't travel on a train carrying a cake that big, but he did want to take back a few pieces with him. The cake was cut and wrapped in seconds and Dad, Pat, and I were off to catch a train.

It seemed to me that we were always hurrying to catch some train. It would be really nice to be married and not have to catch a train after our date was over. Being married would also be far less complicated than trying to carry on a relationship once a week from so many miles away. We arrived just in time for Pat to catch his train. Since we only had two minutes to spare, our goodbyes had to be quick. As Dad and I rode home, I was thinking about what a beautiful day it had been but also, where the heck I was going to put all our shower gifts in my parent's tiny house.

As I said before, our separate lives went on as before with Pat and I meeting as often as possible. His graduation was coming up and we were trying to plan things before he had to leave for Cheltenham. Pat had a two-week leave coming to him between duty stations so we decided he should go visit his parents for a week then come stay in La Grange for his second week. Pat had been given some material about Cheltenham so we already knew what was there. Then the Navy threw us a curve by changing Pat's orders to the Naval Technical Training Center, Corry Station, Pensacola, Florida. We were both happy about that, Florida sounded much better than Maryland. At that point, we had no idea how many more curves the Navy would throw us over the next five years.

It was now mid-August and Pat was visiting his parents in Bellingham, Washington. I so missed seeing him that Saturday wondering how I would make it through not seeing him for the three and a half months before our wedding. Since there wasn't much I could do about it, I just had to live through it. When Pat came to La Grange, we had a whole week together before he had to leave for Florida, so we made the best of every minute we had. We still couldn't spend the days together, I was still working, so Pat hung around the house with Mom and went fishing in the Des Plaines River with Bill.

When I came home, we ate dinner and immediately ran off to a movie or worked on wedding preparations. All that week we didn't get to bed before 2:00 a.m., so I was really dragging by the time Friday rolled around. At work, I was in sort of a daze with everything in the office seeming remote. When people would talk to me, the words didn't seem to want to penetrate my brain, so I was never quite sure what was going on around me.

The one wedding preparation we got settled before Pat left was renting the reception hall. We found a very nice restaurant in Oak Lawn, Illinois, that had banquet rooms for weddings. They had a very nice dinner menu, the price was in our budget, and so we put a deposit down on the hall for December 28. We picked a full turkey dinner. The price included an open bar the entire evening, so I knew that would please a lot of people. In our society, the success of any affair seems to rest on the quality and quantity of the available booze. Some people couldn't care if hot dogs were served as long as their glasses were kept full all night.

When our final day together arrived, it was very hard for the two of us to say goodbye. Since Pat had been staying in Bill's room right next to mine, it was easy for us to have some time to ourselves. There wasn't any serious hanky-panky, just some very, very painful goodbyes. We stayed up practically the entire night hugging and kissing and trying to say all the things that we hadn't said thus far. We did get a couple hours' sleep, but 7:00 a.m. came very fast. It was a rainy day befitting the sadness we both felt. After Pat got the last of his things packed and in the car, he said goodbye to Mark telling him to be good, and gave Mom a kiss and thanked her for everything.

The ride from La Grange to O'Hare Field was very quiet. Pat checked in and we waited with him for the plane to board. In seeming minutes, boarding was called and we said our final goodbye with a last lingering kiss. By the time Pat's plane took off, Dad, Bill, and I were already on our way home. At home, I decided I would go back to bed and try to catch up on my lost sleep. I knew, that the coming months would go by swiftly, because 1001 wedding preparations still had to be made. It's unbelievable how much planning goes into making a single wedding day successful, and how many things can go wrong to prevent that success.

CHAPTER 12
FOR BETTER OR WORSE

After Pat left for Pensacola, Florida, I felt more lost and alone than I ever had in my life. I had to pull myself together, a lot of planning had to be done during the next few weeks. I knew Pat would be just as busy at his end, he had to buy a car and find a place for us to live after we were married. I knew that our letters would help keep us close and, in no time, we would be together again. With these thoughts returned the sadness of leaving my home and my family who also meant the world to me. I knew the time was right for me to marry and make my own home and family. I couldn't conceive of a man more right for me than Pat. When you know it's right, you just have to do it and bear any unpleasant side effects. It was time for both Pat and I to make it on our own and that was what we were going to begin doing on December 28th.

The first thing I accomplished was to select my wedding dress. Mom, Mary Ann and her mother picked their dresses out at the same time, so the female contingent of the wedding party was now taken care of. My dress had a straight skirt with lace top and sleeves, it was simple and reasonably priced. Mom's dress was aqua blue with lace around the collar and sleeves with a straight skirt that showed off her very slim figure.

Mary Ann chose a red velvet dress and her mother a peach dress that cost more than Mom's did, she was really getting into my wedding. Next, Mrs. Mitch began to try to take things over, giving suggestions about things that were my Mom's business not hers. Mom surprised me by not allowing her get away with much. After all, this was her only daughter's wedding, it was up to her to make some of the decisions with no one else's interference.

Dad, Bill, and Mark needed to be measured for their tuxedos. Mark needed one because he was going to be our ring bearer. He was eight years old, cute as anything but so small he looked like he was five years old. Dad had never worn a tuxedo in his life, as his occupation as a truck mechanic seldom called for formal wear.

Gerry suggested a bakery for our wedding cake, so after work one night, Dad and I went to check it out. When we arrived, the owner took us in back to show us some of the cakes that he was working on, they were beautiful. I knew that he had to make our cake. We were there quite some time as he took us on a tour of his entire business, showing us how he made the different decorations. Whenever Dad got together with a talkative, friendly man, unless someone intervenes calling attention to the time, it'll be a long session. I did and we finally got to the purpose of our visit, to select a cake. We settled on a three-tiered cake with red poinsettias with green leaves and lily of the valley scattered here and there. The decoration that would adorn the top would be tiny bride and groom statues standing under a white double arch. I knew he was going to make us a cake to be proud of, with colors befitting the holiday spirit.

We needed to hire some musicians to provide music at the reception. Marie had just gone to a wedding and said that the music was excellent. She got us a card with the musicians' name and telephone number and we made an appointment to hear them play. The band was made up of three teenaged boys who practiced in one of their parent's basements on an accordion, a saxophone, and drums. It seemed an odd combination, but when we heard them play, they were good. Their repertoire included everything from old traditional songs to the very new ones. Their band was named the Top Hats, which fitted them because they were top musicians for their ages. We were so impressed that we hired them on the spot without looking any further.

Next, I selected our wedding announcements. Since Pat's parents couldn't participate, I had to order them. They would be ready in a couple of weeks, so I got busy on the guest list. In between, I got started sorting out my personal things, deciding what would be going with me to Pensacola.

I regularly received letters from Pat, sometimes twice a week. He reported that had bought us a silver 1965 Plymouth Fury four-door sedan. This car would be his transportation to Chicago for the wedding and our transportation to Pensacola after the wedding. He also wrote that he had found a garage apartment for us. A friend and classmate, who was living there with his wife, were leaving just before our wedding. He said that it wasn't much, but it was furnished and the $85 per month rent matched our meager budget. It didn't really matter to me where we lived, all I wanted was to be with Pat. Newlyweds tend to be very idealistic, believing they can easily live on their love, not so much, when the rent comes due and they don't have the money. There has to be a certain amount of reality and practicality or else the marriage suffers because of financial worries. I felt I knew Pat well enough now that I didn't worry about his choices for a car and a place to live. He was very level headed and would not buy or do something without thinking the whole thing through very carefully.

Then, Pat dropped the bomb that none of his family would be able to attend our wedding. Pat's Grandma Clubine had undergone cancer surgery and with her advanced age, she needed a lot of help to recover. I felt bad that things had to work out that way. I had looked forward to meeting them and their meeting my family. Pat said that his Uncle Lincoln Clubine and family from Grand Rapids, Michigan would stand in, so Pat would now have six people from his side. On my side, I was able to accumulate about 100 relatives and Bosler friends, which I thought was just the right amount.

Pat had already given me my engagement and wedding rings, but Pat didn't have a wedding ring. One Saturday, Mark and I went to the Chicago Loop to purchase a ring for Pat. Mark and I went into a jewelry store on State Street which Pat and I had gazed into the window of numerous times. There we had seen a ring that Pat especially liked, so I went there to buy it. The store was owned by a guy whose favorite phrase was, "Have I got a deal for you, you wouldn't believe." With me being so gullible, I figured that that was great, I was always looking for a good deal. I pointed to the ring that I wanted and told him the size needed. The price was posted above the ring, so I knew it was within the price range that I wanted. He led me away from the window telling me that he didn't have that particular ring in the size I asked for.

Back at the counter, he pulled out a huge bunch of men's wedding rings strung on a large metal ring. All of them looked used to me, but he kept after me with his spiel. I looked at most of them, and finally picked out one that was very much like the one in the window. This ring was twice the price, so I told him that it was far outside the budget. He said not to worry, he would knock off $10. I told him again that it was too expensive. He went on and on about the quality I would be getting with this ring that it was, "such a deal." I told him a third time that it was too expensive and started to walk to the door. He asked me to come back, that he would drop another $10. I told him it was still outside my budget and, again, turned to go. He said, "It kills me but, because I like your brother, I'll drop another $10." I told him he had a deal. As I paid him he told me again that he really gave me "such a deal." I told him that I appreciated that. When Mark and I left the store, I had a smile on my face. I knew that even with him dropping $30 off the regular price he had made a profit on the sale. I hadn't worked three years for a Jewish firm and learned nothing. I witnessed every day how good they were at handling money and manipulating customers into believing what a great deal they were giving them.

All of the wedding details were pretty much figured out, except how we would get all the probable presents and my things down to Pensacola with just a car. Pat considered renting a trailer hitch and trailer but, if we got the usual bad December weather, it would probably be too dangerous (especially since Pat had never pulled a trailer before). I suggested the idea of buying a car top carrier and Pat agreed. I ordered one from Sears and solved our transportation problem.

It was now late-November and everything was ready to go. All we had to do now was wait for our wedding day, hoping that everything would continue to go well for us. The Chicago fall weather had been very mild so far. There wasn't a hint of snow in the long-range forecast, so we were hoping that it would stay that way. Since most weddings don't go like clockwork, we were foolish to imagine that everything would for mine.

The first problem cropped up when Mom called Mary Ann's mother to tell her that we needed to go in for our final dress fittings. She told Mom that Mary Ann was very sick, that it might be appendicitis. That was all we needed with the wedding so close. We couldn't get another maid of honor at this late date. Anyway, it would be impossible for her to get a dress made in time. Mom called our druggist (old neighborhood style) and he told her how Mary Ann's mother could check for appendicitis. Mom got back to her and told her what the druggist had said to do. She immediately began pressing on Mary Ann's stomach where the druggist had suggested. From her brief examination, she decided that Mary Ann had the stomach flu, for which we were all thankful (even Mary Ann).

Then another problem came up with Mary Ann. While collecting Bill's dirty clothes, Mom found a picture of Mary Ann dressed in sexy baby doll pajamas. Mom called Mary Ann's mother telling her that things were getting out of hand for two 15-year-olds. Mom told her that she didn't think it was proper for the two of them to be in Mary Ann's bedroom with the door closed. Mary Ann's mother became very indignant and said that she trusted her daughter. Mom told her that it wasn't a question of trust, but of precaution. They were both very young and she didn't want them to get into something that would disgrace both families. The conversation got very heated and when it ended, I was doubtful that I still had a Maid of Honor. Mom thought that we should try to think of someone else just in case. I thought of Pat's sister Tracy, but it would be too expensive for us to fly her in for the wedding. Next, I thought of my cousin Janice next door. Mom talked to my Uncle Jimmy and he thought that she would be glad to do it, if our original choice didn't work out. He said that she still had the dress that she had worn the year before to her sister Judy's wedding.

Mary Ann's mother called a week later to tell us that she would allow Mary Ann to be my Maid of Honor as originally planned. It was obvious that the friendship that had developed between the two families had cooled. It was too bad that it had to happen so close to the wedding, it made things very awkward for all of us.

December was on our doorstep before we knew it, and I was really getting hard to live with. Mom told me that she knew why I was acting this way, I wanted to make things bad so that it would be easier to leave. I realized she was right, Mom was always a smart cookie. She told me that she was happy that I would be seeing and living in new places with Pat. She didn't want me to be like her, not going anywhere outside of Illinois. She refused to let me leave on a sour note. She wanted me to leave with the memories of all the happy times we had had together as a family. By now we were both in tears. I hugged her and told her that I loved her and would miss her most of all. She said that time would go by fast and that we would all be together again soon. I should make the best of our travels, not everyone had a chance like that offered to them. I was glad she and I had that talk, it showed me that, even though I was leaving, my family wished me the best and would be there whenever Pat or I needed them. It was so reassuring for me to hear those words from her. Mom allowed me to see that I wasn't losing my family, merely widening the scope of love in my life. Put that way, it didn't seem such a traumatic change. I was moving to a new State with my new loving roommate and every day would be a new and different adventure. Pat still had five years left in the Navy, so I was sure that we would be living in places that no one would believe. I had no idea how unbelievable they would be.

With much anticipation and stress, the third week of December rolled around, and we were all awaiting Pat's arrival. With all the other preparations made, it seemed the most important element of our wedding still wasn't done.

After all, you can't have a wedding without a groom. With any luck, mine would be arriving any day now.

Friday, December 20, was my last day at Bosler. When 4:45 p.m. rolled around, I started going around to say my goodbyes. It was really difficult, I liked all these people very much. I had spent five days out of each week with them for three years, they were my other family. Everyone knew everyone else's business, like in a small town. When something happened good or bad to one of us, everyone was always there to celebrate or offer help. I would miss these people deeply, but they were a part of my life that was coming to an end. I had to leave them behind to be able to begin a new exciting chapter of my life. My love for Pat made me strong enough to leave everything that had been important to me up until now, to start things anew with him.

When Dad and I were driving home that night, it struck me that this would be our last drive home from work together. He would have to get used to riding to work alone again. All these thoughts hit me at once and I was fast becoming so emotional that one word from anyone made me burst out in tears. I suppose all brides-to-be have similar feelings. What I needed at this point was Pat beside me and I wished more than ever that he would arrive in La Grange soon.

When Dad and I arrived from work, we all went out for our weekly grocery shopping and to have a family dinner. This would probably be my last grocery shopping trip with my family. The next time that I'd go grocery shopping would be as a married woman shopping with her husband. All these last-minute thoughts were driving me crazy. When we returned home, I went upstairs to be alone and cry by myself. I didn't have to cry for long. There was a knock at the door and Mom yelled for me to come downstairs and see who was here. I ran down and there was Pat, in all his worn-out glory, he had driven non-stop from Pensacola to La Grange. My tears stopped and my happiness returned with a bang. I ran into his arms and kissed him like we hadn't seen each other for years instead of months. The wedding could go on as planned, the groom was here! December 28th could now officially be the happiest day of my life.

Pat brought his sea bag in and we went upstairs to say hello more privately without the whole family looking on. We simultaneously tried to tell each other all of the things that had happened while we were separated. We quickly laid out our plan for the week. Since, both of us had had our blood tests, we needed to go to the Cook County Courthouse in Chicago to get our marriage license.

There was very little time left before our wedding, so all we could do was cross our fingers that everything would go smoothly on our big day.

During the week, things, disturbingly, began to go awry. Marie called to tell me that Mr. Neidorf's mother had passed away. That meant that he and the rest of his family wouldn't be able to attend my wedding or the reception. I sent my condolences but that wiped out a number of attendees. Well, we still had enough people left to make a good-sized wedding party. Next, the TV news began reporting that Chicago had a flu epidemic on its hands. This left me very worried over how many would come down with the flu and not be able to attend our wedding. It had been the mild weather that had helped this epidemic spread. I had thought that the weather had been cooperating, now I wasn't so sure.

By Friday, the weather forecast had changed to warnings of a major blizzard, providing the first heavy snowfall of the year. When Mom and I picked up our dresses, a sleety rain had already started to fall. The weathermen were predicting that the temperature would drop sharply during the night and this sleet would turn into gusting snow. When we got the dresses home, we discovered that Mom's hat was missing. With a call to the dress shop, we learned that they couldn't find it. I sat down and said to myself, "Tomorrow is going to be a disaster." An hour later, the dress shop called to tell us that they had found Mom's hat. Well, that little problem was solved, but what could be done about the blizzard and the flu epidemic? The easy answer, nothing!

At about 8:00 p.m., Pat, Dad, and Bill went to spend the night at a neighborhood motel. Mom sent them there so Pat wouldn't see my wedding dress, plus, it would be a lot easier for me to do my final packing with three less bodies in the house. We would all be pacing the floor most of the night anyway. The house became dead quiet as the evening wore on. Mark and Mom managed to sleep, I just couldn't. At 4:00 a.m., I got hungry so I grabbed the only interesting thing left in the refrigerator and sat on the couch to eat a bowl of Jell-O.

When dawn broke on Saturday, December 28, I looked out of the window to see 4"-6" of accumulated snow. I thought, sarcastically, that my wedding day could have had better weather. The snow had tapered off to a light flurry. The gusting wind was whirling the fallen snow into clouds a couple of feet above the ground. It wouldn't have been so bad if it was just snow, but it had been mixed with rain earlier in the evening. The result was a slippery slush that was going to make walking next to impossible and driving even worse. This was my wedding day! The day that I would be wearing my beautiful white wedding dress and white high heeled shoes. The snow seemed to have shown up just to upstage "me," not to provide me with a "white wedding" backdrop.

As the morning progressed more things began to go wrong. The phone was ringing off the hook with calls from people saying that they couldn't attend due to the weather. After ten such calls, I was feeling very depressed. Then, I thought, since I couldn't do anything about the weather, the heck with it. I was getting married! All of the members of my immediate family had been spared from getting the flu, the people who couldn't come because of the flu or weather were incidental to the wedding ceremony. As long as the people I loved the most, Pat and my family, were there, that was all that really mattered. With that thought, my mood picked up and I readied myself for the task of becoming a new bride.

At 11:00 a.m., I went to the local beauty shop to have my hair shampooed and styled. By the time Grandpa Taraba picked me up, the wind was a howling gale. I was sure that I was going to look like the "wicked witch of the North" when the wind got at my hair. I dashed into the house between the wind gusts, so my hair wasn't too tousled. It was now 12:30 p.m. With the wedding scheduled for 3:00 p.m., I decided to get officially dressed. With Mom helping me, it took no time at all, and I found myself wearing a dress that wasn't easy to sit down in. Well, that didn't matter much, I spent most of the time pacing the floor.

In the meantime, Dad called from the motel to say that everything was okay there and that they were getting dressed. Dad and Bill were trying to get into their rented tuxedos while Pat was dressing in his formal Navy dress uniform with medals. For Pat getting dressed was a snap, but Dad was really having his problems with his tux. Pat told me later that Dad hadn't slept the entire night. All he did was walk the floors and chain smoke. When it came time for him to get dressed, he was all shaking thumbs. Pat told me that he had slept fine. In the morning, he and Bill had watched cartoons on TV. As the hours passed, we received calls from Dad asking which way the buttons were supposed to go on his shirt, and how we had put the cummerbund on Mark so he could do the same. Dad was a nervous wreck.

At 2:00 p.m., a photographer arrived at our house and it wasn't the one we hired to take the pictures. The photographer told us that the original photographer couldn't make it for the church service, but would be there for the reception. This guy smelled and acted pickled at 2:00 p.m. in the afternoon! He was slurring his words and making tasteless comments while taking pictures of me getting ready. He told me to lift up my dress, so he could take a picture of my garter. When I did, he told me to lift it higher adding that, "You will be showing more than that to your husband tonight". Talk about tacky! When he was finished, not soon enough for me, we started to bundle up to go to the church.

Mary Ann's father came over in his Cadillac to chauffeur us around for the day. When I opened the front door, and looked out, I wondered if I would make it to the car. Dad said, "Come on, we'll make it." He grabbed me by the arm and had to hold me up all the way. My beautiful new high heel shoes weren't designed for walking in the snow. The wind was blowing stronger now and my veil almost blew off my head. When we reached the car, Dad opened the door and had to push me in.

With everyone in their cars, the possession started for St. Cletus Catholic Church, normally just ten minutes away. The driving was extremely hazardous with very poor visibility. When the three cars arrived at the church, everyone had to be very careful as they made their way into the church. Once inside the church, someone said that the photographer hadn't arrived yet. It was nearing 3:00 p.m. and we'd lost the photographer, why not? Not only that, we couldn't find where the florist had left our wedding flowers: my bouquet, corsages for the ladies and a bouquet of flowers that I would place in front of the statue of the Blessed Virgin Mary during the ceremony. A chaotic mess it was, but the show was going on, no matter what!

Finally, the photographer's car pulled in. When he entered the church, he told us his car had slid off the road and into a ditch a couple of houses from my parents' house. He said that some wonderful people had helped him dig it out. Next, miraculously, my aunt found our wedding flowers stuck under a card table and they were distributed with haste. At this point, the poor priest looked like he was going to have a meltdown. He kept peeking out from the vestibule to see if we would ever be ready to go. All this time the church organist had been playing very softly in the background, waiting for a sign from anyone to start music for our march down the aisle. Suddenly, Bill was running full speed out of the church towards our station wagon. He came back with our wedding rings. He had forgotten them in the glove compartment!

Now we could begin the proceedings. Mark, the Ring Bearer, led the procession carrying his pillow down the aisle, next came Mary Ann, and Dad and I brought up the rear. When I look at the picture of Dad and I walking down the aisle, I have to laugh. Dad and I looked so solemn it seemed we were going to a lynching not my wedding. The church pews were almost deserted, the weather and the flu epidemic had whittled our audience down to some very hardy and loving people. Pat's Uncle Lincoln and family had even made the harrowing drive from Michigan. I had moved beyond worrying about anything but what was about to happen. I had made it to the altar with my Pat, and that was a great accomplishment after all the obstacles.

When Dad and I reached the altar, Pat walked from the right side to stand next to me. Dad lifted up my veil, gave me a kiss, shook hands with Pat and placed my hand in Pat's. Everything went smoothly from then on. As we stood in front of the priest to exchange vows, he whispered, "You can look at each other." We must have been one dazed and scared looking pair. After our vows were exchanged, I placed the bouquet in front of the statue of the Blessed Virgin Mary to the left of the altar, and Pat placed a rose in front of the statue of St. Joseph on the right. After that was done, the priest declared us man and wife, told Pat he could kiss his bride, and introduced us to our family and friends as Mr. and Mrs. Patrick Harrington. We marched down the aisle hand in hand all smiles. Everyone gathered in the church foyer to give us their congratulations, throw rice and see us leave the church. We were actually husband and wife now! We were both ecstatically happy, no weather could dampen that happiness.

The reception started at 6:00 p.m. so we all had a couple of hours to rest and get freshened up. Mainly the freshening was to get the rice out of our hair and from down our backs. A little after 5:00 p.m., we bundled back into our cars to go to the reception hall. The driving was terrible, there were cars that had slid off the road everywhere. Thank goodness, we all made it in one piece. I was nervous entering the hall. I hoped that the cake had been delivered, that the band made it okay and that, at least, some of our guests would venture out to celebrate with us. The cake was there and more beautiful than promised. The Top Hats arrived with wet feet, running noses and their instruments intact. As to guests, it was now after 6:00 p.m. and only a handful had arrived. The room looked ridiculous with so many tables and places setup and so few people. There were 100 guests invited, now it was anybody's guess as to how many would actually show up.

For the next hour and a half, people trickled in. When the trickling finally stopped, we had about fifty stalwart guests. With the open bar, those who showed up were really having a good time, including Dad. He usually didn't drink at all, but by 7:00 p.m., he was already polluted. Mom grabbed him aside telling him that the evening was young, if he didn't take it easy they'd be carrying him out. As the evening wore on it didn't seem he had listened to her, he had a wild, blurry-eyed look about him.

Grandma Taraba seemed to be going the same way as Dad. She began acting as the drink runner for the table she was sitting at. She'd go to the bar with an order for three drinks and on her way back to the table, she would empty the glasses herself. She was soon feeling no pain either. Grandpa Taraba, on the other hand, did no drinking. He was in charge of a silk purse that held any money cards given to us as gifts.

My Aunt Rose always enjoyed parties and drinking. She soon found herself in real need of a bathroom. When she found that the Women's bathroom was at capacity, she entered the Men's. She always did have a great affection for the men, so I was sure that she enjoyed her visit to their john.

Dinner was announced. As soon as everyone was seated, a toast was made to the bride and groom (us!). Then everyone chowed down heartily on their turkey dinners. After dinner, and a couple more toasts, the tables were moved to make room for the dancing. Pat and I danced our first dance together as the Top Hats played "Let Me Call You Sweetheart." After that the Top Hats played every musical request from the guests, from polka to rock.

After some great dancing, it was time to cut the wedding cake. In our pictures, we both look like chipmunks with huge pieces of cake jammed into each other's mouths. Next, Pat threw my blue garter to waiting men and I threw my bridal bouquet to women hoping for marriage. The final ritual at a Bohemian wedding, performed just before the couple leaves the reception, involves removing the bride's veil and tying a white satin apron over her wedding dress signifying that she is no longer a bride, but a wife. My apron had eight tiny babies, a baby bottle, an iron, and pots and pans hanging from ribbons. After the unveiling, I was definitely ready to call it an evening. When Mom told us that she didn't trust Dad to drive home, Pat said he would drive all of us. That was sure a switch, the groom driving the bombed father-in-law home. Hey, everything else had been weird so why not?

As soon as we arrived home, Mom ran into the bathroom to vomit and Dad dropped onto the bed and fell asleep fully dressed. Pat and I decided they needed some time to relax and get calmed down and sober. We quietly slipped out the door and drove to our room at a nearby motel. The room was beautiful.

I told Pat that I was happy everything was over and that I planned to stay married to him forever because I didn't want to go through another wedding. I got undressed in the bathroom and came out dressed in one of my many peignoir sets. Pat undressed in the bedroom coming to bed in his Navy underwear. We kissed and hugged a lot and eventually fell asleep in each other's arms. I had gotten my period the day before, what a surprise, and felt very unhappy about it. Pat told me not to worry about it, he was happy just to be able to hold me for our first night together. He told me that we didn't have to rush things, we had a whole lifetime ahead of us.

When morning came, we bought some donuts and went to the house to see if there were any survivors from the night before. Mom looked terrible and Dad looked even worse. We were hoping Dad would feel better fast, he was supposed to help us pack the car. When I phoned Grandma and Grandpa Taraba to say goodbye, I learned that Grandma had such a hangover that she couldn't get off the couch. I'll say one thing for our wedding reception, it did nothing to promote good family health.

Pat and Dad worked for hours loading our things in the car top carrier. Pat kept saying that he didn't think it was all going to fit. With a lot of maneuvering, they managed to stuff everything either in or on top of the car. I went upstairs to see if anything had been left behind, finding only a lonely bottle of mouthwash. A sudden sad feeling crept over me, all my things had been removed from the only home I've ever known! The moment that I had dreaded for months had finally arrived.

How do you say goodbye to people you have lived with and loved all of your life? How do you thank them for giving up so many things for you? I couldn't think of a worthy way to say it. Mom was in tears when I gave her a kiss and hug goodbye. Neither of us knew what to say but we both knew how we felt. When I kissed Mark telling him to be good, he too was crying. Next came my goodbye to Dad, whose eyes were misty too. Mickey sat up and gave me a big, slobbery kiss goodbye. When Pat came to kiss Mom goodbye, she told him, "You had better take good care of her." We got into our car and with a horn honk, we were off to begin our long drive to our new home and life together.

We did make one more stop to get a fill-up at the gas station where Bill was working. He gave us a case of drinking glasses, shook Pat's hand and gave me a kiss. As we drove away, I saw Bill wiping his eyes with his coverall's sleeve. It took me until we had driven through most of Indiana to stop crying. That had been for my old life, now I could move on to my new life. I had no idea how much strength I would need to deal with it.

PART III
THE MARRIED YEARS

CHAPTER 13
THIS IS OUR HOME?

About the time I stopped crying in Indiana, Pat said that he had had enough driving for one day. We stopped at a motel named The Land of Nod for the night. It was a cute name that went rapidly downhill after we checked into our "honeymoon" room. I knew we couldn't afford to stay in bridal suites, but this room was worse than ridiculous. To call it a room was a vast exaggeration. It was really just an enlarged closet with a bed that had two feet of space around it for walking. To the left of the door was a tiny bathroom with a stand-up shower just wide enough for a person to enter. It was frigidly cold and we could find no heater. We were still in the Midwest at the end of December, so the weather was far from tropical. We undressed quickly, wrapped ourselves around each other and in all the blankets we could find and tried to get some sleep. All night our chattering teeth kept us awake, no sleep for us. With the crack of dawn, we quickly dressed and blew out of there. As soon as we were in our car, Pat ran the car for a bit then put the heater on HIGH. Did it ever feel wonderful a few minutes later! We bid a happy adieu to The Land of Nod forever. No wonder it wasn't in our motel rating book, it only reported on motels with more than zero-star ratings!

As we made our way South, the weather became sunnier and warmer. Soon we were able to shed our winter coats. It was kind of nice being able to do that in December. In early evening, we stopped at a pretty looking motel that we were sure wouldn't offer us another freezing night with no sleep. Our room was spacious with two double beds, a television, a big bathroom and a heater!! The owner brought us ice water and wished us a pleasant night. Now we felt more like newlyweds on their honeymoon. The second double bed was a complete waste for us, but it was nice to have comfort to spare.

We were now in Alabama, so we weren't too far from our new home. This part of Alabama looked very primitive and poor. Down each side of the road were rows of what looked like unpainted sheds. The roofs had gaping holes and dry rotted boards hung from their sides. It was almost inconceivable to me that these were houses where people lived. When a person lives most of their life in early Pilsen and suburban Chicago, it's hard to believe that there are places where people live little better than their animals. I was glad when we were finally making our way into Florida. I figured that things would begin to look less bleak, but I was wrong. Northern Florida didn't look much different than ramshackle Alabama.

We arrived in Pensacola in a pouring rain storm and it sure wasn't what I had expected. When people think of Florida, they picture sunny days, expansive sand beaches, beautiful hotels and palm trees. What I was seeing couldn't be the part of Florida where tourists came, it had to be a part they avoided. Everything looked dirty. The rain soaked outdoor Christmas decorations on stores seemed completely out of place without snow. The sun wasn't shining and it was about 50 degrees with a bone chilling wind blowing off the Gulf. This place didn't resemble any Florida I had pictured in my mind. It was, however, where my husband was and so that was where I belonged. I tried to raise my spirits by thinking of our arrival at my new home.

Pat had written not to expect too much, I wasn't. When Pat drove up to the house, it didn't look all that bad. It was a small two-story building with living quarters over a two-car garage. The house looked kind of cute to me. I had spent most of my life living in a very small, modest house so I felt that it would do just fine for us. Thankfully the rain had stopped as we got out of the car and climbed the stairs up to our apartment.

Pat unlocked the door and showed me in. The first room was a living room furnished with an old couch, a green painted coffee table and a knotty pine bar with a couple of bar stools. The bedroom was the first room through a door in the living room. It included a double bed, two ancient dressers, two windows with pillowcase curtains and a small window mounted air conditioner. Through a door on the right side of the bedroom was a small bathroom with a rust stained footed bathtub, a small rust stained sink, a rust stained toilet and a wall-mounted medicine cabinet with a foggy mirror. The kitchen door was on the left side of the bedroom. It was pretty big with a scratched and dinged dining table and four chairs, a refrigerator, a gas stove, and a rust stained counter mounted sink. Everything was old, but I had confidence that with some major elbow grease, we could make it a comfortable home for the two of us. That night we unpacked and put away all of our things, so by the next day we were completely moved in.

Since Pat had to go back to the Navy Base to watch stand the next day, he said that he would work on the things that would be hard to clean or fix. His first project was to clean the gas stove. The burners were so filthy that two of them were completely plugged and wouldn't light. Pat worked for hours scrubbing away and finally got them all to work. Now came cleaning the oven. Pat couldn't get it to light even after spending another hour cleaning it. Pat decided to stop and show me how to light the burners with a match so I wouldn't blow myself up (Mom had an electric range). After his demonstration, Pat took another look into the oven to see if he had missed something. He put another match by the oven gas jet, which had, evidently, been leaking gas into the oven all this time. The oven lit with a fury throwing Pat half-way across the kitchen. I was afraid that he had been hurt, but only his eyebrows and eyelashes were slightly singed. He got up from the floor very shakily stuttering, "That was not the correct way to light the oven so don't do it that way." Then, we both cracked up laughing in relief.

With Pat working rotating day, midnight and evening watches on the Base, I didn't get to see him much. I used the time between seeing him to do house cleanup projects. First, I painted the entire interior of the house, which made it much cleaner. Next, I tried to do something with that bathtub to make it more desirable for bathing. Since my scrubbing removed little rust, I assumed it wouldn't come off on our bodies when we took a bath. Our little house was improving, but there was only so much that could be done.

We found that the house was heated by small, gas-operated space heaters in each room. They seemed dangerous to us, you could see a pilot flame always burning behind each heater's wide mesh screen. The heater in the bedroom was placed so close to the bed that we were afraid it could catch our blankets on fire when turned on. We decided, whenever possible, to keep them turned off. The poor construction of the house didn't help to keep it warm. You could, literally, look outside through cracks in the corners of the rooms. The living room was evidently a later addition to the apartment. It was poorly constructed with cold drafts blowing through the cracks in the walls. It was no paradise but we had to make the best of it since it was the only place we could afford.

With the cleaning of the stove, I was all set to do "my thing" in the kitchen. Since the only cooking I had done in my life was to bake cupcakes, I was very uncertain as to what "my thing" was. It didn't seem to bother Pat that I had never cooked anything of substance before, but it worried me. Here I was responsible for another person's nutrition! I had never had that responsibility before. I didn't want to fail, making someone I loved suffer from malnutrition or, at least, acute indigestion. I had some cookbooks and time to learn on my side.

Thinking back, there weren't any of the meals that I cooked that were inedible, just a few close calls. Pat never complained once about anything. He ate everything I cooked, perhaps suffering any consequences quietly. I do recall two meals, in particular, that were especially hard to get down. One was my first meat loaf. While it didn't look bad, its main evil surfaced an hour after eating it. It was dry, like eating sawdust held together by eggs. Of the two of us, I was always the one with an iron stomach but this meat loaf even gave me indigestion.

The other meal I especially remember was my "meatball" and spaghetti dinner. This meal tasted pretty darn good, it just looked strange. I don't know why but I only made two meatballs, each the size of a baseball. Each meatball took up half the plate and seemed to still be growing. They probably could have starred in a science fiction movie, *The Meatball That Rolled Over Pensacola*. And they weren't just big, they were tough! None of mankind's weapons could have destroyed them. Poor Pat managed to eat one saying it would fill him up for many hours or, perhaps, days.

After our initial big cleaning, our little apartment stayed quite neat and tidy. I needed to find other things to occupy my time while Pat was in work. Pat said I needed a companion, so we went to the downtown Woolworth's and bought a blue parakeet who we named Peepers. After getting him home, we noticed he had a bent tail but that did nothing to slow him down. Pat decided to try to teach him to talk and found he was a fast learner. The phrase he liked to say most was, "Pretty Peepers." We also found he liked rock and roll music. Every time we had the radio on, he would dance back and forth on his perch, his little head bopping up and down. I couldn't have found a better companion. However, when Pat was home, I couldn't get a word in edgewise between the two of them.

As the weather grew nicer, we were able to do some sightseeing. Pensacola was much nicer looking than when I first saw it. The downtown area was very pretty with palm trees along the sides of Pensacola Blvd. Every weekend, we used to go downtown to buy a *Chicago Tribune* from the news agency. By doing that, we felt that we were keeping up-to-date on what was happening in Chicago, a place that now had special meaning for both of us. We drove out to Pensacola Beach frequently. It was really beautiful with its sugary white sand and sparkling, crystal blue water.

Around the end of March, our sightseeing was interrupted by my catching the flu. It took me several weeks to get over it and get my appetite back. When my flu subsided, the thought of food still nauseated me. Pat told me that I was going to see a doctor, now. My first encounter with Navy medicine was a little scary. I was a modest person and had never been examined by a doctor like I would be now. When the day for my appointment came, I hadn't slept a wink the night before. On entering the medical building, I could see that I wasn't alone. I had never seen so many pregnant women in one place or in every phase of pregnancy. I was just another stomach in the crowd to be processed through as fast as possible.

Eight of us had been separated from the rest of the ladies waiting for their appointments. We all had a suspicion that we were pregnant, we all were here for our first examination by a doctor and we all, except one, were green in knowing what a Navy examination would be like. One woman, who thought she might be pregnant with her second child, told us that none of the doctors here were, "too swift." When it came time to deliver her first baby, her doctor had gone on leave and a dentist had to deliver her baby. We all stared at her through eyes the size of saucers. None of us needed to hear something like that right now.

When my turn came, my stomach wouldn't stop quaking. The last thing the woman had told us was what a monster this doctor was. Before seeing him, the nurse took all my information. I told her that I had had a couple weeks of the flu, had lost ten pounds and had missed a period. I told her that my periods had always been irregular but I needed to know if I was pregnant. She told me my flu sounded more like "morning sickness" and for all intents and purposes I should consider myself pregnant unless today's test proved otherwise.

The doctor was actually very nice. He told me that I was doing very well for someone who had lost ten pounds and that I would probably gain it back as my pregnancy progressed. I came out much relieved and went back to tell the women still waiting for their examination that there was nothing to worry about. Poor Pat had waited for me for hours through all of their tests and 'new mother' training movies. When he finally saw me, he jumped up, asked if I was

OK and told me that no one had told him anything about what was going on. I told him that he wasn't the only one who hadn't known what was going on but that, "We are probably going to be parents." He went from mind boggled to ecstatic in seconds.

With the prospect of becoming new parents looming, we had to make a major decision. Pat was due for new orders in December, upon graduation from advanced electronics school. Our baby was due the first of December. With these two things happening almost simultaneously, we had to figure out what would be the best thing to do. Pat told me that if the baby did come on time, I might not have sufficient time to recuperate before he was forced to travel to his new duty station. If the baby came late, I might have to stay in Pensacola alone with no help or transportation, while Pat left for his new duty station. Pat wasn't even close to sure where that duty station might be or if I could come there with him.

It was a no-brainer for Pat. He thought I should go back to La Grange during my seventh month and have our baby in a civilian hospital. He was absolutely positive that my parents would agree with him. Pat had heard that the Navy hospital was so crowded with patients that a majority of them had to be left in the halls with only screens around them. After hearing this, I was glad to go home, but I dreaded the day when I would have to leave Pat again for another lengthy separation. My parents had agreed with Pat as well and a departure date was set. As the date came closer and closer, I knew it would be like leaving a part of me behind. Once again, we would just have to make the most of the time we had left together.

As spring in Pensacola progressed, we were thankful to have that air conditioner, the weather was unbearable. The night temperatures were running around 104 degrees with extremely high humidity. Even our frequent thunderstorms couldn't cool things off. When it rained, the water came down in torrents so heavy that it was impossible to even see our street. These thunderstorms would quit as abruptly as they started, leaving the sun to blazing down generating an even more stifling mugginess.

Our worst thunderstorm ever was a huge nighttime storm. Pat was home off watch and was I ever grateful. I couldn't have handled things by myself. First the electricity went out with an ear shattering blast of thunder and a burst of lightning so bright it left an after image for seconds. Next, the wind began to howl and torrents of rain poured down. Pat thought he heard water dripping in the front room so he went to see what was going on. Over the bar, the ceiling had spouted at least twenty-five pouring leaks. We realized that if we didn't get all the stuff stored behind the bar into our bedroom, it would be ruined. Those things there were our prize possessions: a reel-to-reel tape recorder, a radio, a camera and loads of paperback books. The temperature in the house was now sweltering as we worked to drag everything into the bedroom and attempt to bale the water out of the living room. It quickly became a losing battle. The number of leaks had increased by two times with water streaming out of the ceiling light fixture, the light switch and the wall sockets. If the electricity were to come back on, it could become a very dangerous situation.

In the midst of our moving things, we realized that the bedroom had become so stifling we thought we would suffocate. The air conditioner had gone out along with the electricity, so our cooling lifeline was cut. With the high humidity, our windows were swollen closed. After attempting to open each and every window in the house, Pat was about going berserk. He yelled that he would get the bedroom window open one way or the other, and he did. He did it by slipping in a puddle of water and putting his hand through the window. He yelled that he thought he was bleeding, he was. I ran into the bathroom searching in the dark for our iodine and a bandage. I found them and ran to Pat to try to feel where the cut was. After putting iodine in five wrong places, I finally found the bulls eye and applied the bandage. With that done, Pat yelled that we were not going into the living room to bail anymore tonight. He slammed our bedroom door and jumped into bed saying that he didn't care if the whole house floated away. We were both so beat that we fell asleep in a matter of minutes, even with the heat.

About two hours later, we were woken by a tremendous crash from the living room. Pat jumped out of bed to see what had happened now. He opened the bedroom door, looked out and closed the door again. He hopped back into bed and told me, very calmly, that the entire front room ceiling had come down then we went back to sleep. The next morning, we found black, fuzzy mold and mildew growing on the fallen front room ceiling tiles and the ceiling. Pat got dressed and went to the corner phone booth (we couldn't qualify for a phone) to get in touch with of our landlord. Pat found out that he was out of town for the next few days. Since, we couldn't afford a motel room, we had to live for three days in a mold and mildew incubator. It was kind of educational to see what new things had grown on the ceiling during the night. When the landlord returned and saw what had happened, he immediately put up a new ceiling and fixed the roof shingles that had been torn away during the storm.

With the hot, humid summer weather, came the host of insects and vermin for which Pensacola is known. As night fell, the neighborhood grass, and our front room floor, literally crawled with bugs. If you had a fear of bugs, Pensacola was not for you. Pensacola was especially known for its large variety of cockroaches, they really liked the climate. One night, lying on the bed watching TV waiting for Pat to come home, I saw a particularly huge roach skittering across the floor. It was too big to step on, so I quietly got off the bed and opened the door to the front room. The roach sensed this and very casually walked out the door, which I slammed behind him. Another time, I noticed a very ominous looking bug in the silverware drawer. Pat said it looked like a scorpion and emptied the drawer looking for it. Somehow it escaped. I was glad, a bug of that size should have never be seen. I don't know where it went, but wherever that was, I hoped it stayed there.

One morning, we awoke to see a chameleon sitting on the top of the air conditioner staring through the window at us. I wasn't afraid of them, but the thought of them crawling all over the garage under our feet was a bit unnerving. Another time, one leaped in my face when I opened the mailbox. It felt like we were living in a reptile house, especially when a Cottonmouth snake was run over with a lawnmower by the owner's son right next to our house. Every time Pat drove past this swampy, wooded area a few blocks from our house, it sounded like jungle sounds from a Tarzan movie. One night, Pat was on his way home from the Base when he suddenly saw something crossing the road in the dark. He tried to avoid hitting it but rolled over it. He was afraid it was someone's pet and immediately got out of the car to see what it was. I know he wished he hadn't, in the middle of road he found a five foot, hissing, snapping alligator. Pat said he didn't spend time asking how it was but jumped back into the car and tore off for home.

As the months went by we were becoming more and more excited about my family's upcoming visit. In January, they sprung the news on us that they were planning to drive down to Pensacola to visit us in August. Going from their first out-of-state trip to Wisconsin a couple of years ago to driving all the way to Pensacola was a major change in my parent's lives. Since Mickey was going to come along, Mom told Dad that they had to have an air-conditioned car for the trip. Dad quickly agreed with her. He wanted a newer car anyway and the long trip to Florida was an excellent excuse to buy one now. The air conditioning would make Mickey and the entire family more comfortable during their long trip.

Dad wrote us that he found the perfect car, a 1967 Chevrolet Impala four-door with a vinyl roof and air conditioning. We were so happy that they were coming, not only because we were lonely, but because they had never gone on a trip so far from home and were really excited. We wanted everything to be perfect for them, so we started looking for a nice place for them to stay while in Pensacola. There were several motels near our house, so we wanted to pick "the best for the least." The motel we picked offered them a two bedroom, light housekeeping cottage that allowed pets, was reasonably priced and was only a few blocks down the street from us.

Pat and I hoped that Dad would find us without too much trouble. As I previously told you, he had never been very good at navigating to new places. It had taken him twenty-five years to find his way around La Grange, so we weren't sure what would happen. Pat drew him a map showing different stores and building's locations, so even if he got confused with the directions, he could use the landmarks that Pat had put on the map. We were both a bundle of nerves on the day of their arrival. We tried to estimate what time they should arrive. When our estimated arrival time passed, we began to worry. We even drove out to the main highway to look for them, but no luck.

It was early evening, when there was a knock on the door. There stood Dad with his eyes bloodshot and bulging. Dad was so anxious to get to Pensacola that he had run himself ragged with too much driving, too little sleep and too many No-Doze. After kissing him hello, I ran down the steps to greet everyone else in the car. Mom was in the back seat with Mickey and a bird cage with two finches. She had been concerned that "Pinky and Dinky" wouldn't eat for anyone else, so here they were with the rest of the family. Mark looked well, but was still tiny and underweight. Bill was now sixteen with acne and a will to do what he wanted. Mickey was stretched out in the back seat, looking none the worse for their long trip.

We had them follow us back to their cottage and we helped them get settled in. I felt kind of conspicuous being almost six months pregnant. The last time my parents saw me, I wasn't. The eight months Pat and I had spent together in Pensacola brought about a lot of changes, the most evident being my bulging stomach. No one dwelled on the subject, so I became more comfortable. There wasn't anything for me to be ashamed of. Our baby was the expression of our love for each other. It was the most natural thing in the world.

The first week of their visit was great fun. We chauffeured them around to show off the high points of Pensacola and at night we went to the beach for picnics. Over the next days, Pat took Dad and Bill fishing and crabbing from the Pensacola Bay fishing bridge. Dad bought a crab trap and had a great time catching Blue crabs. Bill caught a big sea snake and had to whip it against the pavement to get it off his line and keep from getting bitten. They were using small shrimp for bait, so Dad asked Pat where they could buy bigger ones for boiling. Pat took him to a seller that had huge tanks of live shrimp. They were 98 cents per pound, which is almost free compared to their price today. Dad kept buying and boiling them. We ate a lot of fresh shrimp while they were there. Pat was kind of disappointed that we hadn't thought to do this in the eight months we had been living there.

We were all having a wonderful visit, when on August 16th something happened that removed some of that fun. The weather forecasters reported a major hurricane was pushing into the Gulf and moving towards Pensacola. Hurricane Camille had begun its relentless push towards the U.S. coastline. Talk about bad timing, my family's farthest trip out of the Midwest had to be threatened by a hurricane. The only thing we could all do was to sit tight, wait for it to hit or pass us by. We hoped for the latter. After having heard all of the problems we had with our house in a small storm, Mom determined that we should wait it out with them in their cottage. So, we packed up Peepers, our parakeet, and moved in with them.

During the "boarding up" process, local businesses distributed hurricane tracking maps. This allowed you to chart where the hurricane was heading using weather bulletin information. Dad thought this the most exciting thing yet and began to mark his chart with hour by hour locations. Here we sat waiting for Hurricane Camille while Dad carefully plotted its movement for us. From his plotting, it was still heading straight for us! Staying up into the early morning of August 17th, we heard the Florida Hurricane Center announce that Camille had changed its course. It was now going to make landfall near Biloxi, Mississippi and had grown to a Category 5 hurricane, the most explosively violent kind. Pensacola would only be hit with torrential rain and violent winds. We were all very relieved to hear but soon learned they weren't kidding about the violence of our storm.

When daylight came, Dad and Pat drove out to the Pensacola Bay Bridge to see the damage left behind. They couldn't believe how many things had just vanished during the storm. A large part of the fishing pier, where Dad and Pat had fished and crabbed, was gone. Gone, also, were the picnic tables, umbrellas and vending machines where we had our picnics. Later in the day reports came in that many of the homes around Pensacola Beach had suffered vast damage if not complete annihilation. It was quite an experience! My family and I had lived in Illinois all of our lives and had never witnessed a tornado. We come to Florida, and we experience a Category 5 hurricane. There were no casualties reported in the Pensacola area but there were a great many in Mississippi, mostly people at "Hurricane Parties."

With the Pensacola 'All Clear' issued, we had to think about getting Mom and Dad and the rest of the family packed up to go home. We had had so much fun and excitement together during their stay, we were sorry to see them go. I would be seeing them in a month, when I returned home to have the baby. Pat would be seeing them, and our baby, when he finished his training here. Even though we had only been married eight months, we had grown so close. I knew we both would find it difficult to separate in October.

It seemed like our entire relationship was based on goodbyes. I hated the Navy for that! When they issued you an order, that was that, no matter what was happening in your life. It was up to you to handle surviving military orders, your duty stations and being separated for months or even years from your loved ones. I was glad Pat's time would be up in four years. Neither of us could see having our lives controlled by the Navy, telling us where we would live and for how long. If a duty station was especially bad, you had to wait it out and hope for a nicer place the next time around. Many times, the next duty station was worse than the last. Our baby was due December 1, and Pat wouldn't be coming to La Grange until December 15. That meant that he wouldn't be there for the biggest event in our lives together, our baby's birth.

It was now October 7, my departure day. I wasn't sure that I would make it with all the crying I did. Pat had received his orders for the Naval Communications Station, Adak, Alaska and the Navy had packed up our few household goods. Little Peepers, our parakeet, was going with me to La Grange. Before my family came to visit us, I had asked Mom to bring along the little plastic bird carrier that she had. It was going to be Peeper's cage for our trip home. I had purchased a large canvas tote bag to conceal his cage on the plane ride. In 1969, there weren't many airline safety measures, not even x-rays. You could easily carry anything onboard that you could hide. I was going to smuggle a little, blue parakeet, with a big mouth, onboard.

Our ride to the airport was very upsetting. We drove past many of the places that Pat and I had enjoyed during our time in Pensacola. They conjured up many happy memories that weren't easy to leave behind. I wanted to go home very much, but I didn't want to leave Pat by himself. It was a problem with no happy solution, so we both had to make the best of it. At the airport, I gave Pat a long goodbye kiss and took the long walk to the plane with a heavy heart. When I got into my seat by the window, I could see that Pat was crying as he waved goodbye. Seeing him like that tore me up so much I cried halfway to Chicago.

During the plane trip, I put my bag with Peepers inside on the floor near my feet. He was very good for the first half of the trip, then he started to get a little too active. He flapped his wings and began yelling at the top of his lungs! I picked up the bag and started talking into it to quiet him down. He was yelling every word he knew. I was afraid that the stewardesses would take him away from me if they found him. As I was talking into the bag, I noticed a man in the next aisle was giving me weird looks. He must have thought I had gone goofy from the altitude. I decided to put the bag down very nonchalantly and begin reading a magazine. From then on, I was more careful. I stopped talking into the bag, as Peepers had settled down somewhat. With the roar of the plane's engines, I realized it was impossible for anyone to hear him anyway. I always thought that I should have registered Peepers with the *Guinness Book of World Records*. He might have been the only parakeet to have flown from Florida to Chicago at 650 mph without using his wings.

When I deplaned at O'Hare Airport, there was Dad waiting at the gate to take me home. I'm afraid I wasn't much of a companion for him. At home, I walked through the front door to see a big sign that said, "Welcome home, Bonnie." I immediately burst into tears and ran up the stairs to my old room. It was not going to be a happy nine weeks wait for Pat, but I had to pull myself together for my loving family's sake.

As the days passed, I got myself into a routine. As before our getting married, I lived from letter to letter from Pat. Since there were many things I had to do before the baby arrived, I decided that I would focus my attention on getting them done as soon as possible. Mom and Dad bought a baby crib and Dad set it up at the foot of my twin bed. I busied myself making it up and buying all the numerous little things that babies need. I also wanted to get my Christmas shopping done. I didn't want to worry about that after the baby arrived.

By doing these chores, the weeks seemed to fly by. However, every week I found that it was becoming more uncomfortable to move around and sleep. As with all "soon to be" mothers, my disposition deteriorated. I turned into the dreaded crabby hippopotamus. My family had to be very careful what they said to me. I would either burst into tears or start yelling at ear shattering volume. Mom told me, somewhat facetiously, that Pat really knew when to send me back home to them. He had lived with me during the pregnant months when my temperament was the best, now my family had me at my worst. Mom kept saying that it just wasn't fair, not fair at all.

As Thanksgiving, November 27, approached, everyone was making me very uncomfortable. They kept watching me to see if I was ready to go to the hospital. Grandma Taraba would call every hour on the hour to see if I was still at home. When a delivery date is set everyone, especially the person who has been waiting nine months, gets anxious. With something as unpredictable as your first baby's birth, I found it almost unbearable to wait out the last few days.

When Saturday, November 29, rolled around, I noticed that I had started passing some blood. When I reported this to my doctor, he told me that I would be going into labor soon but, I should go about doing what I had planned for the day. He said I should not sit around twiddling my thumbs, waiting for the labor to start. That sounded very sensible, so I started hand painting wooden Christmas tree ornaments.

All evening I tried to act nonchalant, but in my heart, I knew that my time was drawing near. Mom, Dad and I stayed up for the *Late Show* and went to bed after that. I laid down, but couldn't sleep because I was busy timing something. It was a funny sensation but not the sharp pains I expected from watching television shows with women having babies. At 2:00 a.m., I came downstairs to call the hospital and tell the doctor what was going on. He said that I should probably come into the hospital. I worried that the trip would be for nothing. That I would look like a fool for not knowing what labor felt like.

Mom, who had been listening to my conversation, told me that we should go. She woke Dad, grabbed my suitcase and we were on our way to La Grange Community Memorial Hospital. The night was cold and clear with no snow, so the trip was a very quick ten minute drive. Mom got out and carried my suitcase to the door where a nurse was waiting. I got out of the car and started waddling towards the door, when Dad motioned for me to come back. When I waddled back, he told me that I hadn't closed the car door tight enough! I grabbed the door and almost slammed it off its hinges. I believe he wanted to say something else, but nothing came to him just like when I told him I was engaged. It was hard for him to say the right things at the right time. You knew how he felt inside and that was enough.

The nurse ushered Mom and me to a hospital room where I put on a hospital gown and tried to get comfortable for a long night. The nurse examined me to check how far I was into labor. She confirmed that I was definitely in labor, but it seemed to have stopped. She said we'd just have to wait until it started again.

When I came home from Pensacola, I was sent to a practice with four obstetricians. I got to meet each of them on my monthly visits. I liked all of them, especially a Japanese-American doctor. Dr. Kurotsuchi really outshone them all. I hoped that he would be on duty when my baby was born. When I had called the hospital, he was the one I had talked to, so I was happy. However, the shifts had changed before I arrived and I ended up with my least favorite doctor, Dr. Curran. Oh well, I couldn't be fussy. Anything was better than having my baby in the Pensacola Base hospital.

The Dr. Curran came in to see me about an hour after check-in. After examining me he told me that, "You have such a long way to go, I'm going home to watch television." I was glad that he wasn't going to let my condition stop him from watching Sunday reruns. When he noticed Mom sitting by my bed, he sarcastically told her that she should just watch television too, then left. Mom didn't deserve that, she was already a bundle of nerves as it was. It was hard for her to have to be a stand-in for Pat. At 8:00 a.m. Sunday morning, I told Mom to go home and get some sleep. She reluctantly agreed, saying she would leave a note with the nurse to call her if anything started again.

It's was kind of nerve racking laying in a hospital bed for hours, not knowing what is going on or what to expect. Since I hadn't eaten for hours, the nurse hooked me to an ominous looking bottle for intravenous feeding. Shortly after that Dr. Curran, who must have decided that he could break away from his television long enough to check on his patients, wandered into my room. As he was examining me he yelled at the nurse to get something she didn't immediately have at her fingertips. After this rampage, he said that he was going to break my water. When he did, the water squirted all over me and the bed. He left without another word. The poor nurse now had a big mess to clean up.

The morning crept slowly into the afternoon with everything status quo. I decided to watch some television. Maybe something would happen if I didn't pay attention. I watched the Christmas Parade from State Street in Chicago. The weather had been kind to the people in the parade this year. There was no wind to give the marching girls with short skirts frostbite of the knees. After the parade was over, I just laid there in the quiet waiting for my baby to make an entrance. I wished that Pat was here with me to help make the time go by faster.

Around 6:00 p.m. Mom returned, so I had her for company again. She looked more worried than I did. At 8:00 p.m. the doctor made another rare appearance to tell me he was sending me for x-rays. He wanted to see what was going on inside, which worried me a bit. They wheeled me into a freezing cold x-ray room, where I got onto an uncomfortably cold metal table. As I lay there, I realized that I wasn't anxious about the birth anymore, I just wanted it to be over with already!

A couple of hours later, the doctor returned to say all was well. The baby wasn't overly big, so I would be able to deliver it normally. He said he was going to give me something to speed things along. About 11:00 p.m., the nurse added some liquid to the intravenous feeding I was getting. She said that it wouldn't be long now. Wow, was she right! About 30 minutes later, I sat straight up in bed with pains that I couldn't believe. It felt like someone was pushing a knife through my back. It was nearly unbearable. I prayed that it wouldn't keep up like that for very long. Mom started yelling to the nurse that I was ready. The nurse agreed. Finally, the baby was coming after waiting twenty-two hours. They wheeled me into the delivery room while Mom sat in the father's waiting room.

As I lay there, I noticed that things were starting to move very rapidly. The pains had become harder and more frequent. The nurse told me to not to push until she told me, but I couldn't help it. My baby wanted out and it seemed beyond my power to change that. Dr. Curran told me he needed time to make the necessary incisions or the baby could cause irreparable tearing. When he was done, he told me to push. Out slid my long-awaited baby, a boy. We now had a son. Dr. Curran flopped him on my stomach, so I could watch him crying and wriggling. He told me that I'd had many stitches and I'll feel every one of them in the morning. He was so tender and comforting. The nurse said, "She doesn't need to hear that right now, doctor."

Brian Patrick Harrington was born on December 1, 1969, at 12:33 a.m. He weighed in at 7 pounds 3.5 ounces and was 20.5 inches long. Dr. Curran now asked, "Do you want the kid circumcised?" As always, the doctor's phrasing exemplified his moldy personality. When I answered "Yes," he did it in a matter of moments. Brian now lay in my arms as the nurse wheeled us down the hospital hallway to our room. Mom was waiting there for us. When she saw my unwashed baby, it really blew her mind. She told me that she hadn't even seen her own children before they were cleaned up. I thought Mom must have been wearing a blindfold at our births. Shortly after being wheeled into the recovery room, I fell into the sleep of the dead having just finished a very exhausting job.

I woke up the next morning at 6:00 a.m. to the delightful smell of stewed prunes. I didn't care what they gave me to eat. I was starving after not eating for so long. After breakfast, the nurse told me to get up so she could change my bed. Get up! I wasn't even sure if I could. I hadn't really taken an inventory of what was there after "Dr. Nimble Fingers" had stitched me up. When I did it didn't seem too painful. I thought that maybe it wouldn't be as bad as the doctor had predicted. The nurse told me that I could take a shower if I wanted to. I thought she was nuts as that was the last thing I had on my mind. I really didn't feel like walking, bending, or being drenched with water. Hospitals offer you little pity for what you have gone through.

Later in the afternoon Mom came to visit me. She told me that she had let Pat know that he had a son. She said he had about done cartwheels over the phone. On hearing that, I became very depressed and lonesome for him. I guess I had fallen into post-partum blues that were made even worse by my husband's absence. To cheer me up, Mom and I walked over to the nursery to see the very new Brian Patrick Harrington. He was the only boy in the nursery, and was the quietest baby there. All of the other babies seemed to be going berserk, but good old Brian just snoozed on peacefully. Mom said that he'd probably make up for his lack of crying after we got him home.

For the next five days, Mom and I walked over to see him and each and every time he was sacked out. Mom wished he would wake up so she could see what color his eyes were. As the days passed, I was in more and more pain and that added to my depression. I kept worrying about how I was going to take care of Brian properly when I could hardly walk. I was not about to complain about it to the doctor, I wanted to go home. Before I could leave, Mom had to make four trips home with the flowers that I had received. Grandpa and Grandma Taraba transported Mom, Brian and me home that Friday.

It was wonderful to be back home again! Mickey was very excited over Brian. She had sat on my lap when I was pregnant and was kicked over and over by the baby. We set up Brian's buggy in the living room. Every time he cried, Mickey would jump up on the couch, look into the buggy to see what was wrong, then, run to me or Mom to let us know to come over. She watched over Brian as if he were her baby.

As the date of Pat's arrival came closer, I began to come out of my depression. I was hoping to feel completely better in two weeks. I wanted to enjoy Pat and our baby for the three weeks Pat would be on leave in La Grange. I couldn't wait for Pat to see Brian in person. I had sent Pat, Brian's hospital picture, but that didn't do him justice. He had a scowl on his face, one hand clenched and looked like he was after somebody's hide. I wanted to make the most of our time together because Pat's duty station had a six-month housing wait. It seemed like our baby would be practically grown before Pat would see him again. I did feel fully recovered by the day Pat came to La Grange. When he saw his son laying there, he picked him up, kissed him and said he wanted to feed him his bottle. I could tell right then and there that Pat loved him long before Brian was even born. He didn't have to meet Brian to love him, he was the result of the love we had for each other. What could be more beautiful?

Pat really got initiated into what being a father is all about during those three weeks with us. Pat took over Brian's 2:00 a.m. feeding, which was always an ordeal. Brian would suck on the bottle for an hour, swallow only an ounce and then fall asleep. About an hour later he would be up crying because he was hungry again. Since Brian was suffering from a bad cold at the time, we thought that his eating problem was connected to the cold. We returned to the doctor, who had seen him for his cold, to see if she could suggest anything to help. After careful analysis, she said that Brian was suffering from the dread "hole-too-small-in-the-nipple" syndrome. She told us to make the hole bigger in his bottle's nipple and the little guy would take care of the rest. She assured us that he could handle more than a drop of milk at one time. It worked.

Pat and I had gotten the chance to enjoy a few movies on his leave, but, on his last day, we decided to go into the Chicago Loop for a movie and a special dinner. Unfortunately, the weather just wouldn't cooperate. The temperature went down to a bone chilling -40 degrees with the wind chill factor. We thought we'd freeze to the pavement. We would have if it hadn't been for a few stores being open. We got to sit for a while in the Palmer House Hotel which had a special significance for us. It was where we would wait for Dad to pick us up after our dates.

So many things had changed in my life. I had worked as an executive secretary, I had met Pat, I had gotten married and, because of our marriage, I had brought a new person into the world. The Navy sent us to Pensacola, Florida for adventures most people wouldn't have. Now, I would be travelling to Adak, Alaska to live in a place few others had even seen. Life truly was interesting.

CHAPTER 14

WHERE'S SERGEANT PRESTON?

Pat left us for a week's leave with his family in Bellingham, Washington in the third week of January 1970. Here I was saying goodbye to him again but this time it would be for six months or longer. These family separations were the way of life for Navy families. The short time we had been able to spend together since our marriage made this separation really hard. The six-month wait would have been an eternity if it hadn't been for Brian keeping me busy and Pat's letters. Every time I looked at Brian, I felt that Pat wasn't that far away.

There was one thing, however, that happened during those six months that still haunts me all these years later. One beautiful spring day, I decided to take Brian out for a ride in his buggy. It was one of Illinois' finest days; warm with a deep blue sky, green leaves sprouting and the smell of new growth in the air. We kept walking and walking until we found ourselves in downtown La Grange. I decided to go to the bank and do a couple of other errands. To get to our bank, I had to get us across a double set of Burlington Northern railroad tracks. We were about half way across when the gates started to come down and a bell began to ring to signal that a train was coming. I froze when this started, thinking that a train wouldn't really run us over.

I began to hurry across when one of the buggy wheels got caught in the tracks. I looked up and could see the train was much closer, but I still figured I had time to spare. Suddenly, a man sprinted out of a crowd of gapers, picked the buggy up and carried it off the tracks. I ran after him and less than 60 seconds after I stepped off the tracks, the train barreled through at 40 mph. Like a flash, the shock that we could have been killed sunk in and I was shaking. I was so thankful that that man gave me a chance to learn from my mistake, by living. It didn't scare me so much that I was near death, but that I had jeopardized the life of my baby. I had nightmares for weeks afterwards. Every time I cross railroad tracks, this incident pops back into my mind. I have become super cautious and very fast crossing them.

As each month passed, Brian was growing bigger and bigger. Pat and I kept as close as possible by writing letters and my sending Pat pictures of Brian and me. At the beginning of June, Pat wrote to tell me that he had found a place for us to stay until housing became available. Pat's superior, Charlie, and his wife were going on leave in the States for a month. They were looking for someone to stay in the house and look after their cat, Pokey. Pat had immediately volunteered for the job. This meant that Brian and I would be coming to Adak a month earlier than expected. After the month was over, we would move to the "Adak Motel" until we were assigned a house of our own. It sounded kind of complicated, but we would be getting together as a family sooner than expected.

Two weeks later, I received our plane tickets and schedule: Chicago to Seattle, Seattle to Anchorage, and Anchorage to Adak. I was now solely responsible for getting myself and our six-month-old baby from Chicago to Adak, Alaska! That realization scared me half to death. I had only ridden a plane once, from Pensacola to Chicago with a parakeet, and that had been a straight through flight. Now I had to make three plane connections with Brian and our baggage! I questioned myself about my ability to accomplish this one. I had had trouble finding my way around downtown Chicago. I had even been leery about riding buses for fear of getting lost. Now I was faced with the task of getting to Adak, Alaska, a tiny island that was part of the Aleutian Island chain 1,200 miles out in the North Pacific Ocean from Alaska. As frightening as the prospect of this trip was, I wanted to be with my husband and I would have done anything to accomplish that. I would have even tried to swim the Pacific Ocean, even though that would have been fatal as I can't swim.

I phoned my never seen or met in-laws, to let them know our scheduled arrival time Sea-Tac Airport in Seattle, Washington. They told me that they were very excited to meet me and their new grandson, Brian. I was nervous about having to meet them for the first time without Pat being there. I was the daughter-in-law that they had never met after being married one and a half years to their son. I wasn't totally alone though, I had their never-before-seen grandson with me. I just wanted us to make a good impression.

As our departure from La Grange neared, I had to go through the agony of saying goodbye to my family again. Brian had been crabby for weeks with teething. Mom said that he better cut a tooth before leaving after putting her through all his crying. I remember dressing Brian for our long plane ride, with

Mom watching from the sidelines knowing she wouldn't be seeing us for who knew how long. Our plane was scheduled to leave Chicago O'Hare at midnight. I knew that when this trip was over that I would be exhausted beyond imagining. I tried to leave home with better controlled emotions than my first time. I had many details to keep in mind if I was to get us both to Adak safely.

When time arrived for us to leave for the airport to start our journey, Mom was holding Brian checking his mouth to see if a tooth had come in. Low and behold, the long-awaited tooth had materialized! Mom had gotten to see Brian's first tooth after all. It made me sorry that she would have to miss a lot of the other firsts in his life, but I knew we would make up for that after this Navy business was over. But for now, we had to say goodbye to Mom, Mark, and Mickey and be on our way to Chicago O'Hare with Dad and Bill. I was glad they didn't all go, it would have been doubly hard to say goodbye there.

Once at O'Hare, I checked us in. We were assigned a seat on the bulkhead, as it had more leg room for the diaper bag and the other paraphernalia that mothers with babies carry. When the boarding announcement was made, I kissed Dad and Bill, and told them to take care until we could be together again. Then, I swiftly turned away from them and boarded the plane. I knew that if I had turned around to look at them, I would have lost control and I couldn't risk that. I had to be strong and that was what I had to continue to be. I had no idea what I was going to find on Adak except for Pat. I figured anything would be bearable as long as Pat was there.

When the plane reached Sea-Tac Airport around dawn, I was already worn out. I felt like I looked a mess, yet I had to meet Pat's parents for the first time. I had wanted to look my best, but after five hours on an airplane, I looked very disheveled, felt punchy from a sleepless night and was sure my bloodshot eyes added to my elegant look. Since we had only arrived at the first stop before our final destination, there was no time to worry about appearances. What I looked like now was what Pat's parents were going to see.

After collecting my travel stuff and carrying my bundle from heaven, I made my way out of the plane. Since it was 5:00 a.m., there weren't many people waiting to meet the plane. As I stepped into the airport, I saw three anxious faces and I knew that they had to be my new in-laws; Mom (Jane), Dad (Lee) and daughter (Tracy) Harrington. They looked just like they did in the pictures that Pat had of them, and turned out just as nice as I had hoped. At this point, I really needed to meet some friendly faces. After the round of kisses and hugs were over, Pat's Mom said that they had reserved a motel room where we could freshen up before we continued on our journey. They had thought of everything and I was so grateful to them for that.

We made our way out of the airport terminal to a shuttle bus that took us to their parked car. From there we continued to the motel. Brian was ready for his breakfast and I was overdue for some rest. Once inside the motel room, I felt renewed strength and tried to catch my in-laws up on all of the things that had happened in our life together so far. Pat's parents hung on every word. The time flew by and before long we had to return to the airport, so we could continue on our journey.

I, for one, didn't know how to do this. At O'Hare, Dad had taken care of seeing that I got on the plane. Now I was in an alien airport and nearly on my own as Pat's parents seemed as lost as I was. After making a few wrong turns, we were at the Alaskan Airline "Gold Nugget" flight gate. It was supposed to leave at 7:45 a.m., but the ticket agent told me that it had been delayed. I took advantage of the delay to visit longer with Pat's parents. As hours passed, I realized this was a "long" delay. I began to worry that it would botch up our connection in Anchorage for the flight to Adak. I decided I should just worry about getting out of Seattle first.

After three hours, the plane arrived. Brian and I said our goodbyes to everyone. There was no inside boarding ramp for the plane, so I had to carry Brian and our belongings outside to board the plane. Pat's Mom tried to go with me to help carry my stuff, but she was stopped and told it wasn't allowed. When I finally reached the steps to the plane, I gave a final wave to my newly acquired "family," who were waving from the window of the airport. With all of my stuff, all I could manage was the wave of a few fingers, a smile, and a nod of my head

So, Brian and I were off into the wild blue yonder again. We had only seen a tiny piece of the Pacific Northwest, now we were heading for Alaska, "Home of the Midnight Sun," Eskimos, igloos, and gold nuggets. Most important of all though, the place where I would be reunited with my husband and Brian with his father. It was exciting to be flying all over the place. It seemed all of the fun I had missed out on in my teens while I was fat, was being made up for in grand style. If only some of the girls at Nazareth Academy could see me now. It seemed that in a sudden rush, I had acquired; a loving husband, a beautiful son, and the chance to see places that few people ever did.

As I slipped back into reality, I realized that our plane was ascending and we were on our own again. I kept talking to Brian, telling him that it wouldn't be long and we would see Daddy again. It was a nice enough flight, but I really felt out of place. The décor of the plane was "gold lamay and red velvet casino." The seats were mainly filled with men in business suits on their way to Anchorage. I was the only female with a baby on the flight. The people on board were in for a rough flight. Brian was in full teething mode with long periods of crying. Dirty looks abounded. I had no idea what they expected me to do about poor Brian. I couldn't just get up and walk with him up and down the plane's aisle. I was relieved when Brian wore himself out and fell asleep. I hadn't wanted to cause a disturbance but, if Brian needed to cry, that was his prerogative as a paying customer. With that thought firmly in mind, I felt much better. When dirty looks came, I just ignored them and thought that if they don't like it, they could get out and walk. Had none of these people been a baby with sore gums?

As we neared the Anchorage Airport, one of the stewardesses announced that those of us continuing on to Adak would be able to make our connection; Reeve Aleutian Airline was holding their plane for us. I was relieved to hear that. The stewardess said that we would have to really hurry though, that the Reeve flight wouldn't hold for long. As we disembarked, Brian and I raced down the terminal with Navy men who were on their way to Adak, too. At a door with a waving stewardess, we exited the terminal to board the plane via an outside ramp. After we were seated, I noticed that the Reeve Aleutian Airline plane was a far more utilitarian plane than the more luxurious Alaskan Airline "Gold Nugget." This plane looked more like a WWII cargo plane with seats bolted in. It was beat up inside and was powered by twin "turbo" propellers. The interior was really confining with the ceiling about two inches above our heads. The seats were very close together with very little leg room. It was a very different flight than my previous two jet rides but I was still thankful that we had made it in time. I didn't care what means brought us to Adak, only that we got there.

It was supposed to be a little over two-hour flight, but the weather got so foggy that the plane was forced to land at a place named Cold Bay, Alaska, until the fog lifted. I looked out the plane's window as we landed and could hardly believe someone had actually bothered to name this place. As far as I could see there was no vegetation of any kind, just fields of snow and a single dilapidated building. The crew announced that we all had to deplane and led us into that single dilapidated building with its sign announcing: Cold Bay Trading Post. I figured that it couldn't possibly be as bad inside as it was outside, I was wrong. It was worse. The only seats were roughhewn, hard wooden benches. The wind continuously howled through broken windows panes haphazardly repaired with sheets of plastic. It was a cold, dark, awful place. I was positive that Sergeant Preston of the Yukon would soon sled by with his dog, Yukon King. After a seemingly interminable wait, we were led back on to the plane to resume our flight to Adak. I truly prayed that Adak was a better place than Cold Bay but I wasn't holding out much hope that Adak's surroundings would be better.

When the plane landed on Adak, I didn't look out, I just began getting Brian ready to meet his Dad. Since I hadn't shed any of my hand baggage, I was still loaded down and had to make my way down the ramp steps very carefully. I saw Pat trying to get to the ramp to help me, but he wasn't being allowed to come out to the plane. Some Navy brass was on our plane, so they didn't want any one on the tarmac until he got off the plane. A nice sailor on the plane helped me with my bag. When Pat and I finally hugged and kissed, all the weariness of our trip just faded away. I had accomplished my goal! I had gotten Brian and me here safely and we were a complete family again, even if it was on Adak. Pat sat Brian and me down in Adak's clean, modern terminal, while he collected our baggage. When he had everything loaded in our car, we drove off to our temporary home.

Pat's parents had bought the car Pat was driving and the Navy had shipped it from Seattle to Adak for him. It was a car worthy of the place: a light blue and cream, 1956 Chevrolet Bel Aire four-door sedan. Pat said it was built "like a tank" and should stand up to anything Adak could dish out. The driver's door had been deeply dented while in route to Adak, but when you only pay $250 for a car, a dent here and there isn't so bad. We all rode in the front seat of the car, which was a good thing since the back-seat floor had a large drafty hole with a sheet of plywood covering it.

In no time, Pat deposited us in front of a water-front placed duplex house. From the outside, it looked pretty nice. This was where we would be living in for a month, until Pat's boss, Charlie, and his family came back from leave. The interior of the house was very nice with all the conveniences and two bathrooms. I had never lived in a house with two bathrooms before. I decided that even if Adak didn't have much else to offer, we would have a nice house to hibernate in. Besides taking care of the house, we were supposed to take care of their cat, Pokey. He was a very affectionate and personable cat, who liked to sleep on the bed clothes in the linen closet.

After a couple of days of settling in as a family again, Pat decided to take us on a tour of Adak as I hadn't seen much of it on the way from the airport. It really was a curious place with colossal mountains that seemed to enclose the entire island. As we drove from the house, Pat pointed across the bay to Mt. Sitka, the area's active volcano, located on Sitka Island. It just seemed to float out on the bay. Next, we drove around the island's Traffic Circle. The Circle's center consisted of an Aleut totem pole and a small patch of green grass. Driving around Adak, I realized that green grass was something missing from the rest of Adak. Most of the ground was covered by tall, brown tundra grass. Pat took us to do some shopping at the Commissary and the Base Exchange (BX). Both were small, carrying the bare essentials and even some of those were missing. Pat told me that the twice a month supply ship wasn't due for another week. This meant we had to buy either frozen or powdered milk for Brian. The only way to get enough fresh milk to last between supply ships was to get in line at the Commissary while they were unloading the ship. As I came to quickly learn, every purchasing experience on Adak was based on the principle of first-come, first-served until it's gone.

During the month that we watched over Charlie's cat, Pokey, he supplied us with funny experiences that made Adak a little more bearable. One day, as I was filling Pokey's food from a lower cupboard, I noticed that he was missing. When it was time for him to eat, he was always prancing around me. I went through the whole house looking for him, beginning to worry that somehow, he had gotten out of the house. I heard a faint meow, and began to, frantically, track down the sound. It was coming from the lower cupboard where his food was kept. I whipped the door open and out shot one, wide-eyed, terrified cat. Apparently, he had climbed into the cupboard when I wasn't looking and I closed him in. After that, Pokey was never curious about what was in any of the cupboards.

Shortly after we moved in, Pat went outside to give me a demonstration of how to dump our garbage. There was a huge dumpster a little way from the house, placed to accommodate all of the houses. I started watching Pat's demo from the window, but left when Brian started crying. When Pat came in, he asked if I understood what to do? I said, "Oh, sure." A few days later while Pat was on watch, I noticed the garbage was piling up. I decided I would take it out to the dumpster myself. I walked over to the dumpster and realized I had no idea how to get the bag inside of the dumpster. After walking completely around the thing and finding no door, I decided the opening must be on top. The only solution I could see was to throw the garbage bag up into the dumpster. The problem was that the top was about three feet above my head. I wasn't sure if my throw would be strong enough to get the bag up that high. I took a deep breath and threw the bag up in the air as hard as I could. Plop, it came down on my head. I was covered with everything from dirty Pampers to leftover food. I got mad, repacked the garbage and threw it even harder. My second try proved successful, the bag made it up over the top of the dumpster. I stepped back and realized that the top wasn't open like I thought. There was my garbage bag sitting on top for all to see.

When Pat came home, I told him what had happened. He said that all I had to do was open the door on the side and throw the bag in just like he had demonstrated. I had obviously missed the 'open the door' part of his demo. I was so embarrassed I told him to climb up on the dumpster to retrieve the bag. I didn't want to be reminded how stupid I was. He said that it wasn't possible, I would have to wait until the dumpster was emptied for my mistake to go away. Pat was no help at all! Every time he looked out the window, he would turn away laughing. There sat my garbage bag, eight feet in the air, a monument to man's fallibility.

Another thing that happened during our stay in Charlie's house was the capture of two South Korean fishing boats. The boats were captured fishing within U.S. Territorial waters by the U.S. Coast Guard. The boats were taken into custody and then towed to Adak. For nearly the entire month, they were anchored in the bay in front of Charlie's house with marking lights on every night. The U.S. and South Korea settled things and we watched them leave just before we did.

As the month drew to a close, we got ready to move out of the house and into Adak's, Totemtel Motel. It would be a three week wait there until a house would be available for us. We obtained some Navy loaner household goods before moving in, so it wasn't going to be too unbearable. After all nobody had ever died of discomfort at a Holiday Inn. In my naiveté, I hadn't taken into consideration what a motel would be like on Adak. When Pat parked in front of it, I was shocked. It was an old, decrepit, corrugated metal WWII Quonset hut.

Inside, it was easy to see it was temporary living accommodations. There was some old furniture, a washer and dryer, a kitchenette, a bedroom, a bathroom, and a tiny living room with a heater in the corner. After living in a nice house for our first month, we were spoiled, this place was the pits! The refrigerator was a little bigger than a Coleman ice chest. When I looked inside and saw how small it was, I turned to Pat and yelled, "How are we ever going to keep any food in this thing?" He said, "Don't worry, we'll just take out the ice trays to make more room." The ice trays were stuck and when Pat gave them a hard pull freezing water splashed all over my feet.

I hadn't cried for a while, so I broke down and let the tears flow. The sun-less, dreary, grey days of Adak were enough to make a sane person go nuts after a while. Living in a nice cheery home with a cat had helped me through it. Now we had to live in a metal mole hole. There was nothing good to say about it. The only excitement came when I did the wash the first time. The machines vibrated the whole hut so much, I was afraid the whole place would collapse. During the time we lived there, I did an excessive amount of wash in the hope that the stupid place would collapse and we could move out. No luck. We were stuck with a metal mole hole that leaked cold air from every seam and had a bathroom more like an attached outhouse. The water was always cold, so taking a shower consisted of throwing a few drops of water on your face, then running out to warm yourself by the heater.

At last, the news that we were so eagerly waiting for arrived. We were being assigned a house of our own! It wasn't any too soon either. A very terrible thing had happened, our Quonset hut didn't seem that bad anymore. When some-thing like that happens, you know that your brain has slipped a gear.

Our assigned house was a duplex unit with three bedrooms, a bathroom, a full kitchen, a utility room with washer and dryer and a living room with an attached dining area. The hallway to the bedrooms and bathroom had an entire wall of closets and cupboards. Our stuff couldn't even fill a small portion of that. When they did deliver our stored household goods from Pensacola and La Grange, we were in for a shock. In the Pensacola shipment, the portable black and white TV my parents had given us as a wedding gift was broken, as were many of our "unbreakable" Melamine dishes. In the La Grange shipment, many of the jars of baby food I had shipped were broken and rotted. We bought some new dishes and Charlie gave Pat the time and Navy parts and tools to repair our TV.

Brian was now seven months old, and had been an awfully good baby for all the travelling and rigmarole he had gone through. Now he would have a stable home on Adak for at least another ten months. Brian had a nice bedroom next to ours with a crib and a chest of drawers. After he learned to stand up, he really liked to jump in his crib. One morning we heard a loud crash from his room. When we rushed across the hall to see what had happened, we found Brian sitting on his crib mattress on the floor beneath the crib. He had jumped so hard that the crib's bottom spring latches had let loose. His eyes were as big as saucers and since it happened so fast, he wasn't quite sure if he should cry. This changed quickly. When he noticed us, his waterworks went into full gear. After Brian calmed down, Pat fixed the crib latches to ensure that this wouldn't happen again. It never did, because Brian never attempted to jump like that again.

Our house's master bedroom wall was also the master bedroom wall of the attached duplex unit. The family next door always provided us with 'entertainment' to keep things from getting boring. They were a strange family, who we only heard at the crack of dawn. At that early hour, they would start singing at the top of their lungs, I guess for their little daughter. She must not have had ears to like caterwauling like that. Pat always got furious, especially when he was trying to sleep after standing a mid-watch to eve-watch turnaround. Pat's work schedule was two day-watches (8:00 a.m.–4:00 p.m.), two mid-watches (12:00 a.m.–8:00 a.m.), two-eve watches (4:00 p.m.–12:00 a.m.) and two days off. Pat kept saying that he was going to pound on the wall if they didn't shut up. Luckily their concerts never lasted long enough for Pat to carry out his "ultimate" threat of dynamiting the wall. He said that a mere pound on the wall wouldn't do anything to stop a noise like that.

As the days passed, we got more and more used to our life on Adak. My earlier statement about obtaining fresh milk identifies the #1 thing we did on Adak: wait for the supply ship to come in, then hurry to the Commissary and BX to buy what had come in. If you waited until the day after the ship arrived, everything worthwhile had already been bought and everything that wasn't worthwhile was pretty much gone, too. You could never afford to be picky when buying things on Adak. You bought up whatever was shipped in, even if you were uncertain you needed it, or you went without altogether.

Usually, after our supply ship shopping was complete, Pat would take us for a drive. Since Adak had only 23 miles of roads, our drive was pretty much the same each time. Pat's favorite place to go was the Adak dump. It was always guarded by about 100 huge black ravens. Every time we went there, it made me think of Alfred Hitchcock's movie, *The Birds*. They were an ominous looking bunch, but were more afraid of us than we were of them. Brian and I would usually wait in the car while Pat would survey the debris. Sometimes he would make a real find. Lots of worthwhile things ended in the Adak dump when families received surprise orders. The best thing Pat found was a LP record rack on wheels. He sanded it and I spray painted it gold. It looked like new when we finished with it.

Another place we usually drove around was Lake Andrews. It, too, was eerie looking, like a marsh with perpetual low fog. Every time we went there I expected to see some prehistoric monster emerge from the fog because it looked like we had gone thousands of years back in time. We tried fishing off the shore there, but got nothing but cold for our effort. During WWII, Navy men stationed on Adak planted a small cluster of evergreen trees as there were no other trees. When we saw them in 1970, they were still only a small cluster of four-foot tall Douglas Firs. The cluster now laughingly had an official looking marker declaring: Adak National Forest. There was also a green, 20-gallon barrel marked with, "Please Keep Adak Green." When Pat stood among the trees he looked like Paul Bunyan.

The most depressing thing about Adak was the weather. We were lucky if the sun came out once a month, even if only for a couple of hours. Every day when we got up, Pat would look out the window and say, "Well, it's another beautiful day on Adak," which meant that it was already raining, sleeting or snowing or getting ready to. This would either cause us to cover our heads and go back to sleep or send Pat off to work and then cover our heads and go back to sleep. It was critical to check outside every morning, you did not want to miss the sun, if it should appear.

Winter on Adak was long and more treacherous than depressing. A blizzard locally called a Williwaw could come up in a matter of seconds and heaven help you if you weren't sheltered. Such a fast-moving blizzard would cause a "white out" condition, which meant there was near zero visibility. Sometimes the blowing snow was so heavy that you could hardly see your car's wiper blades. If you got caught in one, as Pat did several times on his way to work, you just pulled to the edge of the road and stayed there until it passed. A few years before we got there, some men who left the barracks to go hiking were caught in a "white out." The next day, their frozen bodies were found just yards from the entrance to the Naval Station barracks from which they had left. This incident caused everyone on Adak to have a deep respect for the weather.

Another natural event feared by Adak's inhabitants were our frequent earthquakes. The first time I experienced one, I thought that the entire house would collapse. Everywhere I looked in the house, things were moving. There is almost nothing more frightening than to feel the earth shaking beneath your feet for minutes. Some days we'd get three or four small earthquakes in a row, followed by multiple tremors. After a couple of months on Adak, I had adjusted to earthquakes as a routine life event, proving that people can get used to anything if they have to. There were only a handful of earthquakes that rated a call from Pat, at work thirteen miles away, to check that Brian and I were okay.

Even though Adak was such a desolate, isolated place, the military tried to make it a home for the people who were unfortunate enough to be stationed there. It had its own AFRTS (Armed Forces Radio Television Service) TV station, which offered the luxury of watching 1950's TV show reruns and movies from the '30's–'50's, just like back home. The station did present their own live shows such as a children's program, which was so bad that kids had to be forced to watch it. Sometimes they would also present a live introduction to an afternoon movie. Everyone's favorite program was the news and weather, because it was more of a variety show. With all the mistakes that occurred during the half hour show, it was obvious that these folks broadcast careers would end after Adak. One weather report had to be cancelled because the weatherman was caught in a "white out." It was funny watching the news anchor trying to speculate on the weather, "Ah, gee it must be bad out if our weatherman couldn't get here." Near the end of the show, the weatherman, a disheveled mess of ice and snow, did show up. When the news anchor asked him about the weather he exclaimed, "Don't go out in it!" At times, the weatherman wasn't able to get temperatures for the lower 48, so he would report that, "The lower 48 aren't having any weather."

Aside from "that was all we had," another reason for watching Adak TV, especially on Monday, Wednesday, and Friday, was because everyone was waiting for them to flash the "Mail Call" message. You can imagine how important mail was to everyone on the Island, when TV programming was immediately interrupted to inform people their mail was in. It wasn't just mail from home, it was all the other stuff that people had ordered from mail order catalogs. It was hard to survive on what items Adak had to offer. A Sears catalog was a valued possession on Adak, God help you if you were caught thieving someone's copy. That theft would probably be punishable by having to eat only military rations for the rest of your time on Adak, inflicting terminal indigestion. Pat even mail ordered four new tires for our car from the Sears catalog. It took two postal workers to help him get them in the car.

Pat added to our Adak entertainment choices by building a mail order, Heathkit AM/FM/shortwave radio receiver. If it worked as well as he hoped, we would soon be able to listen to "Larry Lujack" on WLS Radio, Chicago. He strung up a long, wire antenna for it in our backyard. It worked better than he hoped, not only did we listen to "Uncle Larry" but we became acquainted with "Wolfman Jack" out of Mexico. Pat even purchased a few Wolfman Jack "oldies" LP collections from the Wolfman.

We were able to call home from Adak by means of the White Alice Communications System, run by the U.S. Air Force. This system connected us back to Anchorage and then to anywhere in the lower 48. I was so glad we could call, hearing voices from home, really helped to make Adak more bearable for us. The phone was invaluable to us when we found out that Mom had to have immediate surgery for a ruptured navel. I couldn't believe that I had lived at home for twenty-one years and Mom had never needed surgery. I leave and she does. We wanted to be with her, but that was impossible. The next best thing we could do was to call her in the hospital to let her know that she was in our thoughts and prayers. We synchronized our watches then called Grandma Taraba to let her know that we would be calling Mom at such and so time. It was a big deal at the hospital. When Mom told the nurses that her daughter and son-in-law would be calling from Alaska, they made sure that the hospital operator knew to put the call through as soon as it came in. We talked with her for about an hour and that helped ease the fears on both ends of the line. She knew we loved her and would have been with her if we could. That was what she needed to hear and what I needed to say to her.

As Brian grew older, I wanted a pet for him. All of my life I had been surrounded by pets. I felt that Brian was now old enough to have fun with a puppy. There were always ads in the Base newspaper for Adak puppies. All of these dogs looked pretty much the same: medium length hair and big crystal blue eyes. When Pat asked around, his new chief petty officer told him that his dog was going to have puppies and that we could have one. I was very excited and couldn't wait for our puppy. When they were born, we went over to the chief's house to select the one we would take home after it was weaned. They were all cute but we picked a caramel tan and white female and named her Taffy.

When we brought Taffy home, she was a major mischief maker. Pat built her a nice wooden bed with carpeting for a mattress. Within a week, she had eaten half of the bed and was starting on the carpeting. After she had her fill of the bed, she moved on to eating the baseboard molding in the utility room. After nine months with us, she had never learned a thing and was still not housebroken. As she had grown older, she looked more and more like the "Flub-a-Dub" character from the 1950s *Howdy Doody TV Show*. Taffy wasn't like any of the dogs I had grown up with, and I felt bad that she wasn't.

To switch gears a bit, one morning I woke up with excruciating pain in my back. Pat called in to work to get let his chief know that he was taking me to the hospital. We got there and waited for over an hour behind sailors and other dependents for our turn. Pat helped me into the doctor's office and was told to wait outside. The doctor listened to me for a few minutes, then told me that I was a "goldbricker" and handed me a prescription chit. I went out to Pat, handed him the paper and told him what the doctor had said. Pat started to go back but I said, "Please Pat, can we just get the prescription filled?" When Pat read it, he really got mad. It was a prescription for a "bed board," a piece of plywood to put under our bed's mattress!

Pat took me home, put me in bed to rest and called his chief. When Pat explained what had happened, his chief became furious as well. He told Pat to stay put while he talked to the division officer. A few minutes later, the chief called back to tell Pat to take me back to the hospital, that this time I was going to see the hospital's head doctor. He was a very nice, considerate, full commander. After hearing my issues, he had my urine tested and determined that I had a severe bladder infection. A "bed board" would not have cured that! He apologized for the earlier doctor's "error" and prescribed an antibiotic to clear up my infection. Within a week I was back to my non-goldbricking self. This health incident more than cemented our belief that Navy healthcare was not the best.

OK, so far, I have been only relating the negative aspects of Adak to you. Aside from the frozen milk and brown lettuce, Adak did have another side. The Island did take on a new look when the sun appeared. It looked kind of pretty in a frontier sort of way. During the short summer months, the tundra grass grew to five feet tall and turned bright green, the winds didn't blow so ferociously and a 65-degree day seemed swelteringly hot. It was on these days that the three of us took hikes and drives around the island. It was wonderful not feeling trapped in the house by the weather and getting to breathe some fresh air.

Most of Adak's sights consisted of junk left over from World War II. There were dozens of abandoned Quonset huts and tons of other rusted metal hulks all over the island. Looking at these relics gave you an eerie feeling. You could imagine soldiers living in the huts during WWII, waiting for the Japanese to attack. And, when it came, the frenzy and activity that might have taken place on the spot where we were standing. Adak had a lot of past history, and only a small part of it could be realized by its visual remains.

On one of these forays, we found updated WWII boat docks and a docked North Pacific King Crab processing ship. Pat decided to go onto the ship to ask if he could buy a King Crab. The Captain said, "Yes," but Pat had to climb into the hold to collect his own "live" King Crab. Pat fearlessly climbed down into the hold, dodging dozens of snapping claws to select our crab. He grabbed it by the back legs and flipped it onto the steamer belt. After about 30 minutes, Pat climbed down from the ship with the biggest crab I had ever seen! After we cleaned it, we had about ten pounds of delicious, freshly steamed King Crab to enjoy.

Something that Pat enjoyed doing, which made Adak more like home, was to barbeque. On one of our many trips to the dump, Pat collected most of the parts he needed to build a barbeque. I couldn't believe that he made it himself and that it worked even in Adak's harsh weather. It was then that I realized that I had married a very creative man. He mounted a large metal radio cabinet on four metal-rod "legs" then attached wheels from a laundry cart to them. The grill was a shelf rack from an old refrigerator. The top of the cabinet had a hinged door, that could be opened or closed depending on how the wind was blowing. It was ingenious, and it allowed Pat to barbeque whenever he felt like it even though the wind was howling outside. He got a few gawkers when he was out cooking in the rain or snow. He didn't care, we would be soon enjoying the taste of a charcoal broiled steak.

On Adak, a good cookbook collection was critical to the preparing of imaginative home cooked meals. The near daily nasty weather was enough to keep most people in, so a restaurant, other than the main Base cafeteria, would have never survived. We went there to get a soft ice cream "treat." It was strange tasting stuff, made from powdered milk. When they started selling it, everyone rushed over to buy it. We had really missed the ice cream treats we would buy from the Tastee Freeze in Pensacola. This stuff was only in demand because, you guessed it, "It was all we had!"

On our first visit, we ordered two strawberry sundaes. What we got was quite unbelievable. The woman making them had no idea what she was doing. She oozed ice cream out of the machine that had the consistency of chunky buttermilk, plopping it on a large paper plate to overflowing. She covered this with two huge ladles of strawberry preserves. They looked a mess and tasted almost as bad, but it gave us great pleasure just to be able to go out for a sundae. When you are really isolated, you miss things that you had taken for granted. Most of the time people don't truly appreciate even small pleasures until they don't have them readily available.

The other good thing about Adak was that it really made a family much closer. With nowhere to go and not much to do, families had more time for each other. Adak gave Pat, Brian and I the perfect opportunity to really get to know each other and to live together as a family. Up to this point, our lives had been unsettled by lengthy separations. Adak gave us a time to be alone and to watch Brian grow day by day. I didn't have to write Pat to tell him what his son was learning to do, he was there. We were together now and could share in the joy that Brian brought. We had a good foundation to our marriage, but we realized it more than ever from living those months on Adak. Everyone there said that, if your marriage could survive Adak, it would survive anything. There were a number of couples that weren't quite as lucky as we were, many marriages ended in divorce because of Adak's stressful living.

It's hard to believe that anything exciting could happen on Adak, since it was occupied by the military and a few insane civilians, but Adak did have its moments. I mentioned the first event when discussing living in Pat's boss's house: three South Korean fishing boats captured by the U.S. Coast Guard for fishing in U.S. water and were moored offshore from our house.

The next incident was an attempted rape. A male forced his way into one of the Navy housing units, after the husband had left for work, and tried to rape the man's wife. He didn't get very far. She stabbed him in the arm with a butcher knife causing him to run out of the house. Adak's commanding officer ordered all of the men on the island checked for a slashed arm. After three days of searching, a Marine was turned in by his buddies. The reason why they turned him in: they thought he was going to die from blood loss not because of what he did.

The last incident was Adak's commanding officer and his family deciding to go on leave just before the U.S. government planned an underground nuclear test on a small island near Adak. He made a special TV broadcast to assure everyone on the island that we were in no danger from the test and that his leave had been long planned. His telecast convinced everyone that he and his family were deserting the island like rats leaving a sinking ship. He was completely wrong about the effect we would feel. Adak suffered a "trivial" earthquake followed by a tsunami that washed over most of the housing units located along the beaches, including the house we had originally stayed in. No one was injured, as the houses had been evacuated. Adak's commanding officer was reposted while on leave and never returned to Adak. No matter how many people live in a place or where it is, you always have scandals, gossip, and crime.

Through hard studying, Pat passed his tests for petty officer first class with just over three years in the Navy. With his new petty officer first class rating and no four-year "hash mark" on his uniform, the Base commander ordered Pat to stand-down from all inspections. At this same time, Pat's team received a Unit Commendation Medal for their "Top Secret" communications work. In mid-March 1971, Pat received orders to the Naval Security Group Detachment, Misawa, Japan. We were very happy. Originally it had been rumored that one of the Adak crew was being sent to sea aboard the U.S.S. *Pueblo*. Pat had also been looked at to fill an electronics instructor job in Pensacola, Florida or Great Lakes, Illinois. Misawa, Japan sounded like a very exotic and thrilling place to go while recognizing that most military bases are located in the armpit of wherever.

Soon after the receipt of Pat's transfer orders, we had to begin sorting out our household goods. They would be packed up and shipped to Japan while we were on leave in the U.S. We also had to plan our month leave (two weeks with each of our families) and clean up the house. The house had to undergo an inspection on the day we were leaving, and if it didn't pass, we would be detained until it passed. You knew you would pass if everything in the entire house was spotless. The refrigerator had to be crumb-less, the stove spill-less and the washer and dryer lint-less. All in all, it had to look like no human had lived in the house. It was a very unnerving job.

We were assigned two 'pack out' dates. The initial date took place a month before our departure leaving us with only essential items. The Navy loaned us bed clothes, pots and pans, dishes, and utensils, just like they had when we lived at the Totemtel Motel. Our possessions were packed by two women, who were a marvel to watch. They were so fast and efficient that we had to make sure that there wasn't anything out that we didn't want shipped. They told me that if I didn't keep Brian out of their way, they might pack him up, too. I felt confident that our things would arrive in good condition this time. As I wrote earlier, many of the things shipped from Pensacola and La Grange to Adak had arrived broken. The Navy would pay a minimal reimbursement for things broken in transit, but, that couldn't compensate you for broken items with sentimental value.

Leaving Adak was very exciting, we were going to civilization to visit our families! The saddest part was that we would have to give up our dog, Taffy. It was impossible to ship her into Northern Japan and neither of our parents could take her. We tried to find her another Adak home but with all her terrible qualities and habits, it was difficult. At the last minute, we did. When it came time to deliver Taffy to her new owners, Pat put her dog dish and toys in the car then came back for her with tears in his eyes. He picked her up, put her in the car and drove her away. When he came home, he said that she would be alright, he had left her with her nose in her food dish. To this day, I think about her and regret having had to leave her on Adak.

We realized that we were a bit sad at leaving Adak. We enjoyed many good times there together. We knew the island and how to survive it. Now we were pulling up our roots and moving even farther from our families. On Adak, we could phone home regularly via White Alice to keep in touch. Misawa didn't support phone calls to the States, so we wouldn't be able to hear our family's voices for thirty months. We planned to regularly mail cassette audio tapes back and forth to fill in that lack. As isolated as Adak had been, it seemed that Japan might be even worse for isolation and loneliness. Well, we weren't going to worry about that until we got there. We had an entire month of leave to look forward to and we planned to make the most of it.

The trip leaving Adak was a lot easier than it had been when Brian and I flew up all alone. We sailed through Anchorage and were back at Sea-Tac airport meeting Pat's family with no glitches. It was so good to see my new family again. I had heard so much about Pat's family, now I was going to meet all of them and show off our one-and-a-half-year-old son. It was a two-hour ride from the airport to the Harrington home. By the time we turned into the driveway, we were feeling pretty worn out. There wasn't much conversation after we entered the house, just a lot of activity hauling in our luggage. Poor Brian didn't know what was going on. He was so far off his schedule that he didn't know if he should be eating breakfast or dinner, or sleeping. For me, the first thing to do was to get him bedded down for the night. Pat's Mom had a crib set up in our bedroom, so Brian could feel the familiarity of us all being in the same bedroom.

The Harrington home was exactly as Pat had described it, so I felt very comfortable in it. Pat's Dad had designed and started building the house just before Pat was born. The outside was constructed of cinder blocks with a cedar shingle roof. It sat half way up a very steep hill. That was the first thing I noticed about Bellingham, it was very hilly. Most of the land in Illinois is flat, the only things pushing into the clouds are skyscrapers. In Washington State, every-thing seemed built on an incline and there were giant snowcapped mountains. It seemed that on Bellingham streets, none of the houses were built side by side. One might be on a hill while the next one might be built in a gulley. It seemed so odd to look 'down' out of a window to see the "next door" neighbor's house.

When morning came, we were all excited to get things started. Pat's Mom had a lot of things planned, most of which revolved around meeting the rest of the family. When Brian woke up, we brought him into bed with us. Pat started tickling him and soon he was laughing and waving his arms. When I sat up in bed to watch them, Brian accidently gave me a hard poke in the eye. It hurt and didn't seem a good way to start our visit. Pat jumped out of bed and asked his mother if she could find something to put on my eye. It throbbed and teared like mad, I could hardly open it. Pat's Mom found some eye drops and that relieved my malady for the moment. I was thankful that I could now see out of the eye again. It would have really been embarrassing to meet Pat's relatives for the first time looking like a cyclops.

After breakfast, Pat's younger brother Denne, his wife Meredith, and their son Gahan came to visit. Since their son was four months older than Brian, we thought that they would have fun playing together. Unfortunately, babies that age tend not to play nice. They didn't even want to stay in the same play pen together. They must have figured that the other was a threat to his being the center of attention. Pat's sister, Tracy, and Meredith were close to the same age, so I had them to talk to, while Pat was busy telling "sea stories" to Denne.

Our visit went pretty smoothly that day but the next day Brian woke up with a bad chest cold. We figured the mixture of the weather change and leaving germ free Adak had caused it. Brian was really scaring us because he seemed to be having trouble breathing. We rushed him to the emergency room at nearby St. Joseph's hospital. There, after waiting for hours to see a doctor, it seemed Brian's was breathing better. When the doctor saw Brian, he said that he just had a cold and would give us some medicine for it. Oh well, so much for profound diagnosis.

In a couple of days, Brian was doing much better. So much so, that we took a short trip to pick up Pat's grandma, Florence Clubine, who lived in White Rock, British Columbia, Canada. White Rock was located just across the U.S.-Canadian border from Bellingham. She had moved there from Eastern British Columbia after losing her husband, Lincoln Clubine. The White Rock location allowed Pat's Mom to look after her and see that she had all she needed. Florence was 83 and lived by herself in her own apartment. When I first met her, I was a bit afraid of her. She was a very tiny, frail lady who talked in a very abrupt manner. I wanted her to like me because Pat loved her so much. As I talked with her more and more, I began to feel more comfortable with her. She was a very honest woman and would tell you how she felt no matter how it sounded. At 83, she was an incredibly intelligent woman who was current on everything in the U.S. and Canada. She loved to talk politics and had her own opinions on how things should be run. I noticed a loaded bookshelf in her apartment and was kind of shocked to see a copy of Jacqueline Susann's book "Valley of the Dolls." She told me that she liked to read everything and that book proved it.

Pat had told me that his Grandma Clubine had always been daring and had done what she wanted. Now I had the opportunity to hear about her life directly. Florence Bertha Benthey been born on March 26, 1884, in Chicago, Illinois. Her father was a prominent commercial florist who worked on the 1893 Chicago World's Fair. Her mother was a descendent of a branch of the "Lee" family. She grew up learning how to ride a horse so well that she picked up the nickname "Bill" after Wild Bill Hickok. She talked her father into allowing her to learn to type (a man's job at the time) but that was still too tame for her. Next, she got on a train to Spokane, Washington to "visit my sister," but with high hopes of becoming a bareback horse rider in a circus. While visiting her sister, she got a job as a cafe waitress. She soon met her husband to be, Lincoln

Rhodes Clubine, a Canadian gold prospector and miner. She told her father back in Chicago that, "He has great prospects."

After they were married, Lincoln took her to live in the wilderness of Eastern British Columbia, Canada. She set up housekeeping in a small cabin on the side of a mountain with no roads. She fascinated me with her stories of trying to raise three children and fight off bears at the same time. For years, she had hand pumped water from a well, cooked on a wood burning stove and used an outhouse. If she wanted to bathe, she had to heat water on the stove and dump it in a metal tub on their enclosed porch. That made me think back to my early Chicago days. Grandma Clubine and I had a shared history of using portable metal bathtubs.

The first night that Grandma Clubine spent with us was so hectic that I bet she wished she had stayed home. From when we had arrived at Pat's parent's house, I had changed Brian's disposable diapers and flushed them down the toilet. After I flushed another diaper, the water in the toilet started to rise and rise finally stopping at the rim. I got Pat's Mom and when she saw it, she reflexively flushed the toilet again! That caused the toilet to overflow everywhere. Even the bathroom rug starting floating out into the hallway. When Pat's Mom saw this, she started laughing hysterically. Between her laughing fits, she managed to say that she always laughed whenever anything went wrong and she got nervous. I couldn't see anything in the least funny and I was sure that Pat's Dad wouldn't either. I was feeling very guilty, I was sure that I had caused it with the diaper.

When Pat's Dad came and saw the mess, bingo, he was not remotely happy, but he had to do something before the bathroom floated away. He went into the basement and tried to unplug the clog from a cleanout there. He yelled up that the clog was so bad that it was solid for a few feet. He and Pat worked on it for a couple of hours and when they still couldn't unplug it, they decided to give up until the next day. Pat's Mom had to tell Grandma Clubine that she was going to have to use a port-a-potty for the night. To me it looked like a toilet seat hooked to a wastebasket. Grandma, being a hardy soul, didn't break a sweat in using it.

Pat's Mom told Grandma Clubine that she would be sleeping in the bottom bunk in Tracy's room. Grandma said goodnight and went into her room. A few minutes later she came out and said there was a cake in her bed. Pat's Mom apologized telling her that she had forgotten about the birthday cake she had made to celebrate Pat's, Denne's, Grandma's, and my birthdays. There hadn't been room for it in the refrigerator, so she had put it in the coolest location in the house, Grandma's bunk bed. With the cake removed, we all thought that Grandma was finally settled down for a good night's rest. We were wrong. A few minutes later, she was up again and made her point clear, "If that damn cat isn't taken out of my bed, I'm going to sleep outside." I, for one, was very puzzled. Even I knew that Pat's parents didn't have a cat. It turned out to be the neighbor's cat. He liked to sneak into the house and sleep with Tracy, who was normally in that bed. I bet after that night, poor Grandma would have given anything to be back on top of that mountain fighting bears again.

When morning came, the men went back to trying to unclog the drain. After hours more work, they got it unstuffed. I apologized for clogging the toilet with Brian's diapers. Tracy added to my apology by saying that when she had cleaned the bathroom the other day, she had flushed paper towels down the toilet. Then, Pat's Mom confessed that she had recently flushed a bowl of mashed potatoes down the toilet. After hearing their confessions, I didn't feel quite as bad. It was decided that it wasn't anyone's fault, just the cumulative result of all the weird things that had been flushed down the toilet during the last few weeks. Everyone was glad that it was repaired, Easter Sunday was coming up and all the other relatives were coming over. It wouldn't have been very nice to escort them to the port-a-potty when they had to go. With this crisis over, I think we were all hoping that everything would go smoothly during the final days of our visit.

My hopes were squashed the next day, when Pat and I woke up with chest colds. It might have been more an allergy attack with Pat, he began to sound better as the day progressed. I, on the other hand, began to sound worse and worse. By the next day, I was really feeling bad and looked the same. A great way to be presented to a bunch of new relatives! By Saturday, I looked better, but still felt terrible. On Sunday, I came to realize that I needn't have worried, most of the relatives who came to visit were Pat's geriatric Aunts. After Brian and my introductions, they seemed to forget us, got into their own little group and talked amongst themselves all evening. Pat's Dad retrieved Grandma Mosa Harrington from her nursing home, so she too was with us for the holiday. She had been the parish housekeeper for Sacred Heart Parish's priests until stricken with a stroke ten years earlier. Her left side was paralyzed, so whenever she went any place she had to be moved in a wheelchair. She was unable to speak, but I was glad I'd met her so that I could tell her that I would take good care of her favorite grandson.

After the holiday was over, we had to get ready to travel on to Chicago. I was so excited to see my family that my energy was renewed in spite of my cold. I was going home! I knew that the days there were going to fly by like they had in Bellingham but I was not going to worry about that now. I was going to enjoy each and every day with them to the fullest and face the goodbyes when I had to and not before.

We started our homeward journey with a very tearful farewell to Pat's parents at the Sea-Tac Airport. They had made me feel part of their family and that's what I wanted most. I cried when I left them, it felt just like leaving my own family. I had come through the family inspection pretty well considering that my eyes had been watering, my nose had been red and I was stuffed up much of the time. Our United flight to Chicago O'Hare was crowded, every seat on the plane being occupied. On take-off, I thought that my head was going to explode from my congestion and the pressure. I felt awful but I would have gone through anything to get back to Chicago. Our excitement level grew when we heard the pilot announce, "Welcome to Chicago's O'Hare International Airport where the weather is…." It was music to our ears! I couldn't wait to see everyone and for them to see how much Brian had grown.

As the plane landed, we hurriedly got our son and belongings together to disembark the plane. When we exited into the airport, they were all there; Mom, Dad, Mark, and Bill! Everyone looked fine, even Mom. We hugged and kissed all around, then made our way to the car and to La Grange. It was so nice to see that old house again, where so many of my memories had their beginning. This house was our home base, where we could always return. Wherever they would send us, we knew that there was a home back in La Grange, Illinois, that would be waiting for us with open arms.

As I entered the house, I noticed few things had changed, except for Mickey. She had put on many "extra pounds" since we last saw her, now she weighed 55 pounds. I would bet that those pounds made her a near record sized beagle. She didn't let her weight slow her down, she greeted us by sitting up on her hind legs and giving us each a kiss. When she saw Brian, you could tell she knew him right away as the baby she used to look after. She had been so serious about that job that we all use to call her "Auntie Mickey."

There was a new pet addition to the family, a large turtle named "Alexander the Great." He had one eye and Mom kept him in one basin of her kitchen sink. Bill found him walking across 6th Avenue, so he brought him home to stay with the family. He was very intelligent, as far as turtles go, with good taste in food. He wouldn't eat anything but fried chicken and smoked ham, so proved to be one of Mom's more expensive boarders.

As the days passed, we tried to do as many things as we could together. We visited a lot with Grandma and Grandpa Taraba and had dinner together as often as we could. Pat and I missed Chicago take-out foods, so we tried to eat as much Italian beef, Italian sausage, Polish sausage, Chicago Pizza, etc., as we could. We were sure that Japan wouldn't offer most of the food we enjoyed eating in the U.S.

A very special event that we got to participate in was my parent's 25th wedding anniversary renewal of their wedding vows. It was a very sweet and beautiful ceremony. We were so happy that they scheduled it for when we were home.

As hard as we tried to make each day pass slowly, it just didn't work. Before we knew it, our departure day arrived. It seemed that Chicago O'Hare was a place for either sadness or great joy for me. On that day, it was sadness. Brian would be almost four years old when everyone saw him next! Once again, we had a very tearful send off. I was positive that our trip to Japan wouldn't be as bad as going to Adak, since we had Pat along this time. Boy, was I ever a naive, wishful thinker! Our trip to Japan fit Murphy's Law to a tee, every possible thing that could go wrong went wrong. It seemed to me that only through God's grace and Pat's perseverance did we make it to Misawa, Japan.

CHAPTER 15
NO YEN FOR JAPAN

After a nearly five-hour night flight from O'Hare, we arrived at the San Francisco International airport around dawn. We knew it was going to be a long trip, but we had no idea how long it would really be. Neither Pat nor I had slept a wink on the airplane, so we were already feeling exhausted. After Pat collected our luggage, we made our way out of the airport to locate the bus that was going to Travis Air Force Base. Pat helped the driver load our baggage in and we were off for a two-hour ride in a Greyhound bus.

Upon our arrival at Travis AFB, I stood with Brian while Pat got all our things together and checked us in with his orders. He was told that our plane to Yokota, Japan would arrive in about four hours. Waiting in an airport is no joy, but when you are waiting with a one-year-old, it can be chaos. Children at that age have no sit-down ability, so most of the four hours were spent running after Brian.

When our Braniff jet arrived, we joined a group of other families who were more than ready to board, sit down and relax. As soon as everyone was seated, the pilot announced that we would be making two stops along the way: Honolulu, Hawaii, and Wake Island. We were kind of excited about getting to see Hawaii, but what was at Wake Island? It seemed like we had been traveling for an eternity when we landed in Honolulu. With changing time zones and constant meals being served, it was hard to know what day it was or how long we had been in the air. Brian was being very good because he had slept most of the way. I knew that the next lap of our trip wouldn't go as easily because a baby can only sleep so much.

We really didn't get to see much of Hawaii during our one-hour layover, just the airport. At least it was long enough to stretch our legs and soak in the beautiful trees and flowers inside the airport. Pat bought us ice cream cones at premium prices and I bought post cards to send back to our relatives at home.

It was a wonderful hour but soon we were back on that cramped plane on our five-hour flight to Wake Island. Pat and I were both getting punchy from lack of sleep and the constant daylight. Brian, on the other hand, was very spunky and amused himself by attempting to crawl up the wall of the airplane, over the seats, and all over us. It was like trying to keep a snake on hot sand still.

The only thing that offered a break in the monotony, was the frequent meal and soft drink service. As we spent more and more hours on our trip, even those seemed to be getting worse or maybe their novelty had just worn off. Whatever it was, the plane trip was turning out to be almost unbearable.

When we saw Wake Island on our final approach, it looked like a white postage stamp! When the plane touched down, the captain immediately announced, "Please don't be alarmed by the water under each wing. Our jet needed a bit longer runway and just the front wheels had gone in the ocean." A few minutes later, the plane was pulled backwards by a tractor and turned around for our takeoff. The captain next announced that all of the passengers had to deplane so they could wash off the saltwater and refuel. As we were led down the ramp, I felt like I was half conscious of what was happening around me. I was in a daze state brought on from lack of sleep, the 110 degree temperature and 90% high humidity of the island. I felt like I was going to fall over because a steaming wet blanket had been thrown over me. I wanted to get back in that air-conditioned plane as quickly as possible. We were all led into a poorly air-conditioned, cramped military building to wait. Thank God, it was only a twenty-minute refueling stop over.

Once back in the plane, Pat told me that he had overheard someone in the building say that we were almost there. That news gave me a renewed enthusiasm that lasted until the pilot announced that we had a six-hour flight to Yokota. Right then and there I could have chewed my seat to shreds. I tried to stay composed but I felt if another tray of food was served, I would throw it in the server's face. My rotten thoughts helped ease my frustration and anger at the Navy for putting us through such an ordeal. Sadly, I didn't understand what an ordeal was until our journey progressed a little further.

When the pilot announced that we had only two hours left to our seventeen-hour flight, all the families onboard were overcome with joy and renewed energy at the prospect of finally reaching Japan. Then they announced a final meal would be served. We hoped that maybe this one would taste better because it was our last on the plane. Every previous meal tasted the same no matter what they claimed it was; steak, pork chops, or lunch meat. It was all undefinable, tasteless, and rubbery. The beverages hadn't been too bad; soft drinks, coffee, milk, or fruit juice. Pat and I decided to try some fruit juice with this meal instead of soda. We should have known not to drink it with the discoloration around the rim of the cup. At the time, we really couldn't think of anything, except that we would be on solid ground soon.

As we were down to the last thirty minutes of our flight, we experienced some unexpected, heavy turbulence. Suddenly, the plane took a dramatic and sudden major drop in altitude, causing everyone's stomach contents to lurch into their throats. I was looking kind of green, so Pat asked if I wanted an air sickness bag. I said, "Of course not," then the plane took another sudden drop and my apple juice decided to make a return appearance. I frantically yelled for Pat to give me the bag, now! I was embarrassed to be using one of those things in front of other passengers, but many of them were too busy using theirs to look. While filling up the bag, I began to choke on my own vomit. A thought flashed through my mind that this really was going to be my final flight.

Poor Pat turned white and tried desperately to get the attention of a stewardess. His poor wife was choking to death here! All of the stewardesses were fastened in their seats because of the turbulence so they couldn't help me. By this time, I was really gasping for my life. Pat, not knowing what else to do, gave me a hard whack on the back. That whack handed me a reprieve from the Grim Reaper's hand; I could breathe again! I didn't feel much better, but I was now able to complain about it. When I looked at Pat through my watering eyes, he looked putrid. I asked him if he needed an air sickness bag. He said what he needed to do couldn't be relieved in an air sickness bag. When we finally landed in at Yokota Air Force Base, Japan, we were one messed up feeling pair checking through U.S. customs.

I was feeling semi-alive, so I stayed with Brian while Pat raced off at fever pitch to find a bathroom. After what seemed an eternity, Pat found his way back to where we were waiting. He said that he felt a little better, but not much. We both decided that what we needed was some sleep in a bed in a dark room for about a week. We hadn't experienced any darkness or sleep for about twenty-seven hours.

When we checked through U.S. customs, Pat was told to check-in with Navy liaison to find out what we were supposed to do next. We both were hoping that they would find us a place to stay for the night on the Base, we both desperately needed sleep. When Pat came back, he hurriedly grabbed our bags and said he was told we had to board a waiting Navy bus. Pat's orders said that we had to check in at Tachikawa Air Force Base before proceeding to Misawa. The Navy liaison guided us over to a waiting bus.

After dragging ourselves and our bags into a rickety, grey Navy bus (first clue), along with fifteen single Navy men (second clue), we set off for Tachikawa Air Force Base. That bus ride was the scariest I had ever been on. Everything rattled from the windows to the seats. It was like sitting in a blender. After half an hour, I just couldn't stay awake any longer. I leaned on Pat's shoulder and fell asleep while Brian slept on Pat's lap. It was a two-hour "road to hell" ride down roads that were no wider than alleyways and all unlighted.

When we arrived at Tachikawa Air Force Base, Pat unloaded our bags and went to ask the Navy Master-at-Arms at a front gate that said, "Naval Security Group Kamiseya" (third clue), where we were supposed to check in. He inspected Pat's orders and he said that we weren't supposed to be here at all; we were supposed to be at billeting at Tachikawa AFB. He phoned over there and was told that billeting was full. He told Pat that the only thing we could do would be to go to Yokohama in a taxi and stay in a Japanese hotel. When I heard that I turned to Pat and screamed that we couldn't go any further without some food and sleep. Pat went nose-to-nose with the Master-at-Arms, telling him that we had been travelling for almost 30 hours and weren't going anywhere else tonight. Pat told him that they had better find a place for us to stay, before his family died from exhaustion. Since Pat outranked the Master-at-Arms, he called the quarter deck and talked to the Officer-Of-The-Deck, a full commander that night.

When Commander Cross arrived at the gate, he was the most under-standing and compassionate person I would meet while Pat was in the Navy. He took one look at us, listened to our plight and decided that we would spend the night in the Bachelor Officer's Quarters (BOQ), a Navy mortal sin. Enlisted men or women are not allowed to stay in the BOQ. We added to the sin by having a little boy with us as well. For one night, the commander said that no one should worry about it. While Brian and I were settling into the room, Pat went with Commander Cross and came back with some turkey sandwiches, crackers, and milk. We were all so hungry by that point that even the crackers tasted like a gourmet feast. After eating, we all fell asleep snuggled close to each other in the same bed.

When morning came, all hell broke loose for us. The phone rang early in the morning. It was the officer whose room we were occupying. He was really hot about us staying in his room, especially since he had just come in from a flight. The bottom line was that we were to vacate his room as quickly as possible or he would come down and vacate us himself. Our heaven-sent commander called a few minutes later to tell us that we needed to pack up quickly. He had a Navy van ready to take us to Billeting at Tachikawa AFB. He asked if Pat had gotten paid in the past month. Pat told him that he hadn't, that we were traveling on very skimpy funds. The commander said that by the time we were at the van he would have an advance on Pat's pay waiting. He was a kind, caring and thoughtful person who was wasted in the Navy.

We weren't too upset by our sudden forced departure. We had gotten some sleep, something to eat and a pay advance to help us cope with the rest of our trip to Misawa. The day was sunny and mild. This time we enjoyed our van ride to Tachikawa AFB. The van driver was friendly and even helped Pat carry our baggage to our room. We had tried to carry everything in at one time, but couldn't. The driver thought we had everything so drove off with our coats on the back seat. My God, what else?

When Pat realized our coats had driven off without us, he was a bit beside himself. I couldn't blame him, I was feeling the same way. After he calmed down, he went to find a telephone to contact the commander. Pat wasn't able to reach him, but he did talk to a chief who said he would track down the coats and have them routed to us in Misawa. Then he told Pat that he really felt no sympathy for us, we didn't seem to have the brains to handle even simple travel. He went on and on telling Pat how he was a complete idiot who wasn't worthy of being in the Navy. Our problems made him happy that he didn't have to deal with a family. When Pat returned to our room, his spirits had hit the pits. Obviously, the chief didn't care anything about us or how difficult the past few days had been. The Navy wanted its people to deal with their own problems, not to bother important people with issues that the Navy had caused and abetted.

Pat and I collapsed on our bed, trying to nap like Brian was doing. We managed to sleep for a couple of hours. When we woke up, we found the weather was looking very threatening. Pat jumped up and said that he'd better go look for something for us to eat before the rain started. After an hour, there was no sign of Pat and the storm appeared ready to hit in full force. I hoped that the rain would hold off until Pat got back but it didn't. About ten minutes later, Pat walked into our room totally drenched and carrying a cardboard box with soggy hamburgers, french fries, and half-spilled cokes. I felt bad for him and I began to have fears about the next thirty months we would have to live in Japan. Everything was starting our horribly wrong and I prayed this wasn't an omen of how things would continue.

After we squeezed the water out of our supper and ate it, we decided to try to get as much rest as we could before we left for Misawa. It was Friday. Our flight to Misawa was due to leave early Monday morning. We would have two days to rest and go crazy in our little room if the weather didn't improve. We hoped it would so we could walk around the Base and find where the BX was located, in case Brian needed more baby food.

In the end, the weather did improve and we were able to get around a bit, which was very good for Brian. Most babies don't take too well to being in a crib all day in very small room. Pat phoned our sponsor in Misawa to tell him that we would be arriving Monday morning. When a Navy family travels overseas, they are provided with a sponsor to help get them settled in and acquainted with their new duty station. We were truly hoping that things would go smoother for us in Misawa with our sponsors' help.

When Sunday night arrived, I started packing us up again. We were to be checked out of Billeting by midnight and at the airport by 1:00 a.m. The plane was scheduled to leave at 2:00 a.m. and arrive at Misawa around dawn. This schedule had not made our sponsor, Chief J. O. Cox, very happy. He would have to get up very early to pick us up. When everything was packed, we sacked out early. When we went to bed, Pat asked me if I had set the alarm clock. I told him I couldn't find the alarm clock anywhere. Going to bed with that worry, neither of us slept a wink. It seemed that every half hour one or the other of us was popping up to look at our watches. At check-in, no one had bothered to tell us that we could have requested the Billeting office send someone over to wake us up. Things would have been made so much easier if we had known.

Around 10:30 p.m., we gave up trying to get any sleep. I woke Brian up to feed him and get him dressed for our plane ride to Misawa. Babies don't usually take kindly to being woken up in the middle of the night, but Brian had been on such a weird schedule that he took everything in stride. When we were ready, Pat checked us out of the room and we waited for the airport bus to come by. The night was very eerie looking. A dense fog was beginning to appear and the air felt very damp and chilling. I was glad that we had sweaters to wear as our coats were still Absent Without Leave (AWOL).

After a forty-five minute wait, the bus pulled up and we boarded along with other families who were bound for Misawa. The bus ride was quick, as there was little traffic at that time of night. At the airport, Pat checked in our baggage while Brian and I found a place to rest our weary bones. Pat told me that everything was taken care of and that the plane would be here in about an hour. We began to do what everyone enjoys most, sitting for hours in an airport. We had really been lucky on this trip, that's all we seemed to be doing.

After forty-five minutes, an announcement came over the loudspeakers, "All flights out of Tachikawa are cancelled because of fog." All baggage had to be reclaimed as they had no idea when flights out would be resumed. Oh joy, more happy news to cope with. Pat got our luggage and we made our weary way back to Billeting.

When we arrived, we and the other families requested our rooms back. Of course, that turned out to be a much bigger deal than any of us had expected. The office manager, a lowly Air Force Airman, told us that he couldn't check us in until the next day! Since we had all had checked out after midnight, by Air Force regulation, we were not allowed to check back in on the same day. A ridiculous situation made worse by military regulations. Now none of us had a room to stay in. Pat, in his usual logical and calm way, had a nose-to-nose discussion with the Airman. Pat told him that if he didn't assign us rooms immediately, he and the other men were going to shove his face down his throat. It's a marvel how closely people listen to such reason. The manager was even able to assign all of us our original rooms. After some congratulatory handshaking, Pat got us into our room, where we flopped on the bed like the dead and stayed that way until early afternoon. I found it incredible that we had gone through such a rigmarole only to be back where we started.

Pat said that he'd better call our sponsor in Misawa to see if he knew when the next plane was scheduled for Misawa. When Pat got Chief Cox on the phone, Cox was fit to be tied that we hadn't come in when we were supposed to. Pat told him that a heavy fog had rolled in and no aircraft had been allowed to take-off or land. Chief Cox hadn't seemed to listen and kept complaining about how early he had to go to the airport to pick us up and we hadn't bothered to show up. He told Pat that the next scheduled Misawa flight was Wednesday and that we had better be on it or else. What a pleasant human being to have to rely on to get settled in Misawa.

At this point, I felt like telling Pat that I just wanted to go back home. Obviously, I knew I couldn't do that, and anyway, a trip back at this point would probably kill me. OK, I also remembered that in my wedding vows I had stated that I would stay with Pat, "through sickness and health," but was that sickness his or mine? Right now, I felt that my mental health was on the wane. I couldn't desert him while I was going insane, that would be nuts. Come to think of it, I wasn't sure that Pat's sanity was holding up much better than my own.

On Wednesday morning, we went through the same routine that we had on Monday morning, pack up, checkout, ride the bus to the airport, and wait. If we had had to go through it again, we could have done it with our eyes closed. This time the plane was leaving later and was scheduled to arrive at Misawa around 10:00 a.m. By 2:00 a.m., we actually boarded the airplane and were feeling pretty good that we had gotten that far. The plane taxied down the runway, stopped and we sat for a half hour. Finally, the pilot announced that there was heavy fog in Misawa and that no planes were being allowed to land there until it burned off. He said that we would have to wait for the all clear and that might take several hours. He taxied back to the terminal where we deplaned and trudged back inside. I knew it had been too good to be true! We sat there for another hour before the "all clear" announcement came. We headed out to the plane with the thought that we might actually take off and land in Misawa today. We did and the flight was uneventful, thank God!

As we deplaned in Misawa, we were met by our "congenial" sponsor, Chief J.O. Cox. He was a man in his 40s, who looked like he was going on 65. Seeing him made me realize that, after enduring Pat's watch standing at two Navy stations and the uprooting and travel between those duty stations, this could be what Pat would look like if we didn't get out. My God, J.O. looked a lot like my Grandpa Taraba. J.O. wasn't in the best of moods when he met us. He had had to wait an extra two hours for us because of the fog delay. He said everything was arranged for temporary housing until we were assigned a house. I was so glad to have something that we could call our home for a while.

J.O. drove us to the temporary housing quarters. It was a very nice-looking building with four large bedrooms, each with its own bathroom and kitchenette, and a common living room area. Three of the bedrooms were already assigned to other families. The family members were very nice but they told us they were all leaving for the States in the morning. I thought that was kind of odd. Were we the only family in the building that had just arrived? I was just too tired to think about it anymore, so I set my mind to unpacking. It felt good to not be living out of a suitcase anymore. At least, we would be living here for long enough to hang up our things in a closet.

Towards evening, J.O. took us to the Non-Commissioned Officers (NCO) Club for dinner. He told Pat that he would pick him up early in the morning so he could get checked in at the Naval Security Group Detachment. I felt like our luck had shifted, that things were now going smoothly. Boy, was that a premature assumption! When we woke the next morning, everything was strangely quiet compared to the night before. When we opened our bedroom door, all of the other bedroom doors were open and everyone was gone. I wished that it had been us going too, but we still had 30 months standing between us and home. J.O. was true to his word and came by early to take Pat out to the Navy Base.

After Pat left, I fed Brian and put him down for a nap. Since I wasn't going anywhere at the moment, I decided to stay comfortable in a duster. I took everything from the bedroom that I might need for the next couple of hours and closed the bedroom door behind me. I listened at the door and everything was quiet, so I knew Brian had fallen asleep. I continued on with some chores and an hour later, I needed to go back in the bedroom for something. I turned the doorknob and found that the door was locked. Brian was locked in the bedroom! Panic set in. He must have been fooling around with the doorknob and now it could only be opened from the inside. I tried to calm down and figure out how I was going to unlock the door before Brian woke up.

I got out the Base telephone book and found the number for the Billeting office. A Japanese man answered in very broken English. I tried to explain to him what my predicament was. He finally caught on and said that he had a duplicate key, all I had to do was come and pick it up. After I hung up, I realized that I couldn't walk two blocks to the office in a housecoat and slippers. I looked out the window and saw a bunch of kids playing nearby. I called them over and asked if one of them could pick up the key to our bedroom at the office. They were all very polite and said they would. I was so relieved that I could have kissed every one of them. In a few minutes, they were back with a key, but when I tried it, I found that they had been given the wrong key.

I called the boy who had gotten the key over again and explained that he had been given the wrong key. He said he was sorry and returned quickly with another key. His mission was successful this time and I thanked him profusely. When I opened the door Brian was still in a deep sleep. I was so grateful to that boy that I offered him some money as a reward. He declined saying that his parents wouldn't like him taking money for doing someone a favor. I was really impressed with him, and I hoped that Brian would act just as nobly when he was his age.

After this crisis was averted, I settled into a kitchen chair and tried to soak in some peace and quiet. My serenity was shattered when a mob of Japanese maids, each carrying buckets, brooms, and bottles of cleaner barged in. They quickly scattered into different rooms like ants pouring out of an anthill. They seemed so hurried that I got the impression that my being there was throwing a monkey wrench into their works. After a brief huddle, one of the Momma-sans approached. With her meager English, she made me understand that they were supposed to clean up the entire unit and that we would have to pack up and leave.

I couldn't believe what I was hearing. I would have to pack everything up again after getting everything unpacked? With thoughts of pure hatred for the Navy, I started packing things up with a vengeance, tears of frustration streaming down my face. I remember saying to myself, "Dear God, how much more will we be shoved around before we can settle down and get this damned Navy tour over with?" I had tried to be patient, but this torpedo sank that ship. There was nothing I could do to get back at the Navy, so the next best thing I could do was to take it all out on Pat. He was the closest extension of the Navy that I could get my hands on. After I packed all of our things up, I calmly waited for Pat. It was the calm before a tornado strikes, I waited to pounce.

When Pat and J.O. arrived and came inside, there I sat with Brian and our packed suitcases. Pat looked surprised and a bit worried asking me what was wrong? Restraining myself no longer, I burst into tears and screamed, "I was told that we have to pack up and get out. This is temporary housing for those leaving Japan and right now I would give anything to be leaving." J.O. looked really uncomfortable as it all pointed to him as being the source of the problem. Pat shot daggers at J.O. as he said, "Come on Bon, don't take it out on me; I didn't do this. I didn't want us to have any more hassles than we've already had." He gently held me in his arms and said that everything was going to be alright, that he and J.O. would work this out. J.O. jumped right in, declaring that he would personally get this screw up fixed immediately!

In a couple of hours, everything was straightened out and J.O. drove us to our "new arrival" temporary home. It was a little cottage with a living room, a bathroom, and a bedroom. A crib had even been set up in the bedroom for Brian. With the crib's position, we could only get out of bed on one side. It was a tiny place for the three of us and a crib. I suddenly realized that it had no cooking facilities and said so. J.O. blurted out that he would loan us a radio and an electric fry pan. I doubted that a radio and fry pan would make living in this "house" more bearable but what could we do? J.O. said he had to leave but would be back in a couple of hours to take us shopping.

Whatever else J.O. was, he was a man true to his word. He returned later with a fry pan, a radio and his wife. She was a real eyeful. She was very short, weighed over 300 pounds and had hair styled like an electric mixer accident. As she talked, I discovered that her mouth was as big as her body. She told us that she had come along to show us what downtown Misawa was like. We snapped at the chance to get out of our closet for a while.

Misawa City lay just outside the main gate to the Misawa AFB, so it only took a few minutes to get there. At first glance, Misawa's main street looked a lot like my childhood Southside Pilsen neighborhood with tiny stores of all kinds, outdoor fruit stands, and narrow alleyways. What Southside Pilsen did not have was open sewerage ditches running alongside the narrow sidewalks and down the alleyways. Being novices to Japan, we were very leery walking along these smelly "Binjo Ditches." I supposed that we would become as used to them as Misawa's inhabitants but seeing a man squatting over an alley ditch in broad daylight was a little much.

Mrs. Cox led us into the few shops that had graciously covered the ditch with a plank. The way she ordered the shopkeepers around, she seemed to think she was royalty. She was very rude, picking up merchandise and loudly announcing its poor quality, then throwing it down with disgust. We learned from others later on that her behavior was "tolerated" because she was a big spender. It seems people everywhere will put up with almost anything for the sake of money. To us she was definitely an "Ugly American" and we were embarrassed to be in her company.

As we progressed on our tour of Misawa City, we saw a number of restaurants, "B" movie theaters, suit tailors and china shops. A long side street full of bars known as AP (Air Force Police) Alley branched off the main street. It was the favored hangout for military personnel with time on their hands and for

Japanese police raids. Misawa City wasn't as pretty as I had imagined a Japanese city to be. Some of the pedestrians were dressed in kimonos, like I had pictured in my mind, but most were dressed in regular street clothes.

We saw many older people who were dressed in shabby, dirty clothing. Their deeply lined faces spoke of people who worked hard in the hot sun all day and were proudly Japanese farmers. We learned that these people lived in homes with sod roofs and packed dirt floors. Their diet mainly consisted of the rice they grew and the fish they caught. There was little affluence here. Misawa was located in a very old, rural section of Northern Japan. Most of the people in the area surrounding Misawa (Tohoku), kept the ways of their ancestors, except for two modern items. Even if you lived in a sod roofed lean-to with a packed dirt floor, there was a new Japanese car parked in front and a large color television set inside. It was very common to see a large TV antenna mounted on a home's sod roof with a grazing goat alongside. It doesn't matter how traditionalist a people are, there is always some irresistible temptation that draws them into some part of the modern world.

The last stop on our tour was Misawa's one and only four-story supermarket. From its exterior, it looked much like an American supermarket, a closer look brought out many differences. There were no large shopping carts, only small hand carry baskets. In the dairy section, there were no gallon containers of milk, only very small containers which sold for over a ¥360 (about a dollar). Items that were extremely expensive included all canned goods and breakfast cereals. Even tins of mandarin oranges marked "Packed in Japan," were outrageously expensive.

These differences were tiny in comparison to the fresh meat and fish section. First, the smell was nauseating from as far as ten feet away. The smell might have kept others away, but our curiosity drew us in. The store did try to mitigate the raw seafood smell by burning incense sticks, but that just added burning sandalwood to the smell. Huge fish were on display layered on top of chipped ice, not smelling too bad. The really rank smell came from sea slugs in a bucket on the floor. Women were picking through them like they were fresh flowers, placing bunches of them on the counter for wrapping. It seemed that everything you bought in Japan was wrapped like a present and this wrapping job was no different. I have to say, it was a lot nicer than slopping everything into a non-descript brown paper bag like we Americans do.

When I turned away from the sea slugs, my eyes landed on a bucket of small, live octopus sitting alongside a bucket of squid tentacles. To my distinctly American palate, this all looked disgusting and I questioned why anyone would eat such things. It was then I realized that I was seeing and thinking of things through my American prism. Seafood like this was a protein necessity. Beef and pork were not abundant in Japan and so were very expensive. There just wasn't the space or feed available to raise large food animals, so the Japanese had to turn to the sea and poultry to provide them with protein. When we left the store, I promised myself that I would never, ever take for granted the abundance we Americans have!

When J.O. dropped us off at our cottage, he told us that he would be back the next morning to help us find a car. Pat had been tested for and received an international driver's license when he checked in at the Navy Detachment. The Detachment was located about thirty minutes from Air Force housing. Since Pat would be "watch standing" again, a car was a necessity. Used cars passed from one service member to another in Misawa. Always purchased from service members who were transferring to another duty station. The Japanese never purchased used cars, only new ones. This was because of the horrendous taxes on such a transfer and the expensive yearly inspection testing of cars. It was much cheaper to pass with a new car.

Many of the available used cars were pretty worn after going through four or five different owners. A buyer needed to be careful in selecting the car, a really low priced one might not make it through a duty tour. After consulting the Base newspaper, J.O. took us to look at a few different cars. Pat settled on a 1967 Nissan Cedric. The body was in great condition for its age and it ran smoothly even with tens of thousands of miles on it. It was a mid-sized car that looked something like the 4-Dr. Chevrolet Bel Air we had in Adak. It was a 'dazzling' shade of gray with black and silver cloth seats that had seen better days. J.O. said that a Cedric was like an Japanese Cadillac. I could understand that. It was a larger-sized car with a deluxe interior that included a real burled walnut dash and accessories like a rear window defogger. The price of $550 was in our price range, so we became the proud owners of a Nissan Cedric.

With a car of our own, we could break our tie with J.O. (a win for both sides). We were now free to come and go as we pleased. That did an awful lot to boost our morale. Now, the only thing we had to wait for was the assignment of a house, where I would have cooking and clothes washing facilities of my own! For now, our new car was a good start toward a happier life in Japan. Our first trip was to the commissary and Base exchange (BX). They were both much larger than the ones in Adak, but this commissary had many of the same problems as Adak's had. The heads of lettuce were still limp and brown, but in Misawa, they included insects, which the sign above them said, "aren't harmful if accidentally eaten." Potatoes were packed in bags with so much dirt that, after you washed them, you lost about a pound. In this commissary, there were piles of green colored, unlabeled canned foods that could be bought for a song. These were a deal as long as you didn't mind eating whatever you found inside, fruit or vegetable, peaches, corn, or whatever.

At this point, we purchased roach traps and groceries that I could cook in the electric frying pan or by using heat from the living room radiator. We bought canned vegetables, stews, soup, chili, hash, and meat that I could fry. We actually did pretty well for ourselves. If I put a can of vegetables on the radiator in the morning, it would be heated through in time for dinner. We had a few dishes and pieces of silverware which I washed with a bar of soap in the bathroom sink. Many nights I just wiped the dishes off with a paper towel. Sometimes, you just do the best you can with what you have.

After two weeks of surviving in that roach infested shelter, we learned that we had been assigned a house. Japan was beginning to look better every day. This time I was happy to be packing up again; we were moving into our very own house. We hoped it would be nice. In our enthusiasm, we had forgotten that if you expect too much from the military, you will be disappointed every time. We weren't totally disappointed when we saw it, but it was far from being as nice as the housing was in Adak. Misawa Air Force housing consisted of dozens of four-unit townhomes. Each townhouse had a single-story unit on either end and two, two-story units in the middle, all roofed in red medal. Our unit was the first two-story in the townhome. Each unit had its own lawn, bushes, and clothes line. Our unit had a small, covered front porch allowing us to sit on the steps when the weather was nice. Also, there was a playground not too far away where Brian could occupy himself.

The interior of the house was small, with everything painted the usual white of military housing. You entered the living room through a small front door foyer. The back third of the living room served as the dining area. To the left of the dining area was a kitchen stuffed with appliances: a refrigerator, a stove, a washer and dryer, and a double sink mounted in a wooden counter top running halfway around the room. The back door was in the kitchen next to the stove. A stairway to the bedrooms was located to the left as you entered the front door. At the top of the stairs was the bathroom with a deep, oversized tiled tub, the one item that was always king sized in Japan. Turning right into a short hallway, Brian's bedroom was directly ahead and our bedroom was to the right of his. Both bedrooms were large, but closet and storage space was minimal. The rugs throughout the house were gray. The house was heated by radiators covered by white painted wooden covers with sections cut out to let the heat out. Like all radiator heating systems, this one drove you crazy with its constant hissing and clanking.

The day after we moved in, our household goods arrived and we got busy unpacking and putting things in their place. This was a task that we were both getting more and more proficient at with each move we made. That night, when almost everything was put away, there was a knock at the door. It was our neighbor from the first unit, John Baker. John was an Air Force tech sergeant who worked in the commissary. He was a small man with a brush top crewcut and a slight Southern accent. He said that he and his family had arrived a week earlier from North Charleston, South Carolina, that we should come over sometime and meet his wife and three daughters.

A few days later, after our lives had settled back into Pat's routine of watch standing, I decided that it was time to get cooking again. Now that I had all of my cooking equipment and some free time, I decided I would bake some chocolate chip cookies. Halfway through my baking, I heard a knock at the front door and there was John and his wife Rosemary. When they came in, I noticed that Rosemary was wearing a very tall boot on one leg. As I was to learn later, she had been born with her legs backwards, and had had to undergo numerous operations to get them turned. She told me that most of her childhood had been spent in hospitals. The doctors were successful turning one leg so it would bend properly, but the other leg was a problem. They could not get it to bend, so it was always straight and much shorter than the other. This situation was partially remedied by her wearing a special built-up shoe, which allowed her to walk evenly. I knew from the moment I met her, that she would be a woman whose friendship would enrich my life a hundredfold.

Her first words, as we introduced ourselves were, "Something smells awful good. What are you cooking?" When I told her that I was baking some chocolate chip cookies, with an infectious smile, she said, "How about giving us a few if you end up having too many?" That was Rosemary—a frank, honest woman whose bubbly personality hadn't been dampened by all of the pain and misery she had suffered as a child. Any fun that she might have missed as a child, she more than made up for in her adult life. She had an enthusiasm for living and a curiosity that made her enthusiastic about anything new she tried doing. She never felt sorry for herself, but made the best of what she had. After you got to know her, you would never think of her as handicapped, there was so much more to her than a mere imperfection.

Rosemary was about ten years older than me, and at times she reminded me a lot of Mom. I felt that I could confide in her about anything and the same was true about her. When Pat was watch standing all night, Rosemary would come over and we would gab into the early hours of the morning. We exchanged recipes, and shared each other's triumphs and disasters in the kitchen. As the months passed, Rosemary got more and more involved in Base activities. Through her, I became informed of all the Base's hottest gossip. Who was being unfaithful to whom, who was the Base's worst alcoholic, and who had what surgically removed or added. Rosemary knew it all. She was the Rona Barrett of Misawa Air Force Base. The other information that she passed along to me concerned what products would be coming into the BX and when. This was really vital information! Just like on Adak, if there was a "hot item" coming in, you had to be waiting at the BX door before it opened or it would be gone in minutes.

John was very shy and retiring compared to Rosemary. To me, they seemed exact opposites. I asked Rosemary how and where she had met John. She told me that, when she was a teenager she had a lot of pen pals among the military, John being one of them. Since they were both from the east coast, she developed a special affection for him. In his letters, he offered her the love and devotion that she craved from her family and never got. She told me that he came into her life at her darkest moment. He gave her a reason to believe in herself and her worth, while ignoring the suffering that she had endured in her life. His love dulled much of the rejection that she always felt and gave her belief that being handicapped didn't make her any less of a person.

Before John and Rosemary were married, her doctor told her that she would probably never have children because of a pin in her hip. What a wonderful surprise to them when they had their first daughter, Mary! Rosemary's determination seemed able to surmount anything that doctors could predict about her life. Not long after Mary, she bore their second daughter, Rosanne. It must have been a strain on her keeping up with two little children. She carried on in fine style, even when raising them alone while John was stationed in Turkey. After John's leave from Turkey, she found herself pregnant with a third daughter, Debbie. That fact would have probably sent any other woman up the wall, but Rosemary accepted the fact willingly. As you may have concluded already, military life is very difficult for anyone. Stepping up to the responsibility of getting three children and your household goods packed while having difficulty getting around, made Rosemary even more worthy of admiration. Here I was, a younger person with no handicaps and one child who sometimes felt I was drowning in the pressures of military life. What a wimp! With the friendship of Rosemary, life in Misawa took on a smoother, more normal flavor. Accomplishing things became easier for us, so we became more at ease in the country that our parents and grandparents had fought during World War II thirty years earlier.

Something that made it seem like we were still on Adak was the constant earthquakes. These differed from Adak's. Here they started out like a big explosion, then lost momentum. On Adak, they began slowly and worked themselves up to their peak. In both cases, earthquakes were scary. The worst one, that I recall, occurred a couple of months after our arrival in Misawa. Pat had just left to stand evening watch, I was at the dining room table doing some sewing and Brian was playing peacefully in his playpen. Suddenly, there was a huge explosion. Everything started shaking with a force so great that I was afraid the house would collapse before it stopped. The walls seemed to be moving from side to side and records were being thrown across the room from their rack. I grabbed Brian and ran out the front door onto the lawn. It was even more frightening outside! All of the townhouses around me were shaking as if they were made out of cardboard. Right after our evacuation, Rosemary ran out on the lawn holding a sandwich and yelling for her daughters to follow her. It was such a comical sight that it relieved a lot of the tension that was bottled up inside of me. When Rosemary saw me laughing, she said, "I didn't want a perfectly good sandwich to go to waste. The house might have collapsed on it!"

As the months passed we found ourselves watching more and more Japanese television. The Base's Armed Forces Radio and Television Service (AFRTS) station offered the pits in TV programming, just like Adak's had, so our only alternative was Japanese programming. Although we could only understand a little of the dialog, we could almost always figure out the plot. Japanese television consisted mainly of Samurai soap operas, cartoons, superhero series, and NHK's Japanese voice-over episodes of Sesame Street and Bonanza. There was nothing funnier that hearing deep voiced "Hoss" Cartwright speaking in a higher-pitched Japanese voice.

We enjoyed the superhero series the most. Main characters like Ultraman, Kamen Rider and Lion Man would change themselves into giant heroes in times of disaster, especially when monsters were levelling Tokyo. It was interesting to see what kind of monster they could dream up from week to week, each with its costume zipper showing. The most ridiculous one we ever saw was a giant violin monster that drove people crazy by playing itself. You have to admit that that was really stretching it, but we enjoyed it, even though it was impossible to take seriously.

Brian really enjoyed watching Sesame Street. It was funny listening to Big Bird speaking Japanese, but entertaining even if it was spoken in another language. Brian also liked watching Japanese cartoons. With these, we had to carefully monitor and, at times, shut them off because of their ultra-violence. It was a bit shocking, at the time, to see cartoon characters with blood gushing out of them after parts were chopped or blown off. Cartoon violence, like Road Runner, is child's play when compared to theirs. If there wasn't at least twenty-five sword slicings and stabbings an hour in a show, it wouldn't become popular. It got to be too much for even Pat and me at times.

The one TV show that Pat and I watched whenever we could was the *11:15 Show*. It was hosted by a short, chubby Japanese man with a bad complexion, a piano key smile and big horned rimmed glasses. It was kind of like a U.S. talk show but dealt with almost any subject and guest. One night the entire show was devoted to toilet seats; where to buy them and what style to buy to match your personal tastes and needs. To us, the point of this particular show seemed a bit off, every Japanese toilet we had ever used had NO seat! The Japanese toilets we were familiar with consisted of a hole in the tile floor with rails on either side to support yourself as you hung over the hole and did your business. The show made it seem that toilet seats had a different import in Japanese society (a luxury item or a fetish?).

Another *11:15 Show* dealt with the Japanese communal baths. Their live TV cameras moved right into the baths to photograph and interview the completely naked men and women using the baths together. In Japan, TV wasn't censored from showing the upper half of a woman's naked body. Was that because most Japanese women had such small breasts they didn't look that different than a man?

The overall weirdest *11:15 Show* featured a guest who brought a glass box which held a live King Cobra. The snake kept striking the glass box on the side near the host, making him jump and babble. The guest then took a mongoose out of a carrier, opened the top of the box, and dropped the mongoose in. The cobra struck at the mongoose, which ducked and then attacked the snake. The cobra wrapped him up in coils and bit him over and over until he was obviously dead. The guest became crazed. He opened the box, grabbed the cobra with both hands and began ripping it to shreds with his teeth! The host and the audience began heading for the exits screaming and the show ended. Japanese TV was really interesting.

The most important thing that helped us to survive our thirty months in Japan were audio tapes and care packages from my family in La Grange, Illinois. At least once a month, a big cardboard box would arrive filled with new products popular in the States and things we had asked them to send because we couldn't buy them in Japan. There were always toys for Brian, paperback books for Pat and me, and dozens of other things to remind us that we had a family who were constantly thinking about us.

One month, the box's arrival was weeks late and we got worried about my family. To our relief, it finally arrived at Misawa. When Pat went to pick it up there wasn't a cardboard box waiting but a large plastic trash bag. The box had accidentally been routed to Subic Bay, Philippines, where it was smashed. The Subic Bay Navy Post Office salvaged what they could, packed it all in a plastic trash bag and sent it on to us. The Misawa Air Force Post Office said luckily there were no perishable items. Otherwise, we would have received a smelly, pre-packaged mess of garbage ready for disposal.

The audio cassette tapes we sent back and forth with my parents were a Godsend. We loved hearing everybody's voices, but you had to wait weeks to get a question answered. Sometimes we would wait a month for an answer and, by the time we received it, we had forgotten what we asked. Whatever it was didn't seem as important after the long lapse of time. Besides their voices, sometimes Mom would record a favorite song from some TV program. At Christmas, we would start our tapes off with a Christmas carol. Never before had I truly appreciated the wonders of electronics until it enabled us to stay close to the ones we loved.

CHAPTER 16
MAKING THE BEST OF IT

On the whole, living in Misawa was pretty ordinarily unless you used your imagination to come up with things you wouldn't normally have done. One such thing was having Pat pierce my ears. His mother had sent me a pair of pierced earrings, and since my ears weren't pierced, I could never wear them. I didn't want to go to the hospital, I knew a woman who had gotten an infection from them doing it. I figured that no one would take more care than Pat, so he was the most likely candidate to play Dr. Welby. When I first approached him with the idea, he said that I was crazy. After some coaxing, he finally said that if I trusted him enough to do it, he couldn't refuse.

He began by keeping everything as sterile as possible. He sterilized a needle and thread with iodine, and got a bowl of soap washed ice cubes ready to provide the anesthetic. At the last minute, I thought he was going to chicken out. I told him that since we had gone this far, we might as well carry on. And carry on Pat did! He held ice cubes on both sides of one earlobe and let it numb. He hit his first obstacle when he found out how thick an ear lobe is. It's not easy to penetrate it with a needle. He got halfway through and found that the needle wouldn't go straight through, it kept going off in other directions. I was getting worried, the numbness was starting to wear off. When I told Pat as calmly as I could that it was beginning to hurt, he made a mad dash for some more ice cubes. When it was deadened once again, he resumed his trek through my ear lobe. After a seemingly interminable length of time, the needle came through my earlobe and were we ever relieved.

The bad part was that we still had another earlobe to go. I desperately hoped that it would go easier now that Pat had some experience. Luckily, it did. In a few minutes, the other earlobe was pierced. Pat stepped back to look at his work, turned white and yelled, "This hole isn't even with the other ear." I thought he was going to faint, he was perspiring from every pore. I felt sorry for us both. The only logical decision was to make another hole in the right place. Pat yelled, "But then you'll have two holes in one ear." As calmly as I could I said, "So what's one more hole in my head? You have to correct your mistake. If I can go through it, so can you." He calmed down, numbed the earlobe and made the new hole in a few short minutes. The extra hole eventually healed, leaving one hole in each earlobe. I was glad that Pat did it for me, it was something unusual that we would remember and laugh about for years to come.

As our first Christmas in Misawa drew near, everyone on the Base was eagerly waiting for the BX's Toyland to open. Rosemary told us that we had to be in line long before it opened or there was a good chance that everything would be gone. When shopping at the BX you always had to be there early, grab everything you might want, get in the checkout line and then decide if you wanted what you had grabbed. Since we wanted Brian to have a nice Christmas, we got there an hour before Toyland opened and found that a long line had formed already. Looking back, it seems silly that everyone was so rabid about shopping. The longer you were in the military the more rabid you became. You took on the attitude that if you didn't look out for yourself, no one else would.

During the last twenty minutes of our wait, it started to drizzle. When the doors to Toyland finally opened, there was a two-block line of very wet and very tired people in the ugliest of moods. As we slowly inched our way into the building, we tried to quickly eyeball everything. Our reaction time had to be razor sharp, or we wouldn't be fast enough to grab much. It was a very small building compared to the amount of business it would be handling. The BX people forced us into a single file line that slowly moved around the merchandise and toward the exit. There was no going back, if you saw a potential gift you weren't sure about, you had to grab it and carry it around with you until you could make up your mind. If you decided you didn't want a toy you had been carrying, all you had to do was to discard it and it would be immediately snatched by someone behind you in line. I had never seen so many people carrying around so many toys.

I'll never forget Rosemary standing in the thick of the crowd with a giant stuffed St. Bernard dog held over her head. It looked like she was trying to save it from drowning in the sea of shoppers. Rosemary always accomplished what she set out to do, and wherever there was chaos and confusion, we'd be sure to find her! It was a very nerve wracking experience, but it was well worth the struggle. Brian got some nice presents from Santa that year.

Aside from the BX, another good source of shopping came when local merchants entered the Base to sell their wares. This was called a Bazaar, and everyone waited anxiously for their dates to be announced. Just like Maxwell Street in Chicago, almost anything you could think of was sold at real bargain prices. A favorite merchant named China Pete specialized in what his name indicated, China. We bought a 45-piece set of stoneware china from him for $10. No one knew how or where he got his merchandise, but most were made for American companies. Our set of china had the Montgomery Ward name on them, others had the Sears name on them. China Pete also carried crystal stemware, ceramic figures, vases, and various brass items. Other merchants sold fabric, radios and TVs, woodenware, cuckoo clocks, and even clothing that bore labels from J.C. Penney, Sears, and Wards. Pat and I bought and stashed away a lot of things for when we could use them in our very own home "back in the world."

Something that we realized, as our stay in Misawa lengthened, was what a shame it was that there weren't more people like John and Rosemary and their daughters on the Base. Most of our neighbor's children were obnoxious little brats who took advantage of their father's rate or rank in the Air Force or Navy to get what they wanted. They saw their parents do this, so they figured it was the way of the world. It seemed that the next step, as the children became older, was to become loiters around the Base, getting into trouble whenever and wherever they could find it. Also, since partying and slot machine gambling ranked high on the list of adult activities on the Base, most of the kids were left on their own. Their parents were just too busy hobnobbing with the Base's social elite at club meetings and parties to be concerned about their children.

Neither Pat nor I wanted our family life broken up because of the Navy. We kept to ourselves, occasionally having a friend or couple over for dinner. This freed us from the pressures of accepting invitations we didn't want or having people over to our house we didn't like. It was a time of close family unity for us, neither Pat or I wanted to miss the enjoyment of watching Brian grow and learn. We geared all of our outings and activities around Brian, and always had a terrific time.

There was a family who lived across the court from us that had eight children. The youngest, John, was about the same age as Brian. John and Brian played together from time to time but every time they did, Brian would come home crying with deep teeth marks on his arms. John enjoyed biting other kids. His parents would scold him for doing it but he wouldn't stop. One day I was talking to his mother and she said, "Oh, by the way, John likes to bite, so you should watch out for him." We already knew and I felt like telling her she should keep John muzzled and on a leash. I found it hard to believe that she had such a cavalier attitude concerning her son hurting others. After that, I kept Brian away from John as much as I could.

One day, Pat watched Brian while I went to have my hair cut. Somehow Brian and John got together and Brian came home crying from a vicious bite. Pat, not being one to pull punches, called John over to our back door. When he came, Pat told him that it was wrong that he bit and hurt his playmates; how would he like it? John asked Pat why it was wrong so Pat bent down and bit John lightly on one finger. John took off for home in a flash crying all the way. Pat said that he fully expected John's father, a chief petty officer, to come pounding on our door to seek revenge, but nothing was ever said. John never bit Brian again, and I think it held true with the rest of the neighborhood kids. Sometimes a child needs a little more than a few scolding words to understand when a behavior is wrong.

I also experienced an unfortunate life lesson a few months after our arrival. While we were shopping in the commissary, Pat pushed Brian in our shopping cart to the next aisle while I went back to grab a couple of items. When I rejoined them, I realized that I had left my purse laying on some canned goods while I picked up my items. I immediately ran back but my purse was gone. When we located the commissary manager, he had my purse in his hands. He gave me a ten-minute lecture on how stupid I was to have put it down and forgotten it, then handed it back asking if anything was missing. Of course, there was. My wallet was gone and I felt crushed.

The manager said that he would alert his staff to be on the lookout for my wallet, but he didn't hold out much hope of them finding it. He said he hoped that I had learned a lesson from this. Pat tried to console me, but I found it hard to erase the manager's harsh words and my own embarrassment for doing something so stupid. I didn't want Pat to think I was an irresponsible feather-head. I prided myself on my level-headedness and dependability; now I felt that my foolishness outshone everything. I had only lost $17, but it might as well have been $100s for the depression I fell into. About a week later, John called to tell me that he had found my wallet thrown behind some canned goods. I was so relieved, I could have kissed John! The money was obviously gone, but my treasured pictures and important ID cards were still in it. I came away from this situation $17 poorer, but much smarter. I had learned a life lesson: certain people will steal from you if you give them the opportunity, so you must always closely guard your possessions from them.

As we became more familiar with the Tohoku (back country) area surrounding Misawa, and heard more about Tokyo, we felt very lucky that we had been stationed in this area of Japan. The Tohoku area was very rural and retained much of its natural beauty. There weren't millions of people packed in millions of cars causing traffic jams and polluting the air like there was in Tokyo. As Pat grew more confident in his driving, we began to travel around the Tohoku area to see what the different cities and sights around Misawa were like.

Our first trip in our Cedric took us to the city of Hachinohe, a large fishing port about forty miles southwest of Misawa. Hachinohe was far more modern than Misawa and much larger. There were no Binjo Ditches, the sidewalks were wide and the downtown area was filled with modern looking stores and tall buildings. I guess we should have been a little anxious going to a new Japanese city with our few words of Japanese, but it seemed that it wasn't all that important. The Japanese people were friendly and kind to us wherever we ventured. They especially loved Brian. He left every store we took him into with a gift. When we went into a bakery he was always offered a donut. He was too small to realize just how very popular he was.

Something Brian did understand was how much he enjoyed going for electric toy rides on the roof of Hachinohe's largest department store. They were coin operated and cost ¥10 (about 36 cents) for a three-minute ride. Brian got to ride on the backs of some of the superheroes he saw on Japanese television. Along with these, there were monster rides and rides in the shape of frogs and hippos. After going on as many rides as he could take, we would take Brian into their snack shop.

Generally, people all around us were not eating hamburgers or hot dogs but a Japanese snack food called Soba noodles. We didn't order Soba. Like true Americans, we ordered their incredibly beautiful, full fat content, ice cream desserts. These delicious mountains of ice cream were served up with fresh cherries, watermelon, or bananas, with a dab of whipped cream to top the whole thing off. Since he still couldn't order in Japanese, Pat would ask the waitress to come outside the snack shop so he could point to the window samples and tell her how many we wanted. Most Japanese restaurants were wonderful for new-bies. They displayed life-sized samples of their menu items (along with prices) in their front windows. Even if we didn't know what exactly what each thing was, we could point to something that looked interesting and we never starved. We did this a lot while we were in Japan.

Japan is a country with many traditional festivals, and Misawa had a won-derful one the first summer we were there. The Tanabata Festival of Star Crossed Lovers was held each year. The festival originated from an ancient myth that two stars, very much in love, were separated by the King of the Sky when they forgot to accomplish their duties. The Milky Way was placed between them and only once a year, on the evening of July 7, were they allowed to meet. The entire city of Misawa was decorated to the hilt for this festival. The Main Street was shut down and every store celebrated by hanging long colorful strips of paper outside on bamboo branches. People from the stores would write their wishes on the paper strips. It was thought that the reuniting would grant wishes.

The merchants also built large, beautiful decorations of crepe paper for the front of their stores. The one we liked the best was a taxi cab. All the deco-rations were so detailed and intricate that it was evident that the merchants prepared all year for this festival. Their street festivals reminded me of the car-nivals held during the summer in Chicago, but with no carnival rides. As we walked down the street, there were at least a hundred concession stands trying to lure you to spend your Yen with them. They were selling everything from elephant beetles in little cages (to bring good luck) to Fuji dogs (pieces of bat-tered, deep fried sausage on a stick). I laughed to myself when I saw the usual American carnival paraphernalia being sold as well: balloons, inflatable toys, cotton candy and soft drinks. I guess some things are just universally synony-mous with having fun.

Along with all of this excitement there seemed to be an endless, beau-tiful parade flowing down Main Street. It seemed that everyone in the city of Misawa had dressed in traditional Japanese costumes with traditional hairdos and were marching down the street. This was the Japan that I had pictured in my mind when we were told we were going there. In between the marching people there were dozens of colorful, incredibly delicate floats depicting Shinto shrines and various gods of nature. Some floats offered music, others offered a throbbing drum beat provided by a team of men beating five or six huge drums with wooden clubs. The local public schools were represented by colorfully dressed children dancing their hearts around each float. Absent were the high school marching bands that are a hallmark in parades in the United States. Even though the parade was different, it included what every parade includes; exuberant participants and fascinated onlookers. Everyone everywhere enjoys a celebration, but it's the cultural differences that make each country's celebrations unique and interesting to others.

In late August, we attended the Nebuta Festival in the port city of Aomori, about ninety miles northwest of Misawa. This festival is considered one of the most colorful and famous in Japan and lasts for five days. It features a parade of dozens of gigantic, specially-constructed, illuminated paper floats, Nebuta Lanterns. These huge floats are colorfully painted as mythical figures. A team of up to twenty men, dressed in traditional Japanese costumes, carry each of them through the streets as the crowd shouts encouragement. The Nebuta Lanterns originate from a myth about a general who ordered huge lanterns placed on Aomori's hills so that curious enemies coming to investigate them, could be captured. At night, the images are illuminated from the inside making them stunningly life-like, creating a fantastic and colorful sight.

Pat didn't drive us to Aomori, we traveled there with a group on a bus chartered by the Base. Pat's hometown friend, Jim Marquand, who had just been transferred to Misawa from Guam joined us. Since Jim had been studying Japanese, we were expecting to have a terrific time. Festival day was hot and muggy, not the ideal weather for a long trip on a crowded, non-air-conditioned bus. I was hoping that Brian would be in a good mood, it was going to be a long day for him.

The supposed two-hour trip was closer to a three-hour trip. All of us were thankful for our arrival. We were all looking forward to stretching our legs and getting some fresh air, even if it was a bit stifling. Pat, Brian, Jim, and I walked around the streets of Aomori checking out a lot of the department stores and soon became hungry. Pat and I were figuring on eating dinner in one of the many restaurants as we always did in Hachinohe. When we told Jim what we planned, he got cold feet and said that we didn't want to do that. Here we had been happy to have him along for his Japanese and now he didn't even want to make use of it. Pat said, "Then what are we going to eat?" Jim said that we'd just walk around and pick up odds and ends from the different grocery stores. What we ended up buying was potato chips, peanuts, and orange soda. Not even close to what we had planned to eat.

As it began to turn dark, we decided to look for a good seat for the parade. We tried sitting on the curb in front of a few stores but were shooed away each time. Finally, we found a bus bench with one Japanese man sitting on it, so we all sat down next to him. When people began to try to stand in front of us, Pat suggested we move the bench up to the edge of the curb. Jim said, pointing at the man on the bench, "How do we ask this guy to help us move the bench?" The man turned to us and said with a very English accent, "Why don't you just ask me?" We moved the bench as he explained that he had been to school in England. Pat and I were all embarrassed for acting like typical Americans. Yet again Jim had failed to aid us with his Japanese language prowess.

Across the street from us, we saw twin Japanese girls dressed in traditional Kimonos and hairdos. They were so cute that Pat ran across the street to ask the mother if he could take their picture. She was very happy to oblige. After Pat came back, the girl's mother came running over to our bench and asked if she could take a picture of Brian. We thought it funny that a Japanese woman would want a picture of our son in traditional Sears Roebuck shorts and a t-shirt. I guess everybody has their own idea of what they want to remember in pictures.

As the parade began passing in front of us, we were awe struck at the immense size of the illuminated floats. Some of the figures were 30 to 40 feet tall with ferocious expressions. They didn't frighten Brian, he had seen worse on Japanese TV. Like everything else, he just took them in stride, fascinated with the colors and lights. Unfortunately, adding to the heat and humidity, the constant drum beating by parade participants got your head throbbing.

Halfway through the parade, Brian began fidgeting, so I told Pat that Brian needed a little more to eat and drink. Pat left with Jim saying he would be right back. It was so crowded, I was afraid that he and Jim would never find us again. After a very stressful fifty-minute wait, Pat and Jim came with warm cans of apple juice and roasted ears of corn. That satisfied Brian for the meantime, so we settled down to watch the parade.

As the hours passed, the men carrying the Nebuta Lanterns were getting drunker and drunker from the sake that they were constantly drinking. All of a sudden, a group of ten men left their float, came over to us and tried to grab Brian. Our new Japanese friend said that they wanted Brian to march with them in the parade. Pat was holding Brian when I heard this, so I yelled, "Don't let go of him." It was like a tug-of-war for Brian until they realized that Pat wasn't about to let Brian go with them. They let go, smiled, and returned to the parade to resume their journey. I was really scared and Pat was holding Brian tighter than ever.

At 11:00 p.m., the parade ended with a whimper; a disheveled, insane looking American walking along with a sandwich board that said, "Repent! Your time draws near!" and screaming, "Repent, Repent!" at the crowd. How embarrassing! We were glad it was time for us to find our bus. I began to worry that if we missed the bus, we would have to spend the night in this sake crazed city. I had enough Nebuta Festival and its incessant drum beating. I wanted to get to the Base and listen to some quiet.

When we found the bus, I thankfully settled myself in for the long ride back. Brian was asleep before the bus driver turned the ignition key. It was still stifling in the bus, and after the first hour, I began to feel sick. Not just sick but deathly sick. From childhood, I had had a very sensitive stomach to the motion of driving, but I thought I had outgrown that. To add to this, I was starving and had a pounding headache. That was the longest, most hellish bus ride I had ever been on. When we got off the bus at the Base, it felt like my legs were made of rubber; my head was a spinning top and my stomach was a volcano about to erupt. When we arrived home, Brian was still fast asleep, so I dressed him in his pajamas and put him in his crib. The fact that he hadn't had much to eat either, didn't seem to bother him at all. All he wanted was sleep. Pat went to the Enlisted Club to get us a couple of hamburgers that he told me would, "fix us both right up." I found that very hard to believe but they did!

After the unpleasant memory of our excursion to Aomori had faded, we became itchy to strike out on our own and see new scenery. Everything in and around the Base held no special appeal anymore. You get to the point that if you don't venture outside the safety of the Base, you will go goofy. One of the first signs of this is standing outside of the BX, after hours, with your nose pressed against the window hoping to see if some new merchandise had been brought in while you weren't able to be in the BX. I'm not exaggerating when I say that, for many people, it was an obsession to be at the BX when new merchandise was brought in. Many people's free time was spent in the BX looking for something to purchase that would break the monotony of living on Misawa AFB.

Through some friends, Pat had heard about a beautiful place called Lake Towada. It was a favorite Japanese location to visit if you were looking for natural beauty and serenity. It was, also, a favorite "chill out" resort for people from Tokyo wanting to get away from the bustle of big city living. So, with our meagerly expanded knowledge of the Japanese language, we set out to see the wonders of Lake Towada, about two hours from Misawa.

Lake Towada is a round, crystal clear, volcanic crater-lake with two fingers of land extending into the center, surrounded by trees down to the water's edge. The three-mile park drive to get to the lake was incredible. The road was very narrow and wound around each and every tree. The road was built in the Shinto manner so as not to interfere with the natural beauty of the park. The road curved so much that a sign with a picture of a blowing horn was posted at every curve, so much for tranquility. Every time you approached a curve you had to slow your car and sound your horn in case there was a vehicle coming from the other side. It was like riding a roller coaster through a forest preserve, thank God for Dramamine.

Before we arrived at the lake, we stopped along the road and hiked down a trail that took us into a little canyon complete with picnic benches and a waterfall. It was a bit chilly down in the canyon but very beautiful. While we ate our lunch, we got to wave at Japanese tour buses as they passed us on the road about twenty feet above us. When our lunch was over, we walked back up into the sunlight and decided to walk around a bit more before proceeding to the lake. You had to really look closely to see all the hidden beauty. Although we weren't there during the fall, when the scenery is even more breathtaking, we were impressed with what we did see. Everywhere we looked there were mounds of variously colored moss, miniature waterfalls and running streams dashing against odd shaped boulders that stood in the way.

Our entire day could easily have been spent hiking in the forest but we did want to get to see the lake and go on a lake boat tour. We didn't know the boat schedule or the tour cost, so we were worried that we might not be able to purchase a ticket. We hoped that we could make ourselves understood. We were always able to do so in Misawa City and Hachinohe. What we didn't realize was that we had invaded a truly Japanese resort that was far out of the way for most Americans to visit. The Lake was surrounded by hotels that catered specifically to the Japanese customers. Japanese visitors were here looking to get back in touch with nature, not to stay in some elaborate room with a vibrating bed that took yen. To go with the quiet and scenery, Lake Towada offered many spas with natural hot springs baths offering the curing powers of certain minerals that are claimed to do wonders to the body.

We found that it was easy to figure out the times and cost of the boat tours, they were posted on a huge sign. All Pat had to do was hold up three fingers, point to the boat and he got three tickets. I don't know why we were worried, there was nothing to it. On our way onto the boat we got very pleasant smiles and slight bows from the other passengers on the boat. The boat itself had two accommodations; the first was unpadded benches out in the open and the second was in the boat's upper level closed off from the weather. Seating in the upper level was individual red velvet covered chairs that allowed you to see in all directions because there was glass on all sides. We believed we had purchased upper level tickets and so sat there.

About ten minutes into the tour we became uncomfortable as we noticed that we were the only three people sitting in this area. When we looked out of the glass, all we saw were Japanese people looking in at us from all sides, like we were on exhibit. Pat and I began to wonder if we were really supposed to be in there but decided to stay until someone threw us out. We didn't have to wait long. One of the boat's officers entered, bowed politely and tried to explain that we were not supposed to be in there. Apparently, this particular tour only sold outside seating. With our faces as red as the chairs, we exited as gracefully as possible. That's pretty hard to do when thirty people are staring at you and giggling.

When our boat trip ended, we were very happy that we had gone. It was a beautiful day, the lake water was a brilliant crystalline blue and perfectly calm, and the surrounding forest was gorgeous! It's fun to take a boat ride, especially when the scenery doesn't need much explanation. Which was good because the tour guide only spoke Japanese.

Once off the boat, Pat took out his trusty Japanese map and decided that we could add a side trip through the surrounding mountains on the way home. It was fun when we first started, but then it got damp and clammy feeling, and it seemed there was hardly enough air to breathe. With the winding roads and the increasing elevation, I began to get car sick again. This was our second trip on Japanese roads and the second time I got car sick. As I soon found, I could never travel for long distances in Japan without getting car sick. The roads always seemed to be too winding for my stomach and our Cedric didn't have the greatest shock absorbers. After this trip, whenever we left for a long drive, I made sure that I didn't leave home without my Dramamine. After all, I was a flatlander from Chicago who was used to driving on flat, smooth, straight roads and expressways.

We took many car trips before we left Japan. Our last major trip was to find the grave of Jesus Christ, which, per local legend/myth, was hidden in the Japanese countryside. After reading about this legend in the Base newspaper, we had to go see it for ourselves. It was pretty bizarre to hear someone say that Christ's grave is located in northern Japan. Aside from anything else, it's hard to imagine how Christ could have gotten to Japan.

The legend of Christ in Japan is told by people living in Nozawa Onsen, a small village located near a beautiful hot spring in Northern Japan. Christ, while wandering in this area, came upon a steaming hot pool. In the pool was standing a large eagle whose leg had been wounded by a hunter. When Christ returned to the pool the next day he found the eagle still standing in the pool, but now its leg was fully healed. Christ began using the pool for his bathing. The Nozawa Onsen hot springs have been used by local residents since at least 1191 AD. Its high radium count is said to effect cures for many ailments. This still doesn't answer the questions: How and when did Christ get here and what was He doing in Japan?

The legend says that Christ came to live in and around the small village of Shingo-Mura located in a lush valley with rice and dairy farming. Dairy farming is said to be popular due to Christ's influence. The area was previously known as Herai, reportedly a Hebrew word with no Japanese meaning. Christ's grave is located on a small hill outside of the village. Markers located there, in English and Japanese, briefly tell this story: Christ came to Japan when He was about 21 years old crossing Asia and sailing to Japan. He studied and meditated in the Herai area, then returned to Judea in His early thirties.

Somehow Christ' younger brother, Isukiri, substituted for Him during the crucifixion and Christ escaped across Asia back to Japan. Several years later Isukiri's body was exhumed and sent for reburial in Northern Japan. Christ settled in the Shingo Mura area, married a Japanese woman and lived to be more than one hundred years old. The couple bore several children. This incredible story has been checked by Japanese investigators who have found a wealth of supporting evidence.

One of the more interesting pieces of evidence discovered is a Star of David design on lintels of the older houses in the area belonging to the Sawaguchi family. The Sawaguchi family claim to be direct descendants of Christ. The yearly Kirisuto-Matsuri (Christ festival), includes a Naniya Doyara or ceremonial dance, to honor Christ's memory. Naniya Doyara is another name which is not Japanese and is of possible Hebrew origin. During the Kirisuto-Matsuri the children of the area have crosses inscribed on their foreheads with charcoal to ward off evils. Other proof are age-old stones with non-Japanese script carved on their faces. One of the stones, known as the Moses Stone, purportedly contains the Ten Commandments inscribed in an ancient code resembling ancient Hebrew.

The day that we visited the grave site was sunny and very warm. As we drove down the road, we had to watch carefully for the site's marker. It was a white pillar-like sign with Japanese writing running down the length of it and a Star of David at the very top. It seemed very odd to see a Star of David in the heart of Northern Japan. We parked our car on the side of the road and walked up a short gravel trail to the site. On our right was a small hill topped with a white Christian cross. It was surrounded by trees and bushes shading it from the sun. The site was completely silent, not a sound disturbed the serenity of the place. It felt very eerie to be visiting what local people believed was the grave of Christ.

This story was light years from what I had been taught at St. Cletus and Nazareth, yet who knows what really happened so long ago? Christ does disappear from record from age 12 to age 30, according to the New Testament. We were left with many unanswered questions swirling in our minds. In our hearts, we felt that Christ wasn't buried there, but who is buried there? No one will ever really know. Even if there was a slim chance that Christ was buried there, we had had the privilege to visit Him. You know, it doesn't really matter what we believe as long as what we believe in helps us to be better people. The experience of our visit to that grave, one warm summer day, left us with a sense of awe and a stronger faith that there is someone greater, who can help us when there seems no hope.

CHAPTER 17
I PROMISE I'LL DO BETTER!

We were close to beginning our final twelve months in Japan and things were moving along smoothly. As each month passed, we grew more excited than ever to go home and become civilians again. Then, an unexpected black cloud settled over us, I discovered a lump in my right breast. It wasn't very big and I was only 24 years old, so why worry, right? It didn't mean anything, did it? I tried to forget about it, ignoring it until Pat forced me to see a Base doctor.

During my exam, the doctor examined the lump, then said he would take me to see the surgeon. The way he said it frightened me. He sounded like if it wasn't taken out in the next few minutes there was no hope for me. The surgeon was very abrupt and to the point. He told me that he would attempt to drain it but, if that wasn't successful, he would remove the lump as soon as possible. Of course, it couldn't be drained, thanks again Murphy. I was scheduled to have the lump removed the next week. I was told that the surgeon was excellent, but showed little sympathy or empathy for his patients. I suppose I shouldn't blame military doctors for being callous and unempathetic, they do have to put up with many hypochondriacs and "goldbrickers." Some people do make many trips to the doctor for the slightest reasons: it's free, they are bored and/or they want to get out of working. I had never abused the use of the medical facilities, and now, when I needed some understanding from a doctor, he had used it up on the hundreds of patients before me.

The week waiting for my surgery was one of the worst and best in my life. As I waited, I became convinced that I wouldn't live to see my son grow up. I tried to convince myself that the lump would be benign, but there was this little voice that kept saying, "Sure you're too young, but maybe you'll be the unlucky exception to the rule." In a more positive vein, I really started to live. I wanted to enjoy every moment, appreciate the beauty of each warm, sunny day and pay even closer attention to Pat and Brian. In my mind, I began to relive every good time we had had together and every detail of each of their personalities.

By the time surgery day came, I had learned that I would have my good friend, Rosemary, close by. The doctors had discovered a cyst growing around the tendons in her wrist and it had to be removed. All week she had been telling me, "Hey, don't worry, I'll be there with you. Look at how many operations I've had and I'm still around." Pat, on the other hand, was a nervous wreck, which was not helpful. I was glad this was going to be over in a few hours so all our fears could be washed away.

When Pat and I entered the operating hallway, John was already there. He said that they hadn't started on Rosemary yet, so I was afraid I would have to wait even longer to get this over with. To my surprise the nurse told me to follow her into another operating room, as they had changed the operating schedule. She had me remove my blouse and lay down on the operating table. I faintly heard someone calling my name and I knew it was Rosemary. She was in the adjacent operating room yelling, "Don't be afraid, and good luck!" Hearing her made me laugh, here she was also having more surgery and telling me not to be afraid. She was one exceptional friend!

They gave me a local and told me I could watch my operation in a mirror by the bed. When the doctor came in, I got up enough courage to ask him if he thought it could be malignant. He shot back, "Don't be ridiculous, you're not in the age group for it to be cancerous." Why hadn't he told me that a week ago? It would have spared me from a lot of needless worry. Then again, the wait had gotten me thinking about the importance of those in my life and the beauty of things around me, things I had sort of taken for granted. It had made me realize that nothing is certain and that things can be snatched away from us at any moment.

As the surgeon began the operation, I watched in the mirror as he made his first incision, my skin pulling, then separating with blood spurting out. I decided I had had enough watching. I knew that the part of me he was cutting was deadened, but I felt that if I kept watching what he was doing, it would hurt!

After he stitched me up, the nurse walked me out to where Pat and Brian were waiting. Pat told me Brian had been pretty good for all that time, amusing himself by playing with some swinging doors. Pat took hold of my arm as we walked, commenting on how pale I was. I told him I was not used to seeing so much blood, especially my own. After Pat helped me into the car, he tried to come up with something to say that would make me feel better. He asked if I wanted to look around the BX for anything that I might want. I told him, "I would take you up on that offer any other time but not now. I just want to go home and relax."

When we arrived home, Pat helped me into bed and gave me two pain killers. He said, "Please don't worry about anything today, I'll take care of Brian and everything." He did do a great job, except for washing the dishes in cold water and putting them away with a greasy film on them. After laying down for a few hours, I became very sick feeling, with nausea, dizziness, and headache. Apparently, it was a reaction to the pain killers.

When I came to the hospital the next day for my surgery follow-up, I told the surgeon that the incision didn't hurt but I was suffering from nausea. He said, in his usual caring and understanding way, "All women are nauseated." I thought, what the heck does that mean? Did he mean that doctors like him make all of their female patients nauseous? If so, he was correct. At least he had done a good job of making the incision minimally noticeable. It took one miserable long week for the biopsy results to come back from Tokyo "benign."

Rosemary's surgery had taken much longer than the doctor had expected, over three hours. The cyst in her wrist had broken open when they tried to remove it, so the surgeon had to take it out in bits and pieces. He told her that there was a chance that it could come back because he wasn't sure he had gotten all of it out. She had to have her arm in a sling for a couple of weeks. I felt really sorry for her, every time something was supposed to go simply for her it ended up complicated.

Rosemary had even more surgery before we left Japan. After delivering her third child in South Carolina, Rosemary started having painful gynecological problems. Her gynecologist in Misawa told her that he could do a thirty-minute procedure that would help relieve her pain, that there would be nothing to it. The doctor had no idea how bad Rosemary's luck had always been, the thirty-minute operation took six hours! The doctor told John that he had never seen anything like it before. When he opened her up, he found that almost all of her insides were adhered. Evidently, after her last delivery, she hadn't rested from heavy work long enough to heal properly. The doctor had to separate her different parts and remove what wasn't necessary. It took a complete hysterectomy and massive repair work.

It took Rosemary months to get back on her feet. Thankfully, nothing had been malignant, so she could concentrate on getting well and strong. She and I both knew that, with so much internal damage, the doctor had saved her life. This gentleman was a military doctor who had compassion and empathy for the people he was treating. If this doctor could manage that, I wondered why more of them couldn't. I guess many of these doctors, when discharged from the military, turn into the civilian doctors that we complain about not caring. The only difference being that we have to pay good money to receive their apathy and wrong diagnoses.

CHAPTER 18
OUR DAY HAS COME!

In May of 1973, John and Rosemary found out that they were being transferred back to the States on the first of June. John had secretly decided that twenty-three years in the Air Force was all he could stand. I think Pat might have had some influence on John's decision. Pat had always made no bones about wanting to get out of the Navy as soon as possible. This was a major decision for John and his family. If he stayed in two more years, he would get a full pension. My guess was that leaving the Air Force had been in John's mind for some time. John only told Rosemary about his decision after he had signed his Air Force separation papers! She was not happy about it and, because John had let Pat know about it before her, she partially blamed Pat for John's decision. She had become used to military life and thrived on living in different places. Before they left, Rosemary confided in me that she was terrified that she would "dry up" if they settled somewhere permanently.

John and Rosemary had an immediate decision to make, where they were going to move to? She was originally from New York and John from New Jersey. However, before coming to Misawa, they had lived for six years in North Charleston, South Carolina. After much soul searching, they decided to move back to North Charleston where a military base was handy and they could continue to enjoy their military benefits. John was told that he could probably get a job as a postal clerk on the Base, so more income would be available to them.

Pat and I envied John and Rosemary's returning home, even though they didn't seem very excited about it! We, on the other hand, could hardly wait to get back in Illinois. We, with my parent's happy consent, had decided that we would settle in Illinois. My parent's house was small but they were excited to welcome us all home and help support us until we could get on our feet. Our departure date was still November 1, and that still seemed like years away. It seemed there was so much for us to do when we got out; where would Pat work, what kind of car would we buy, what kind of house would we buy, what furniture would we need, etc.? As of now, the only furniture we owned was Brian's baby furniture, which would do little for us when we moved into our "dream house."

As the Baker's departure date approached, Pat and I became more filled with the "leaving bug" than ever. We had paid strict attention to everything the Baker's had to do before leaving Japan. When our time came, we didn't want anything to delay our leaving. We wanted everything to go smoothly, so our plans would work out. Pat had filed papers requesting a three-month "early out" from the Navy, so with every mail call we hoped to see something saying Pat was accepted. So far, we hadn't and with each passing day not hearing, we felt more and more that we would be stuck in Japan for Pat's full tour.

When June 1, rolled around, we were excited for John and Rosemary, but sad to see them go. We had become good friends and had made living in Japan more bearable for each other. Now they were leaving us behind, and we knew that a lot of our fun was leaving on their plane. True military people do not let such partings bother them. They realize that constant uprooting's are just part of military life. I think that's why many military families didn't seem to get very chummy with their neighbors. It hardly pays, since you or they may be gone tomorrow. This was definitely one of the reasons we didn't belong in the military. Neither of us liked the forced separations, the miserable travel or being told where to live only to be uprooted every few years. We had no intention of spending the best years of our lives moving from one hell hole to another, hoping that the next one would be better, when we knew that the odds were against it.

I was getting Brian ready to go see the Bakers off to civilian life, when one of Rosemary's daughters came running over with our mail. For the past several weeks, they had been checking our mailbox when Pat was working, to see if his "early out" had come in. I think our mailbox was being checked twenty times a day. Rosemary's daughter was carrying a large brown envelope. My heart almost jumped out of my chest. It was from Washington, D.C. and looked like what we had been waiting for! I tried to stay calm but my hands were shaking as I opened it and there were the papers we had been hoping and praying for. I ran upstairs to where Pat was sleeping after his mid-watch and yelled at the top of my lungs for him to get up. When he didn't, I started to shake and pummel him vigorously. He finally got the point that, if he didn't get up, he would be beaten alive. He got up far too slowly for me and said, "What's all the excite-ment about?" All I could say with tears in my eyes was, "We're going home!" Without looking at the papers, Pat shot out of bed like he was jet propelled and started running around in his underwear looking for our typewriter. He had it burned into his brain what had to be done as soon as the papers came. They hadn't arrived any too early, there was just enough time to get them filed so we could leave August 1, instead of November 1. I felt bad but I had to tell Pat to cool his jets, we had get to the airport to see John and Rosemary off.

We got to the Misawa airport in record time, because we were bursting with excitement to tell John and Rosemary about the 'early out'. They congratu-lated us saying that their leaving day had brought us luck, that they just couldn't leave us behind for too long. As the plane arrived and the passengers started to board, we said our goodbyes to our best friends and wished them the best of everything in their new life as civilians.

When we returned home, Pat immediately finished the "early out" paper-work and said he was going in to work to get the wheels moving. We would now be leaving in just two months and there was so much that had to be done! I got my part started by setting up a housecleaning date with the Japanese maid service. When a family knew when they would be leaving, they called in the maids to clean the house so it would be sure to pass final inspection. If the maids cleaned your house, you were guaranteed that it would pass and we wanted that guarantee! This time we wouldn't have to worry that all of the fuzz was out of the dryer or that all of the crumbs were out of the refrigerator. For the low, low price of $10, a great deal of worry could be alleviated, and it isn't every day that a girl gets to call in maids to clean her house.

When Pat returned we started making our final plans for home. First, we decided to think of what kind of car we would buy. During our time in the Navy, all we had owned were old, used cars that had to be sold on receiving orders to a new duty station. Pat said that maybe we could swing a new car as we could order it through a manufacturer's rep in the BX. The rep could order any car you wanted and have it waiting for you at a car dealer near your destination. The problem was he only had a few 1972 car brochures and you needed to tell him exactly what 1973 car you wanted to order. Pat was disap-pointed until I told him that, "This was not a time to lift up your hood and cuss," it was a time to involve my Dad. I sent off a letter asking him to visit different car dealers and send us brochures showing new 1973 cars. Within a couple of weeks, we received envelopes of brochures. After pondering them for two weeks, we decided to buy a new 1973 Ford Pinto station wagon with a four-cylinder engine and a stick shift. It was a reasonable $2,500 and seemed a practical car for our little family. It would provide good gas mileage and plenty of room to haul things. The Ford dealer we selected was pretty close to my parent's home, so pick-up should be easy.

Next, Pat's employment after leaving the Navy was on the agenda. Pat wrote an introduction letter and a resume which I typed up for him. After a few trips to the Base library for addresses, we began mailing them to electronics companies in the Chicagoland area. We figured by doing that Pat would have a step up in the job market, and might even be able to confirm some job interviews.

As our leaving date drew closer, we were excited, but scared as well. We hadn't been civilians for over five years or in the States for over three years! We were wondering what it would be like to live in the "real world" again. Although we were scared, we were also optimistic that civilian life had to be better than what we had endured for the last five years in the Navy. As I said, until Pat got a job we would be living with my parents. Their house might have been small, but their hearts were huge and full of love for us. With us moving in there would be seven people, one beagle, one turtle, and only one bathroom! I knew that would make us an even more close-knit family than ever before.

Our last to-do was to set our "pack out" date, just four days before our departure date. After our 'pack out', with all of our belongings gone and the house clean, we moved into a large, multi-family transient housing unit. We stayed there for four days, long enough to drive a person completely out of their skull! There were so many large families squashed into one building that you had to walk down the hallway sideways. There wasn't anything for the kids to do, so they just sat, waiting as noisily as possible. There always seemed like there were twenty kids yelling, screaming, and crying, while their parents yelled back and forth at each other.

Thank God, we still had our Cedric, so we drove for hours at a time, not wanting to spend one minute more than we had to in that zoo. All we wanted to do was to sleep there, and that was nearly impossible because of the hundreds of mosquitoes that infested the rooms. Brian woke up every morning with at least ten bites. We bought a sticky strip bug catcher to hang up, but with so many mosquitoes, it needed replacement every day. Brian had to endure another uncomfortable situation, a single bed without bars to lay. At least once a night, he would fall between the bed and the wall. It was pretty unnerving the first time it happened. He didn't even wake up, but we did. When we checked his bed, it was empty. We feared that he had been carried away by mosquitoes, but on closer inspection, we found him lying on the floor. I guess since he had lived with earthquakes most of his life, falling on the floor was nothing to disturb his slumber.

When July 30th arrived, it was us who were getting ready to go to the airport. What a glorious day! We were so excited we could have swum home if we had to, but we decided to use the plane. We had been told that the airline we were flying to Yokota was Air America, affectionately called "Scare Air" by its many devoted passengers. All of their planes were old, dented DC3s that had been used to fly supplies over the "Burma Hump" during World War II. We wished that the airline had newer planes. After, waiting for so long to go home, we didn't want to take any chances at the very end. Oh well, we had no other choice so this was the plane we would take.

We arrived at the airport about an hour before departure and checked in our baggage. The next hour seemed to drag by and Brian was getting fidgety, as three-year old kids tend to do. After the prescribed hour, the plane still hadn't arrived. Then, an announcement was made that the plane would be two hours late. Oh well, what can you expect from an airline nicknamed "Scare Air." The only thing for us to do was to wait and try to amuse Brian. Pat decided to take him out to see some Japan Air Self-Defense Force (JASDF) jets taking off and landing. Brian was pretty impressed for a while, but soon that even got old. When Pat brought him back into the terminal, he said that Brian smelled kind of funny. I said that was impossible, he hadn't had an accident in his pants for over a year. Pat said, "That may be true, but I think you should take him into the bathroom and check him out." So, I did and I wish I hadn't. Old Brian had had a whopper of an accident. I had no clothes to change him into and the plane was due to arrive at any moment. I kept thinking to myself, "Brian, why now?"

The only thing I could think to do was take off his undershorts, wash them out and stuff them in my purse until I could get to a washer. His outer shorts didn't smell all that great either, but there was nothing I could do about that. When we came out of the bathroom, Pat said that our plane had just landed. My excitement was renewed. I told Pat, "Brian doesn't smell all that great." Pat said, "Don't worry, maybe he'll air out as we walk to the plane. We'll just sit him down fast and not let him get up until we land. Maybe no one will notice with the air conditioning blowing." I hoped so because if the other passengers got a whiff, I was sure they would have made us walk to Yokota AFB.

After a three-hour uneventful flight, we arrived in Yokota at dusk. We took the bus to temporary lodging, where we would stay until our plane left for the States. The accommodations we were assigned had a common living room with four bedrooms, two on each side of the common room. When we entered, there was already a family sleeping in two of the bedrooms. It felt uncomfortable barging in but this was our assigned room too. That's one of the benefits of temporary housing, you never know who you're sharing a room with. The only thing to do was to pick a bedroom, settle our bones down for the night and delight in the knowledge that the first leg of our journey back home was over.

When morning came, Brian was the first one up and the first to get acquainted with our new room buddies. They were an Air Force family with two boys, ages two and four. They had just arrived in Japan, so Pat and I conveyed some of the important things they needed to know about living in Japan. The wife was very nice and imaginative as she was trying to make her boys an early lunch in a coffee pot. Her husband seemed typical military, nearly always separated from his family or out drinking with his buddies (as he did even in temporary housing). I had always been glad that the Navy hadn't changed Pat like that. From the beginning of our marriage, family had always came first and he always tried to make things turn out right for us.

We spent our stopover at Yokota AFB riding the bus around the Base and doing some last-minute BX shopping. While we were eating our dinner in the Base cafeteria, Pat selected the song "Frankenstein" by the Edgar Winter Group on the jukebox, and Brian started dancing around to it. That was fun! When we returned to our room, we began getting ready for our flight to Hawaii and on to Travis Air Force Base. I don't remember much of that trip, so I assume that we had made it without trouble. When we arrived at Travis, Pat bought Greyhound bus tickets to take us to a Holiday Inn next to the San Francisco Airport. The bus ride was colorful, with the orange setting sun a backdrop to the sights. Unfortunately, it was still the same uncomfortable ride we had taken on our trip to Japan 30 months before. It was much easier to cope with this time because every uncomfortable mile brought us that much closer to home.

When the bus arrived at the Holliday Inn, there was a bone chilling wind that we weren't prepared for. Once we were in our room, we decided to go out for dinner at one of the nearby restaurants. We were all super tired and grumpy. Once seated in the restaurant, Brian became crabby because it was past his bedtime. Pat and I joined him by getting on each other's nerves. All through the meal Brian fussed until he finally spilled his glass of milk all over the table, himself and us. We began to speed eat so we could get back to our room to get some sleep.

Our room was located on the outside third floor, so we had to wait in the chilly wind for Pat to open to the door. The key wouldn't work! I thought, "How can the key not open the door?" I knew that I was going to have a nervous breakdown if I didn't get this fussing kid off to bed. Pat flagged down one of the hotel's drivers and asked him what was wrong. He said that the room must have been locked with the double lock and that we needed another key to get in. He ran to get us the key and we entered before our ears fell off from frostbite. This was our first contact with civilian housing, and it hadn't gone any better than Air Force housing. Unbelievable, while we were living in Japan, even the way motel locks worked had changed. There were going to be a lot of things we had to catch up on. Once settled in our room, we called my family in La Grange to let them know we had made it safely to San Francisco and would be seeing them tomorrow. I can't explain what a thrill it was to talk directly to Mom for the first time in thirty months! Everyone was fine and they would pick us up at O'Hare the next day.

In the morning, we turned on the TV and watched *Captain Kangaroo* with Brian. This was the first American English TV show we had watched since going to Japan. The Captain certainly hadn't changed much. Brian would have to get used to watching only American TV programs, no more samurais and monsters with zippers. We would have to get used to gas costing $1 per gallon. We were happy that we had bought a fuel-efficient car!

After taking the motel's courtesy van to the airport, it really sank in that we were on the final leg of our journey home. Anticipation and excitement were hard to contain as our plane descended toward O'Hare, four hours later. When the pilot announced, "Welcome to Chicago's O'Hare Airport! The weather in Chicago is …," I couldn't believe the flood of emotion that swept over me. After five years, our travelling days were over. We had the privilege of leading a normal life with the freedom to live however we wanted and wherever we wanted to.

We landed and, making our way into the terminal, we saw no one waiting at the gate. Knowing my family, they were there somewhere, all we had to do was find them. That didn't take long, they were off by a couple of gates. Everyone was there including May, my future sister-in-law. Mom and Dad looked the same, maybe a little grayer. Bill had grown fatter and Mark had grown taller. After all the kisses, hugs and tears, we got our bags and drove home to La Grange.

The old Rissky homestead looked pretty much the same, except my parents had turned their backyard into a super playground for Brian with a swing set, a tent and a picnic table. Mickey greeted us enthusiastically by sitting up. She had gotten really chubby and seemed kind of perplexed over who Brian was. She didn't realize that he was the baby that she used to watch over years before. Mom and Dad seemed just as astonished at how much Brian had grown. You can't keep a child from growing. They had missed much of Brian's growing up, but he still had a lot of growing to do and now he would do that here with them.

We drove over to Grandpa and Grandma Taraba's house to visit with them, then came back home. By early evening, everyone was worn out and hoarse from talking, so we all decided to call it a day. Pat and I had the same sleeping arrangement as before, upstairs on my single bed with Brian sleeping on a cot at the foot of the bed. No bed had ever felt as good as it did that night. Neither Pat nor I slept much, we were too excited about the beginning of our new life. Much of our fear about entering the "real world" was gone. We were in familiar surroundings with loving people who we could share our problems with. We felt reassured that, as long as these people were there with us, there was nothing we couldn't overcome. We were living in, "Don't lift up your hood and cuss, call us," territory again and I knew that we would be calling a lot as the years went by.

PART IV
CIVILIAN ADJUSTMENT

CHAPTER 19
WHO'LL BE THE NEXT IN LINE?

After all the excitement of our return home, we had some major issues to be worked out. Pat would be out of work as soon as he was discharged from the Navy and he needed to be able to get to interviews. Pat needed an Illinois Driver's license and car insurance, so we could go pickup and drive our new car. We needed a local bank account to transfer the money we had saved from Misawa. We had no permanent residence. Anyway, even if we had a permanent residence, we had no furniture for it. We were so happy that we could live with my parents until we could get these things all sorted out. It would have been even more difficult for us if we hadn't had anyone to take us in.

During our six-week stay in La Grange, everything went along quite well considering there were six adults and one toddler fighting for the bathroom. Things did get a little crowded at times, especially when Pat would take a bath. He always loved to take baths of one and a half to two hours while reading. He still was able to take his lengthy baths in La Grange but had to wait until everybody else had everything taken care of and had gone to bed.

Pat was able to get his Illinois Driver's license and car insurance very quickly. Soon we were off to pick-up our car. Dad drove us to the dealer and, since they said it would take a while to get ready, we told him to go home. As we finally pulled out of their lot an hour later, the entire backseat, with Brian strapped into it, fell over backwards. Pat jumped out and opened the door to see if Brian was okay. He was but there were no bolts holding the backseat to the floor. The dealer soon corrected this, then handed Pat the rear hatch lift handle saying they had no screws to mount it but would call him when they came in. I just thought, "Why not? Murphy strikes again." Maybe civilian life wasn't going to be all that much different than military life after all.

Pat had to spend one night in the barracks at Naval Station Great Lakes to await his discharge from the Navy the next day. When he drove home, he was officially a civilian and could start interviewing for a job. A company named Tektronix had answered Pat's inquiry from Japan, so he went there first. He was interviewed by an anti-Vietnam War manager who told Pat he didn't hire "baby killers," spit at him, and sent him packing. Pat came back to La Grange very shook up. He said, "I just gave away six years of my life to protect this country; maybe I should have stayed in the Navy!" and started to cry. I told him it would work out; he had never even been to Vietnam or shot at anyone. The next day he went to the Illinois State Employment Office, where a sympathetic, ex-Army employment advisor talked him down. He got Pat an interview and a job offer within a week with Hallicrafter's Company in Rolling Meadows, Illinois, a little over an hour from La Grange.

Our new car and Pat's new job started an awkward part of our stay in La Grange. Bill had begun driving while we were in Japan and had his own car. This meant there were already two cars in my parent's short driveway. Our newly acquired Pinto station fouled parking up big time. It was a long drive to Rolling Meadows from La Grange, so Pat had to leave at 6:00 a.m. to make it to work by 7:30 a.m. Dad left for work at 7:00 a.m. and Bill would leave whenever someone could pry him out of bed. Before a parking system was worked out, Pat ended up barricaded by the two other cars, so he had to wait until we could wake up Dad and Bill to get their cars out of his way. Most of the time, Bill wouldn't budge, so Dad would end up moving two cars.

After this aggravating situation went on for two weeks, Mom said, "I had it with this craziness that goes on every morning. From now on Pat will be the last car parked in the driveway, Dad will be the first, and Bill would park his car off to the side of the driveway on the grass." That simple solution cured the problems in the morning, but with Bill dragging in at all hours and forgetting to park on the grass, many times the cars were still in the wrong place. To me, it looked like a game of checkers using cars. Pat couldn't jump over Dad's car until Bill moved his car from blocking him.

Speaking of cars, Dad's favorite used car was going to the dogs, so he decided to look for newer one. He had gotten a really good deal on the 1967 Chevrolet Impala they had come to Florida to visit us in. He was hoping that he would have the same luck again, so he went out to invade the used car lots. After an exhaustive search that turned up very little that he liked, he found a Chevrolet Malibu that seemed to be the best he could find. The dealer couldn't tell him how much trade-in he could offer until the appraiser saw the Impala and he wasn't there when Dad was. Dad said that he would bring the car back in over the weekend for appraisal.

To improve its trade-in value, Dad decided to clean the car up a bit, and to remove some things from the trunk. Dad was a heavy smoker and not very careful about where his cigarettes landed. While he was cleaning the car, he unknowingly dropped his lighted cigarette on the front seat. After a few minutes, the seat started to smolder and smoke. Since the garage had a door to the kitchen, Dad yelled to Mom, "Get me a glass of water!" Thinking he wanted a drink, she handed him a glass of water without question. Next, he yelled to her, "Give me a bowl of water." Mom gave him the bowl of water but thought something was very suspicious. Next, he yelled, "Fill up this bucket with water quick!" and handed her a large bucket. This got her full attention. When she came through the kitchen door with the bucket she saw that the passenger's side of the front seat was smoking furiously. Dad was frantically throwing water on it and beating it with a rag. After they got the fire out, Mom said, "Now they'll probably give you $2.98 for the car." Dad said, "Don't worry, I'll just cover the seat with a blanket." Mom said she was glad that he would be taking the car in by himself. She said that she did not want to have anything to do with trading in a car that, "smelled like a smoked salmon."

When the day of the appraisal came, Dad was nervous because the car seat hadn't thoroughly dried yet and it still smelled putrid. Mom said that maybe this would teach him to be more careful with his smoking materials. When he drove the car into the dealership, he was greeted by the appraiser, decked out in a three-piece suit. The appraiser was also the dealership owner. He told Dad that he liked to appraise the trade-ins himself to be sure that the cars taken as trade-ins were given the correct value. This was a very important part of any car transaction and shouldn't be left to people who didn't have anything at stake if a mistake was made. This spiel didn't make Dad feel any better, he still had to go through with a test drive if he wanted the newer car. When they got into the car and left on their test drive, the owner commented on how well the car started and drove. Dad told him that he was a mechanic and regularly maintained it. Since it was a warm day outside, Dad kept his window open, so the smell wasn't that noticeable. As Dad pulled back into the dealership, he thought that he had it made. That was until the owner got out of the car and Dad saw that the back of his pants was wet. He turned to Dad and said, "What the hell is this?" Dad told him that there had been a small fire. The owner lifted the blanket and said, "It sure looks like it, but it doesn't matter that much, we have a seat bottom to replace it with." Dad was relieved about that and the fact that the owner hadn't charged him for the cleaning of his suit.

Aside from buying a new car while we were in Japan, my parents had made a major change to the sunroom at the back of the house. It had been converted to a laundry room complete with a washer and dryer. During the years we were growing up, we had used a laundromat for that purpose. Mom told us that they had gotten the washer and dryer from Bill's future in-laws. May's family owned an apartment building in La Grange and when they replaced some of their old machines, they had given these to Mom. They were nice, well-built machines with one drawback, you had to insert a quarter to make them work. Mom said it wasn't a big deal. Since the front of the coin box was missing, she just used the same quarter over and over.

Mom was very anxious for me to try her newly acquired cleaning possessions. I put in all our dirty clothes, inserted the quarter and away it went. When the clothes had finished washing, I opened the lid and a cloud of steam flowed up into the air fogging my glasses. I thought that that was some awfully hot water. When I took the clothes out, I told Mom that they were all wrinkled. She said, "I know and I don't know why." I thought about it for a few days, feeling bad that every piece of clothing washed in that machine had to be ironed. That was a real bummer! Finally, the solution dawned on me. I told Mom that it was because the water was too hot, permanent press clothes had to be washed in warm water. Mom got on Dad's case and told him to figure out a solution. He managed to repair the water temperature mechanism. Now we could get water that was cooler than boiling. After all we were washing clothes not steaming a lobster.

CHAPTER 20
THIS WAY TO THE TENTS

With Pat working at a job in Rolling Meadows, we could now think about finding a home. We looked around the suburbs close to my parent's home but that left Pat with the same lengthy commute he had now. We both felt it would better if we could live closer to Pat's job, so we began house hunting in the Northwest suburbs. Up to this point, I had never been to the Northwest suburbs of Chicago. It made me sad that we wouldn't be able to live closer to my parents, but it was exciting to be starting our lives in a new suburb. Whatever suburb we settled in, it would be "our" suburb, just like La Grange had been my parents' when they moved out of Chicago. Since most of Northwest suburbs were about an hour from La Grange, we would be located close enough to render assistance in case somebody "had to lift up his hood and cuss."

Pat and I were excited on our first trip to look for homes in Rolling Meadows. Our excitement quickly dwindled when our realtor told us that the house we could afford would be much less than we had imagined. Pat's time "serving our country" had dealt us an awful hand. While Uncle Sam had us overseas, house prices and inflation had skyrocketed. When we got married, a new Northwest Suburban, three-bedroom home with a basement or family room, was selling for between $18,000 and $25,000. Now, we learned to our astonishment, you couldn't even buy an older two-bedroom home without a basement or family room for that. We had scrimped and saved nearly $14,000 over our six years in the Navy. We had dreamed that that would be enough to make a good down payment and buy furniture for a nice suburban home we could live in for the rest of our lives. We were tired of moving and wanted our home to be big enough that we wouldn't have to move again. Soaring inflation and the requirement for a 20% down payment proved to us that our dreams had been extremely naive.

After four weekend trips to Rolling Meadows to be shown worse and worse three-bedroom homes, located farther and farther away from Rolling Meadows, we told the realtor that we would like to look at two-bedroom homes. She told us with our present income, a two-bedroom was our only hope over a townhouse, which, after living in Navy or Air Force housing for four years, we really didn't want. The realtor finally found a "fixer upper" located in Palatine, Illinois, just a few blocks from where Pat worked. It was a shabby two-bedroom home with a detached-garage, a single bath, no basement, and a lot of hard work ahead. The interior was just okay. We hoped that lots of soap and water and some fresh paint would make it much better.

So, with an overwhelming sense of defeat and disappointment hanging over us, we made an offer to buy the house for $27,500 (it was listed for $29,000). I have to admit, I was secretly hoping our offer would be turned down, but it wasn't. When the realtor called to tell us we owned a home, I sat down and cried, not from happiness but from the frustration of not having other choices. We set our move in date for around mid-October.

With our home purchased, we had to work at putting some furniture in it, especially beds. We found a Montgomery Ward ad in the *Chicago Tribune* announcing they were running a sale on furniture and appliances. This was exactly what we were hoping to find. When we put together a list of what we needed, it seemed overwhelming! We needed everything: a stove, a refrigerator, a washer and dryer set, a dining room set, a living room set, and two complete bedroom sets. When she learned of our need, our realtor took us to the Ward's store in Mt. Prospect, Illinois, and assisted us in getting a Ward's credit card (we had never used any form of credit while in the Navy). Our new Ward's credit card and the quantity of stuff we needed to buy, helped us purchase everything we needed right then and there. Our Ward's salespersons assured us that everything would be delivered on the very day we wanted. Naiveté struck again. Having never bought much from a civilian store, we believed them. Boy, were we ever suckers!!

On the day of our scheduled deliveries, October 15, we packed up all of our things in La Grange and left for our new home in Palatine. We were really excited to see what the house would look like with the house cleaning and interior painting we had done and new furniture. Pat dropped Brian and me off at the house before leaving for work. We would await the delivery of our new furniture and our Navy household goods. As we waited in the empty house, my enthusiasm began to wane as each hour passed with nothing being delivered. Finally, in the late afternoon, a Ward's delivery truck pulled up in front of the house. Only Brian's twin bed, mattress and dresser, a rocker, and a refrigerator arrived, a far cry from what we had expected. When I asked the driver where the rest of the furniture was, he told me that it was all on backorder and would be delivered at later dates.

To add to this "good news," our Navy household goods hadn't shown up at all. So, here we sat (not on chairs) with no stove, no double bed or mattress, no dining room set, no washer and dryer, and no living room set. Since the "do not haves" far exceeded the "haves," we decided to pack up and return to La Grange until we could get things straightened out. Mom was surprised to see us so soon, I think she was enjoying being alone again. Now she had her boarders back for another round.

After talking it over that night, Pat and I decided we should go back to Palatine and make the best of it. A phone call to Montgomery Ward provided us with a list of the delivery dates that the furniture would dribble in on. When Pat phoned Van Sydow Storage concerning the non-delivery of our household goods, he was put on hold while they checked into it. Then they told him, "Sorry we can't find your stuff," and hung up. Pat found the phone number for the Naval Station Great Lakes Transportation Department on our Bill of Lading, and the fur began to fly. When Pat explained what had happened to the Chief of Transportation, the chief called Van Sydow Storage and started to lean really hard on them. He told them that they'd better find our household goods or the Navy might have to reconsider the renewal of the contract they had with them. He also told them that he "could" contact the Chicago Police Department as he had heard there might be theft problems at Van Sydow Storage. That was what they needed to hear, in no time, our household goods were located and scheduled for delivery. With their arrival, our spirits rose as we started unpacking our things into our new home.

We were only able to provide seating in our home through the kindness of our next-door neighbors, the O'Brien's, who loaned us an umbrella table and four lawn chairs. Montgomery Ward also took pity on us, delivering a loaner stove until our new came in. As for sleeping arrangements, Brian slept on the cot he had used at my parent's house and Pat and I slept on Brian's single bed as we were old hands at sleeping on a single bed!

After our furniture was paid up, we still had a few dollars left to beautify the exterior of the house and it really needed it. When we first saw the house, I thought it should have been named, "The Ma and Pa Kettle Special." Grandma Taraba told me later that when she saw the house, she thought that we must have lost our minds or that both of us had gone blind. The painted wood siding was a mess, the front and back screen doors were hanging off their hinges, there were no rain gutters and the wooden windows were rotting away. The only thing appealing about the house was its large backyard and many fruit trees. Our new house was a fixer upper par excellence!

Pat only stayed at Hallicrafter's Company and their new owner, Northrup Corporation for seven months. He was tired of the forced overtime and the everyday security checks, so he started looking for something better. May's father, whose company manufactured leather portable radio cases for Motorola Inc., lined him up with an interview at Motorola. Pat received an offer for a technical services job and started working for the Motorola Communications and Electronics Division, Elk Grove Village office on June 1, 1974. We hoped this change of jobs would start Pat on a career with Motorola. The job included slightly higher pay and cheaper medical coverage. This provided us with more income to finance our home improvements.

Pat's first exterior improvement was to replace the warped, wooden screen doors with white cross-buck aluminum screen doors that opened and closed properly. When we saw the astonishing difference the new screen doors made, we decided to go hog wild. We would have the house aluminum sided, replace the wooden windows with aluminum triple track storm windows and have rain gutters installed.

We paid cash for half of this project and financed the rest through a loan from the Motorola Credit Union. In 1974, it cost us $1,800 to have all of that done, today we would be lucky to get one side of the house done for that amount. We finished our exterior project by painting the detached garage and mounting aluminum awnings over the front and back doors. A number of our neighbors came over to complement us on how great the house looked. This made us feel good, but after what we had invested, we figured that we might have to spend the rest of our lives in this little house.

With the exterior completed, it was time to finish the interior. We decided to buy kitchen cabinet kits from Sears to save some money. Pat worked on them for weeks, with some prodding from me. It's amazing how fast a person can lose their enthusiasm for a project that takes longer than a day to complete. When the cabinets were hung and finished, it seemed Pat had rebuilt our house just the way we wanted it. He followed the cabinets with a new stainless-steel sink, a self-stick tile floor, colorful wood paneling, and a new fluorescent light fixture. My finishing touch was to add new curtains. Incredible, we had a brand-new kitchen! I was so proud of Pat for the nice job that he had done. I had no idea that he was so handy when we got married. He had had little chance to show off his carpentry side before and it shined.

The next room Pat tackled was our one and only bathroom. His goal was to replace the bathtub, the toilet, the vanity, the medicine cabinet and put self-stick carpet squares on the floor. We had to ask Dad to come out to help Pat get the old cast iron bath tub out of the house. With the tub out, Pat removed the toilet but, before he could install the new one, he was bowled over by the Victoria flu. Over the next couple of days both Brian and I also caught the bug. It felt like we were back in Japan, all we had for a toilet was a hole in the floor. The boys didn't have much trouble with that, but I really had to use my imagination. Pat burned off the last of his flu fever while finishing the bathroom renovation.

With two major rooms remodeled, we decided it was time to relax and enjoy all the improvements we had made. Pat just couldn't sit idle for long. He decided that he wanted to use his GI benefits to take a TV repair course. He said it would be a good backup job if something happened at Motorola. I was kind of skeptical and wondered why TV repair? Pat told me that the course centered around gaining the skills through study material and through building and testing a 26-inch color television. As you worked your way through the various levels of knowledge, you received small boxes of parts to build the TV circuit boards and test equipment.

I hoped that Pat was prepared for what he was getting into because it seemed like a monster, time consuming undertaking to me. Well, prepared or not, Pat enrolled in the course and for months he studied, wired, soldered and adjusted. Our mailman was delivering dozens of boxes of various sizes almost every day. One day, the mailman, sounding very frustrated, asked me, "What's in all these boxes I've been delivering to you?" I responded, "A 26-inch color television set and equipment to test it." He replied skeptically, "Uh huh, whatever turns you on."

The two things we had to purchase separately from the course were the color TV tube and the cabinet. When Pat had everything assembled and in its right place, it looked just like the picture in the study materials. Pat said that he was ready to plug it in. I hoped to God that he was right so it wouldn't self-destruct on plug in. Don't get me wrong, I had confidence in Pat. However, there were hundreds of minute bits and pieces that had to be placed perfectly, and that would be sticky for the best of us. I was already impressed that he made it this far without stomping something or eating his soldering iron. Sometimes things had gotten kind of rough and Pat did have an impressive Navy vocabulary.

Pat plugged in the TV and turned it on. There was no smoke or flames, just a black screen for a few seconds and then a picture appeared. The color was off a bit but Pat assured me that, with a picture on the screen, he could now adjust it. I stood there in awe of what my husband had accomplished, he had actually built a color TV and it worked! It was then I decided that Pat was really worth his weight in gold. I always thought he was anyway, but this was yet another side of him. I had what most women would give their eye teeth to have, my own live-in, "jack-of-all-trades."

CHAPTER 21
SEASON OF CHANGE

My brother Bill's wedding took place not long after we arrived home from Japan. Bill had asked May, the girl he had dated through most of high school, to marry him while we were in Japan. I really liked her. May had even taken the time to write to us while we were overseas and that made her special to us. I think everyone considered her part of the family long before they got married. We got to know her a bit while we were on leave from Adak. She was comfortable to be around and I knew she would be good for Bill.

While we sat in our pews waiting for May and Bill to take their vows, I thought back to Bill's birth. I hadn't much cared for his presence at the time. How time has a way of changing your feelings towards a person. As the years passed, I had helped Bill with his schoolwork and he done a lot for me in return. We had our arguments, but when it came down to needing help, we would always be there for each other. Looking at Bill standing there in his wedding tuxedo, brought back more memories of growing up with Bill.

One summer our cousins, next door, got a wading pool and they were being especially obnoxious bragging about it. Bill, ever direct in his responses, snuck into their yard after they went inside and poked dozens of holes in the side of the pool. There was a big hoopla over this incident, but if Bill hadn't been egged on by their teasing, it would have never had entered his mind to do it.

Another memory of Bill that came to me happened when the neighborhood boys decided to campout in the field across the street. They were all supposed to spend the night in a tent or so everyone thought. At about 3:00 a.m., my parents got a call from the La Grange Police to come and pick up their son. Bill and six other boys were caught wandering around in downtown La Grange after curfew.

This memory was closely followed by one of Bill's high school incidents. Bill was picked up by the La Grange Police while incessantly driving his car past a home whose picture window featured a grown man dressed in diapers and in a playpen. Bill and twenty other car cruising teenagers had been brought to the police station on the complaint of people living in the house. A story had been circulating around Lyons Township High School about this house and the man wearing diapers. Teenagers being teenagers, they just had to check out the story to see if it was true. According to the complaints, the person in the window was their retarded son, who got great joy from looking out the window at passing cars. When Dad went to pick up Bill, the police told him that Bill should stay away from the house. However, he felt that the parents were asking for spectators by having him so "prominently displayed" in their front window.

Last, I remembered all the injuries that Bill had suffered: he was hit in the head with a baseball bat, he had broken a finger playing football, and he had totaled the car Grandpa Taraba had given him. Bill had survived all of these injuries to come to the altar and become a husband. As he said his vows, I began to cry; I knew that our lives had truly changed. No more childish adventures or accidents; we were now adults contending with our own family issues. Bill's marriage ceremony evoked some sadness for the loss of his childhood, but also tons of happiness at seeing the child you grew up with become a man and start life as the head of a new family. I know Mom was joyous for one other reason; it would now be May's responsibility to get Bill up in the morning to go to work! Bill's work tardiness would have to stop, he was now responsible for earning a living for his family.

Mark had been changing as well. He was now a teenager. He had outgrown his earlier virus and was gaining weight and thriving. There had been many times when we hadn't been sure what the future held for Mark. Pat and I were so happy that he loved Brian and that the two of them got along famously. Since there were only nine years' age difference between them, it seemed they were more brothers than uncle and nephew.

A very exciting change in our lives came when we received a letter from Geddes Modeling Agency stating that they wanted us to bring Brian in for an audition to be a model. We were proud as peacocks, we figured that someone must have spotted Brian's outstanding handsomeness. We found later that these letters were sent out randomly to people who had small children. I still prefer to think that he was "discovered." I made an appointment and we took him there on a Saturday. Pat and I both knew that he would do well, he wasn't shy and could carry on a conversation with anyone. He sure wasn't like either of us as children. We were both shy and non-coping. The audition went so well that the agency wanted to sign him up. It was the most exciting thing that had ever happened to us, our own son sought after to model.

Brian wasn't in school yet, so we figured that he had the time to experience something that few kids ever did. He modeled for about two years and appeared in multiple Sears's sale flyers and an S&H Green Stamp catalog. He enjoyed taking the Northwestern train into Chicago and having his picture taken. After the two years elapsed, neither of our hearts were in it anymore. Brian was getting tired of it and the competition for the jobs was more and more ferocious. Brian and I looked at it, not as a job, but as something for fun and for the excitement of looking for his picture in the ads. I brought some extra clothes along with me when requested, but other mothers would come in with garment bags filled with every type of clothing imaginable. These mothers and their children would go to several auditions each day, we would only go to one. I just felt that a three-and-a-half-year-old didn't need to feel the pressures of competitively earning money. The money Brian did earn just about covered the modeling agency fees and our travel expenses. Any left-over money was put into Brian's savings account.

One, near disastrous incident, did occur to Brian during his illustrious modeling career. One day, after receiving a call for an assignment, I noticed Brian's hair had grown a little long in front. I decided to use my electric clippers to shorten it a bit. I didn't notice that his right eyebrow was under the hair I was cutting. Before I knew it, I had both trimmed his hair and removed his right eyebrow. When I saw what I had done, I almost cried. Thinking quickly, I grabbed my eyebrow pencil, waved it magically above his right eye and, ta da, there was a simulated eyebrow. I told Brian that he was good to go, but cautioned him not to look in the mirror. Fortunately, the agency didn't notice a thing because I was too fast for them. Every time Brian rubbed it off, I would draw it back on.

The next big change in my life occurred when Brian entered grade school. As all mothers do, I had mixed emotions about it. On one hand, I wanted to keep him close to me for a little bit longer so he wouldn't have to cope with the outside world so soon. On the other hand, I wanted him to grow up normally and experience all of the things as he should. So, it was with a troubled heart and queasy stomach that I got my only child ready for his first day of kindergarten at Paddock Grade School in Palatine, Illinois.

That first day of school still burns brightly in my memory. It was a warm, sunny day and I wanted my disposition to be the same. As I walked Brian to school, he became more and more excited with each step we took. He told everyone he met on the way that he was going to his first day of school. Everyone wished him well, no one more than I did.

Just as we arrived, the bell rang and all of the children began cramming their little bodies through the doors. I let go of Brian's hand telling him to go along with the rest. He walked up to the door and stopped. I got scared that he was going to lose his nerve and run back to me. We almost had to anesthetize Bill on his first day of school and I didn't want it to be that hard for Brian. Well, the reason Brian had stopped was to wave the rest of the children through the door. Exasperated, I yelled to him to get in there! He entered, disappearing among the other fledglings who had been thrown out of their nests by their mothers. I was glad his first day was over, it had, obviously, been the hardest on me.

About nine months after Bill and May's wedding there was an expansion to the Rissky family. May presented Bill with a son, Bill Junior, to carry on all of the fine Rissky traditions that we could never actually identify. Now parental revenge had started for him. Bill was now going to find out what Mom and Dad meant when they told him, "Wait until you have children of your own, then you'll realize what being your parent was like!" Pat and I had already lived almost five years of that reality with Brian. The reality that being a parent is truly hard. You try not to make the same mistakes your parents made with you, instead, you make new ones. I don't think it's in the human genome to be a perfect parent, all you can do is to be the best parent you can and hope that that saves you from being an abject failure.

Pat and Dad caused a short-term change in our lives when they were bitten by, what I will call the, "Daniel Boone Syndrome." This syndrome causes men to suddenly want to own a piece of our shrinking, isolated wilderness. They thought it would be a great family legacy to own and pass on land in Northern Wisconsin where we could all enjoy weekends and summer vacations. Dad had purchased a pop-up camper and he was yearning to take it some place other than his backyard in La Grange. Since neither family could afford decent property separately, so we decided to pool our money and buy land together.

We perused the Chicago newspapers and found a realty that dealt exclusively in recreational land in Wisconsin. Pat talked to the agent and he came over to our house to show us what he had in our price range. He seemed a nice man who was sympathetic to our desire to own some land in "God's Country." We told him that we only had $800 to spend. He said not to worry, he had a five-acre piece of property with a creek in Eau Claire, Wisconsin, only a six-hour drive from Palatine. That sounded awfully far to us, but he assured us that once we got used to the trip, it really wasn't. He produced a picture to illustrate what the property resembled. We told him that without seeing a real photo we didn't feel comfortable putting our hard-earned money down. He told us that the purchase came with a six-month grace period during which we could inspect the land. If, for any reason, we didn't like it, he would cheerfully refund our money. We decided that we couldn't lose that way, so we signed the contract and gave him our money. Again, I say, naive suckers!

After he left, Pat more carefully read over the dimensions of the property, finding that it was very oddly shaped. It was 418 feet deep and 900 feet wide; in other words, it was shaped like a wiener. We decided that its odd shape must be what had made the asking price so reasonable. We had purchased our piece of the "wilderness," now all we had to do was to wait for winter to end and go see it.

When April came, we came to the sudden realization that our grace period had only a couple of weeks to go! We needed to set a date for our trip pronto. The day we had chosen was warm, dark, and rainy. We hoped that the rain would quit before we got into Wisconsin. My parents came out to our house at 6:00 a.m. and the six of us: Pat, Brian, Mom, Dad, Mark, and I piled into our luxurious Ford Pinto station wagon. It was a snug fit, but everybody managed to get into their assigned space, and off we went. After three hours of travel, rigor mortis was already beginning to settle in. Those three hours already seemed like a long trip and we still had three hours to go! We all started developing a very bad feeling about this place we had yet to see. When the sixth hour rolled around and we still hadn't arrived at our property, I thought that the only way I would make this trip again was by airplane!

When Pat finally turned onto the road fronting our purchase, the rain fall was still at a mini-monsoon level. Pat drove slowly down the road looking for the lot number. Then he pointed to his left while saying, "There's our piece of God's country." Mom and I just stared, not believing that we had travelled all these hours to see this? Pat said that he and Dad would get out and check it out. The property was located across the road from an extremely dilapidated farmhouse.

From its look, our property looked like it was being or had been used as pasture land. It was covered with deep ruts filled to overflowing with rain water and dozens of huge cow chips. A small section of the front was treeless but the rest was covered with trees so thick a person couldn't walk through them. The worst thing about the land was that it was about three feet lower than the gravel road fronting it. There was no access to drive a car and camper onto it without major construction. If a camper were to be put on it, it would be sinking or floating every time it rained heavily. The property was, to say the least, the pits! The only thing we had to look forward to was another six-hour ride back home squashed in our Pinto. Mom succinctly summed up the situation up for us, she opened the door and vomited.

Once back in Palatine, and very thankful to be there, Pat said he would call the realtor on Monday to demand a refund. The realtor was not, what a surprise, as friendly as before. He told Pat that he wouldn't "buy it back from us" unless we paid the Wisconsin property taxes. What a slimy operator. After much arguing, Pat called the Eau Claire County Court House to request they send us the tax bill, about $50. We paid it. When Pat called the realtor to tell him, he began hemming and hawing about returning our money and hung up when Pat started arguing with him.

This impasse ended when Dad called the realtor. Good old Dad came right to point telling him in a language he could understand, "If you don't give us back our money, I'm going to come over to your office and rip out your lying tongue!" That scared the realtor enough to reluctantly return our money without reimbursement for the taxes we paid. That $50 was a very small price for us to learn that things aren't always like you imagine them to be. Sometimes your dreams are not realized and maybe that's for the best. Many dreams far outshine reality. "God's Country" is all around us, even where we make our home every day. Maybe working to improve the quality of our everyday lives is a better choice than always looking for something better.

CHAPTER 22
I REMEMBER YOU, UNFORTUNATELY

When the summer of 1975 rolled around, my parents received a letter that was supposed to be forwarded to me concerning my Nazareth High School ten-year class reunion. I read the letter with mixed emotions, there were a lot of nice girls in my graduating class but many who weren't. I told Pat that I didn't really feel I cared to go. He insisted that I had to go. He said that I had accomplished many things to be proud of, so forget about what it had been like back then. I relented, deciding he was right and that I should go.

Along with the letter came a blank page to be returned to the reunion committee. On it you were supposed to summarize what you had been doing during the past ten years. When I began writing it, I was shocked at all of the things that had happened in the span of those ten years: I had gotten a job I liked and was good at; I had lost sixty pounds through personal effort; I found and married a wonderful man; I had lived in some exotic parts of the world; and I had a handsome son of model quality. I had to agree that I had a lot to be thankful for. I became more and more excited to share my accomplishments with my classmates.

The reunion was held at a country club in La Grange, so Mom could easily watch Brian for us. That night I dressed carefully and made sure that I looked as perfect as I possibly could. We arrived early and were greeted by the reunion committee, who were distributing name tags and biographies. No one recognized me until I gave them my name. The committee members seemed shocked over how much I had changed. Let's face it, the main reason for attending a reunion is to compare each other's deterioration. With me what they saw was a person who, compared to her high school years, had greatly improved rather than deteriorated. I was a mere shadow of my former self. I suddenly realized that this was going to be a very, very enjoyable evening for me!

As Pat and I mingled with the other attendees, I found some of the girls I had been friends with, but not many. Most of the girls attending had been the "back stabbers" and "gossip mongers" of ten years ago. Miss Popularity was there, loved by all and president of everything. Evidently, the best years of her life had been during high school, because, listening to her now, it was obvious they weren't all that glamorous now. All she could talk about were the dances, elections, and boyfriends of ten years ago. She said that all she did nowadays was watch over her three children and cook Italian dishes for her husband, who looked fifteen years her senior.

Since there weren't many of my crowd present, I stayed close to Pat to keep him company, since he knew no one there. When dinner was over, the committee said that they had some awards to hand out: one for having the most children; one for having had twins; one for the oddest career and one for the most travelled. When they announced that the most travelled person had lived in Florida, Alaska, and Japan, I thought that that sounded kind of familiar. It never occurred to me, until they called my name, that I would the recipient of an award. When I rose from my chair to get my little plastic loving cup, I heard a lot of whispering along with the applause. Pat told me that what they were whispering was, "Is that really Bonnie Rissky?" "That can't be the same person," and "I don't believe it." When I returned to my seat, Pat was sitting there with a huge smile on his face. He said, "Now aren't you glad we came?" I said, "Yes I am! It makes me see how great my life is now compared to all those years ago." After dinner, Pat and I danced and talked to a few more people and left early. I was so happy that I think I floated home on a cloud instead of riding home in our car.

The following day, I read through all my classmate's biographies to see what everyone was doing now. I laughed when I read about the girl who had become a stripper and was now a rock and roll singer. We got a chance to talk to her and she was a blast. I was sure hers was not the type of career the nuns wanted us to have. All I can say is, tough.

Another girl, who I had gone to grammar school and Nazareth with, had died from leukemia. I just couldn't comprehend this. She was such an energetic girl, a natural leader at everything. Her father was a doctor and they had lived in a beautiful house near St. Cletus Grade School. We had been very close at St. Cletus, but at Nazareth we had drifted apart because we weren't in many classes together. It seemed incredible that someone like her could die at 24 years old, never having the chance to love a husband or bear a child. She should have been immune to everything since her father was a doctor. Life is not predictable. If it was, I might still be the shy, fat, lonely person that I was in high school.

I was glad we had gone to the reunion. I came away with a feeling of triumph about what I ultimately had made of myself. I had come to the reunion as a thin, seasoned world traveler with a loving husband and beautiful son. I didn't have to do what most of them were trying to do, recapture teenage popularity and relive the "best days" of their lives. My best days are today and tomorrow and I am glad they are. The teen years are unstable, fleeting years. It's a great disappointment for those who had it all as teens and were never able to hold on to it as adults. It must be difficult coming down from a pedestal and having to be an adult who is just one of the masses. I'm one of the masses but that's okay by me. I love who I am and I have the love and respect of my two men, who think I am special. Whenever I, "Lift Up My Hood and Cuss," they will always be there for me.

I have redeemed myself!

PART V
LIFE ON FAST FORWARD

CHAPTER 23
EPILOGUE

I thought that I had finished writing my memoirs when I completed this book in 1976, but life has gone on. I decided I really owed an update to the people who have made my life so full and special, so here goes.

1970s—Moving on Up
In 1979, Pat, Brian and I moved into the type of house we had wanted when Pat left the Navy. It was a split-level ranch with three bedrooms, two baths and a finished basement. It was located about five blocks from our first home in a quiet neighborhood. A creek ran along the back of the property with Brian's grade school located on the other side of the creek. The house quickly became our second fixer-upper home because we had to replace several cracked windows, fix a hole in the roof, repair a deteriorated sidewalk, and repair the furnace. Many improvements have been made to our home over the years and we still love it.

1980s—Not Very Good to Us
On December 8, 1980, we woke to the shocking news that John Lennon had been murdered in front of the Dakota Apartments by Mark David Chapman. It was such an unbelievable and senseless murder. John had always been an activist for peace and love. He had brought so much music and excitement into my life. Now he was gone!

My beloved Grandma Taraba, whom I considered my second mother, passed away on February 10, 1985. I was lucky to have her in my life for so long. She didn't like or trust doctors so didn't see one for over 30 years and still lived to 77. Her passing left a big hole in our family. She had always been there to help our families during hard times.

Grandpa Taraba passed away 15 months after Grandma on May 1, 1986, at age 79. Grandpa had been a hardworking family man his entire life. When he retired from Dean's Dairy, he put his energy into gardening and helping Grandma take care of their pets: a miniature poodle named Bubbles and a pigeon named Clementine, who roosted in their garage. Grandpa would do anything for us and usually did. Our family was devastated again by his passing.

In 1987, Mark moved to Ft. Lauderdale, Florida, to open a sandwich shop with his close friend, Michael. While crossing a street to get to their car, they were hit by a speeding SUV. Mark sustained back injuries and was black and blue over his entire body. Michael's aorta was torn but he survived. Their prolonged recoveries ended their new business but they stayed in Florida.

1990s—Still Not So Hot

In 1991, Brian entered the U.S. Navy and graduated from Great Lakes Naval Training Center, Illinois, as an Aerographer's Mate (weatherman). This was the same Naval Station Great Lakes that Grandpa Taraba, Dad and Pat had graduated from. We now had four generations of Navy. Mom and Dad proudly joined us at Brian's graduation.

Four months after Brian's graduation, Mom suffered a severe heart attack at age 67. I stayed with her in the hospital as did Mark. During her stay, I went to the chapel to ask God to give her a little more time with us, at least until she reached 70. He must have listened because, after a long stay in the ICU and a long recuperation, she made it through.

On Saturday, January 8, 1993, Pat and I went out to see an afternoon movie. On the way back home, we were startled to see multiple local TV news vans in the parking lot of the food store where we always shopped. Pat slowed down and we could see that the attention was really aimed at the Brown's Chicken restaurant at the front of the grocery store lot. When we arrived home, I turned on the TV to see what had happened. They were reporting that on the previous Friday night, the two owners and five of their employees, including two high school students, had been put into the walk-in freezer and gunned down in cold blood. This crime really shook our community up big time. It was shocking and horrific and took place less than a mile from our home.

It took until 2002 for the murderers to be taken into custody. The key to their capture was DNA from a discarded chicken leg and the guilty conscience of an ex-girlfriend. Her boyfriend bragged of doing the deed to her but she had been too terrified of him to come forward. The murders, Juan Luna and James Degorski, are now serving life sentences in prison. Justice was finally served but what a cost to the families of the victims. It was not even a robbery just butchery for the thrill of it. Unfortunately, the mind-numbing violence in our society continues. How did we get to this point?

Later in 1993, Pat and I finally got to go on the honeymoon we had never had. For our 25th wedding anniversary we honeymooned on the Big Island of Hawaii. We drove completely around the island staying on both the Kona and Hilo coasts. We saw magnificent lava flows, a huge volcanic crater and lava tube, dozens of cascading waterfalls, huge cattle ranches, and beautiful flowers of every color. It was worth the 25-year wait.

Mom passed away on February 2, 1995, from respiratory failure, three months after she turned 70. God had been listening to my prayers. Her body was shutting down and she weighed only 85 pounds. Mom had been so sickly all of her life, I was happy that she was in a better place with no earthly suffering. It took Dad a longtime to recover his own life after Mom's passing. We tried to help by taking him on a trip to visit Pat's family in Bellingham, Washington. We took him fishing in the ocean and then at a trout lake. He even got to walk around in the snow near the top of Mt. Baker.

Also in 1995, Brian was discharged from the Navy in Rota, Spain, his final duty station. There he met and married Laura, a governess from South Wales. The two of them opened a bar, The Underground, in Rota just outside the Navy Base. The bar, unfortunately, failed after a time. During a very severe asthma attack Brian overused his inhaler and had to be put in the ICU of a Spanish hospital with a collapsed lung. After recovery, we had Brian and Laura flown to Palatine to live with us for a few months. Ultimately, they decided to move on to make their home in San Francisco, California.

2000s—Still Giving Us Great Sadness

In 2000, Pat won a special award from Motorola for his work, the Encore Award. Pat won the award because his job performance was in the top 1% of Motorola's over 100,000 employees. Aside from a glass trophy, the award included a three day, all-expenses paid stay at Disney World in Orlando, Florida. There we were wined and dined in style. We ate a buffet dinner on the beach with a band and massive fireworks and had breakfast served in bed each day. We were also given spending credits for the Disney store, two days of unlimited rides and attractions and a private dinner with a live performance of *The Lion King*. Motorola really pulled out all of the stops to make everyone attending feel very honored, including spouses and partners.

On May 9, 2004, Mother's Day, Dad passed away at 84. When I called him early in the morning he didn't answer. I became worried, so I called his neighbor to ask if she could check his house. She knocked several times but no one answered. She called me back to tell me that his Chevy Blazer was parked in the driveway. Pat and I left Palatine for his house as fast as we could. When we arrived, I unlocked the front door with a great worry about what we might find. We found Dad sitting on the kitchen floor in front of an open refrigerator, his legs out to the sides. When Pat touched his forehead, it was warm. Dad opened his eyes, looked at us and said, "I knew you would come." I called the paramedics immediately. When they lifted Dad on to a carry board, he went into cardiac arrest and they couldn't bring him back. We had lost our beloved leader.

A few months later, we found ourselves having to sell Dad and Mom's home. In all honesty, the house was falling apart. We had been lucky that it had lasted as long as it had. Dad hadn't wanted to spend much money on upkeep, so it had been up to Pat and me to fix things on a very limited budget. We had made many band-aid type repairs but never sacrificed Dad's safety.

Pat and I got the idea of attempting to sell the house to a developer. Someone who might be looking for a choice piece of property to build on in La Grange. I wrote a letter and we mailed it to several local developers. The property sold in a couple of months for a price Dad would have been proud of. The developer razed the house soon after and replaced it with a three story "McMansion." Dad had lived in that house for fifty-three years and with his passing, it seemed appropriate that the house passed on as well. No matter, I got to keep all of my memories of growing up in that house with my family and our pets.

In late 2004, Mark got a job as a custodian at Coral Glades High School, Coral Springs, Florida.

In 2005, Mark's mobile home and most of his possessions were destroyed by Hurricane Wilma. Mark and his pets hunkered down inside his van, which was parked behind a cement wall, and survived the hurricane.

In 2007, continuing his unlucky run of living in Florida, Mark was involved in a bad traffic accident on the way home from work. Mark sustained head injuries that developed into a subdural hematoma (a blood clot). Mark underwent emergency brain surgery to relieve the pressure on the brain. He came through the surgery fine and is still doing fine.

In August 2007, Pat, who was 62 at the time, was offered an early retirement package from Motorola. It was a retirement offer that he couldn't refuse. So, after thirty-four years, Motorola was no longer part of Pat's life. Pat was given a great retirement party, got a gold Motorola cellphone and I got to give a speech about my life with Pat.

In 2007, Pat's Mom, Jane, was hospitalized just before Christmas with severe diarrhea. She was supposed to have a short stay but things began going very wrong. She contracted a MRSA infection, had a stroke and passed away on February 1, 2008, just shy of her 90th birthday. Eight months after her death, Pat's Dad, Lee, having a broken heart after losing his wife of nearly seventy years, began to have a mental breakdown and passed away on October 8, 2008, at 94.

In 2009, John Baker, our dear friend from Misawa, Japan, passed away. We had remained long distance friends with John and Rosemary for over thirty years and Pat had remained John's constant pen pal through all of that time.

We were really hoping that the rest of 2009 would offer some relief from this continuing sadness and worry, but it was not to be. The "Big C" turned our life upside down when Pat was diagnosed with prostate cancer. We were both stunned to say the least. Pat was referred to the Chicago Prostate Cancer Center in Westmont, Illinois. His doctors determined that radiated seed implants would be the best form of treatment for him. They were right, he has continued to be cancer free for seven years now.

In 2012, Brian and Laura divorced. Brian decided to move back to Palatine and begin his life here over again. We do not know where Laura is but wish her well.

OUR MANY PETS

Like my parent's house while I was growing up, our house has always been full of pets. Our pets have offered us friendship, joy and comfort and have always made us smile. Our house has never been devoid of anything furry, feathered or scaled. What follows is a compilation of our beloved friends.

Trixie was our first shelter dog (all of our dogs have come from shelters). She was a medium-sized, Rat Terrier mix with a curly tail. She was a little devil who ate curtains right off the laundry room window. She loved to run in circles around our yard so fast that her side would almost touch the ground. She was really special because she was Brian's best friend as he grew up. She was born in 1973 and was with us until 1985.

Molly was a large Shepard Sheltie mix. Since she grew to weigh 95 pounds, she was obviously more Shepard than Sheltie. Molly was a loving, gentle dog who would smile on command. She liked to carry around one of Brian's old baby socks and bark at the mailman. She was plagued all of her life with allergies that caused very bad itching and skin rashes. She was born in 1984 and was with us until 1994.

Gracie was a slightly smaller Shepard mix. She was only three months old when we got her, so we couldn't blame her for teething on our kitchen chairs. We named her after Gracie Allen because she was so funny. Dad loved her and taught her to sing along with him. She was born in 1994 and was with us until 2007.

Sophie, our current furry friend, is a Shih-Tzu mixed with Siberian husky and four other breeds. She is our shortest and smallest dog weighing about 23 pounds. She has a beautiful face, a long silky coat, a pom-pom tail and a laid-back personality. She is also an extreme snorer! She's a warrior princess who goes on her daily walks in any kind of Chicago weather, except thunderstorms. I think she'd make an excellent mail carrier. When she is extremely excited, she goes into her "happy dance," sitting back on her rear and whirling around with a happy smile on her face. She was born in 2006 and is still with us.

We have had many other non-canine pets. Many parakeets could be heard tweeting over the years. There was a turtle named Chester, a chameleon named ET and a pair of hamsters named Mork and Mindy.

Alfie was a White Hooded Rat, smarter than any pet I had ever known. When I would clean her cage, she would climb out and go into a wastebasket next to the cage. When done cleaning, I would tap the cage and she would climb back into her cage by herself. She liked to sit next to me on the couch and eat M&Ms. She was born in 1980 and lived with us until 1983.

Louie was a Peach-Cheeked Grey Cockatiel. One Saturday, Pat took Brian fishing and Louie flew down from a tree, landing on our car's hood. The boys caught him and put him in the only container they had, their bait bucket. He survived the trip home in the bucket and lived with us for eight years (1984 to 1992).

Noah, an African Grey Parrot came into our lives in 1992. His price was very reasonable because, unknown to us, he was too old to be trained and was missing part of a toe. For a month, he woke us up at 5:00 a.m. screaming his lungs out and we never knew why. He has now been our constant companion for twenty-five years. He is still a pain because he throws his seeds all over and throws water on my head when I cleanup around his cage. These shortcomings are insignificant when you realize how smart he is.

Noah has become totally integrated to the rhythms of our family. He knows when dinner is ready from kitchen sounds and yells, "Come on Pat," in my voice! He can tell from how I sound on the phone that I am talking to my brother Mark and yells, "It's Mark!" If he hears a loud noise he says, "Are you okay?" If he hears the sound of a package opening he says, "Want some." He knows so many words and how to use them correctly; it's mind blowing. He likes to lure you into a false sense of security by acting friendly, then he lunges at you. He especially likes to grab a sleeve that is too close to his cage and make a hole in it. Oh well, nobody is perfect, but we love him dearly in spite of himself.

HERE WE ARE IN 2017

Pat and I have adjusted to his retirement just fine and keep busy around here most days. We are thankful that we have been blessed with good health allowing us to keep up with our house and lawn chores (I love to mow the lawn).

After all the many trips that we took during and after the Navy and Pat's travels around the world for Motorola, we are very content to be homebodies at this stage in our lives. Perhaps there will be a 50th Wedding Anniversary trip. We'll have to wait and see.

Although our families have gotten much smaller, we keep moving forward carrying the memories of the loved ones we have lost. They will always be part of us. We continue to see and talk to our current family members as much as possible.

Bill runs B&M Service Center, an auto and small engine repair business (lawn mowers and snow blowers) in Lyons, Illinois, and has for decades. May runs a U-Haul rental business from the same location. Billy works as a mechanic for his Dad's business and Angela, Billy's wife, works for Walgreens and is studying to become a pharmacy technician.

Mark was promoted to Head Custodian of Coral Glades High School, Florida, several years ago. He puts his heart and soul into his work and the kids love him for it. The kids know that Mark is there to help keep them safe and their school clean. I think he has found his calling because he has been there thirteen years and has outlasted several principals. We love it when Mark can come up to visit.

Brian is working as a computer technician and lives in a Palatine condo. We are very proud of him. It was very traumatic for him to lose his wife and come back home to start over. Pat and I enjoy having our son back with us and having dinner with him at least twice a week.

Rosemary, one of our dearest friends, continues to survive her husband, John. After John's passing, she had to add heart bypass surgery to all of her other operations. She is now in her early 80s and lives with her daughter Mary. Whenever I think of how much physical pain Rosemary has had to endure throughout her life, it just seems so unfair. Then, when I think of the kind of person she is, I realize I know no one who could have handled all of it with so much optimism, dignity and faith. Rosemary, you will always be our hero!

This year I turned 70 and Pat turned 72. Next year we will celebrate our 50th Wedding Anniversary. I guess time flies when you're having fun. Pat and I are now the Patriarch and Matriarch of our families. We are now supposed to be the elders with all of the answers! Well, I don't know about that but we have had some interesting life experiences. I am hoping that by providing a few of the lessons learned in my life, I might help others maneuver their life challenges. I can hear Dad on my shoulder saying, "Don't lift up your hood and cuss, call us," and that's what this book was all about.

Made in the USA
Lexington, KY
03 November 2017